1st Workshop on Artificial Intelligence and Easy and Plain Language in Institutional Contexts (AI & EL/PL 2025)

Geneva, Switzerland
23 June 2025

ISBN: 979-8-3313-2669-2

Printed from e-media with permission by:

Curran Associates, Inc.
57 Morehouse Lane
Red Hook, NY 12571

Some format issues inherent in the e-media version may also appear in this print version.

Association for Computational Linguistics
209 N. Eighth Street
Stroudsburg, Pennsylvania 18360

Phone: 1-570-476-8006
Fax: 1-570-476-0860

acl@aclweb.org

Additional copies of this publication are available from:

Curran Associates, Inc.
57 Morehouse Lane
Red Hook, NY 12571 USA
Phone: 845-758-0400
Fax: 845-758-2633
Email: curran@proceedings.com
Web: www.proceedings.com

aielpl 2025

1st Workshop on Artificial Intelligence and Easy and Plain Language in Institutional Contexts (AI & EL/PL)

Proceedings of the Workshop

June 23, 2025

Geneva, Switzerland

Message from the Organising Committee

This volume contains the proceedings of the 1st International Workshop on Artificial Intelligence and Easy and Plain Language in Institutional Contexts (AI & EL/PL 2025), held in conjunction with the 20th Machine Translation Summit (MT Summit 2025). The workshop aims to explore technological solutions focused on Easy and Plain Language across various institutional contexts and to bring together researchers from diverse fields, including healthcare, administrative communication, and education. It also aims to encourage multidisciplinary research that both develops and critically examines solutions and challenges related to promoting awareness of Easy and Plain Language, as well as advancing specialised machine translation and translation tools, including applications of large language models (LLMs) for translation.

The workshop received 13 submissions, with 10 accepted following a rigorous review process. The selected papers reflect a rich interdisciplinary engagement with AI-driven approaches to easy and plain language in institutional settings. Topics range from LLM-based simplification of administrative, healthcare, and web texts to the adaptation of numerical expressions and intralingual translation into Easy Languages. Several contributions focus on evaluating linguistic accessibility, including the alignment of professional adaptations with Easy-to-Understand guidelines and computational metrics for word complexity. Others reflect on the social and democratic implications of language simplification. Together, these works showcase a dynamic blend of technical innovation, empirical research, and inclusive design.

In addition to the technical programme, we are honoured to have two invited speakers: Christiane Maaß (University of Hildesheim) with a keynote entitled AI-assisted Intralingual and Interlingual Translation iinto Plain and Easy Language: An Emerging Field of Research"; and Silvia Hansen-Schirra and her team (Johannes Gutenberg University) who will present an Interactive session on Prompt Engineering for Easy Language translation.

We sincerely thank all the people and institutions that contributed to the success of the workshop: the authors of the submitted papers for their interest in the topic; the Programme Committee members for their valuable feedback and insightful comments; the MT Summit organisers for their support.

We hope you enjoy reading the papers and are looking forward to a fruitful and enriching workshop!

María Isabel Rivas Ginel
Patrick Cadwell
Paolo Canavese
Silvia Hansen-Schirra
Martin Kappus
Anna Matamala
Will Noonan

Organising Committee

Programme Chairs

María Isabel Rivas Ginel	ADAPT Centre / School of Applied Language and Intercultural Studies (SALIS), Dublin City University & TIL Université Bourgogne Europe
Patrick Cadwell	School of Applied Language and Intercultural Studies (SALIS), Dublin City University
Paolo Canavese	Faculty of Translation and Interpreting (FTI) & Centre for Legal and Institutional Translation Studies (TRANSIUS), University of Geneva
Silvia Hansen-Schirra	Johannes Gutenberg University
Martin Kappus	ZHAW School of Applied Linguistics
Anna Matamala	Universitat Autònoma de Barcelona
Will Noonan	Université Bourgogne Europe

Programme Committee

Łucja Biel	University of Warsaw
Katy Brickley	Kings College
Luisa Carrer	Zurich University of Applied Sciences
Iria da Cunha	Universidad Nacional de Educación a Distancia
Silvana Deilen	Hildesheim University
Carlo Eugeni	University of Leeds
Annarita Felici	University of Geneva
Itziar Gonzalez-Dios	University of the Basque Country (UPV/EHU)
Silke Gutermuth	Johannes Gutenberg-Universität Mainz
Sergio Hernández Garrido	Hildesheim University
Freya Hewett	University of Potsdam, Humboldt Institute for Internet and Society
Ekaterina Lapshinova-Koltunski	Hildesheim University
Sarah McDonagh	Universitat Autònoma de Barcelona
Joss Moorkens	Dublin City University
Jean Nitzke	University of Agder
Katharina Oster	Johannes Gutenberg-Universität Mainz
Elisa Perego	University of Pavia
Maja Popović	Dublin City University
Caroline Rossi	Université Grenoble Alpes
Regina Stodden	Heinrich Heine University
Jesús Torres del Rey	Universidad de Salamanca
Jan Trienes	University of Marburg
Ulla Vanhatalo	University of Helsinki
Giulia Venturi	Istituto di Linguistica Computazionale Antonio Zampolli"

Opening Keynote

AI-assisted Intralingual and Interlingual Translation into Plain and Easy Language: An Emerging Field of Research

Christiane Maaß
University of Hildesheim

Abstract: AI-assisted translation into Plain and Easy Language–both within the same language (intralingual) and across languages (interlingual)–is an emerging field at the intersection of translation studies, language technology, and accessibility research. This field addresses the growing need for accessible communication, particularly for people with reading difficulties, cognitive impairments, or limited proficiency in the source language. Unlike traditional interlingual translation, intralingual translation into Plain or Easy Language involves not merely simplifying text but adapting content to meet defined linguistic and cognitive standards, which presents unique challenges for automation.

Recent advancements leverage AI-driven tools to automate and standardize translation processes. While such tools increase efficiency and can generate texts that are easier to understand than standard versions, studies show that AI-generated outputs often fall short of fully meeting the nuanced standards upheld by human translators, especially regarding content accuracy and adherence to accessibility guidelines. Furthermore, the lack of one-to-one sentence correspondence in intralingual translation complicates the use of conventional computer-assisted translation (CAT) tools, requiring new approaches for alignment and quality assurance.

Despite these challenges, AI-assisted translation holds significant promise for inclusive communication, enabling broader participation in social, educational, and scientific discourse. Ongoing research focuses on improving model accuracy, integrating user feedback, and developing open-source solutions to ensure continuous quality improvement and wider adoption. As the field matures, it is expected to play a crucial role in reducing language barriers and promoting accessibility across diverse populations.

Bio: Christiane Maaß is a full professor at the University of Hildesheim and Director of the Department of Translation Studies and Specialized Communication. Since 2014 she has been Director of the Research Centre for Easy Language at the University of Hildesheim. She is an authorised expert for the German Federal Government's Accessibility Initiative. She is the Head of the accessible health communication section of the German Network for Health Literacy. She is the author and co-author of several monographical works as well as numerous articles and papers on Easy and Plain Language and co-editor of the Handbook Accessible Communication.

Interactive Sessions

Prompt Engineering for Easy Language Translation

Silvia Hansen-Schirra, Dimitrios Kapnas
Johannes Gutenberg University

Abstract: Similar to interlingual translation workflows, Artificial Intelligence (AI) can also be used to optimize intralingual translation processes by generating Easy Language (EL) translations, which can further be postedited. In order to produce high-quality AI translations into EL, prompt engineering is a way to implement rules, target groups, and other parameters in the instructions to an AI, like ChatGPT. In the workshop, we will introduce and test different prompting strategies (e.g. role-goal-context style prompting). The AI's output depends on how the prompt is formulated, and this has an effect on the postediting effort afterwards. Therefore, we will explain what prompt engineering is, why it matters, and how to do it in a simple way.

In order to test the quality of the AI output or the postedited texts, several methods come into play: Eyetracking, for instance, helps test the readability of the intralingual translations. Ratings and comprehensibility tests shed light on how well readers comprehend the AI-generated texts. In the workshop, we will therefore also show how to test the readability of the AI output by recording and quantifying eye movements, such as fixations (areas the eye stops on), saccades (jumps between fixations), and regressions (jumps back to previous text). Based on the eye-mind hypothesis, we correlate the eyetracking metrics with processing effort. This enables us to evaluate different prompting strategies for intralingual translation into EL.

Bio: Silvia Hansen-Schirra is a full Professor of English Linguistics and Translation Studies and Director of the Translation & Cognition (Tra&Co) Center at Johannes Gutenberg University Mainz in Germersheim. She is the co-editor of the book series Translation and Multilingual Natural Language Processingand Easy – Plain – Accessible". Her research interests include machine translation, accessible communication and translation process research.

Dimitrios Kapnas holds two M.A. Diplomas, one in Translation and one in Conference Interpreting. He finished his studies at the Johannes Gutenberg University Mainz in Germersheim in 2022. He is currently a doctoral student at the Tra&Co Center. His research interests include machine translation, accessible communication, easy language as well as gender linguistics.

Table of Contents

Leveraging Large Language Models for Joint Linguistic and Technical Accessibility Improvement: A Case Study on University Webpages

Pierrette Bouillon **Johanna Gerlach** **Raphael Rubino**
TIM/FTI, University of Geneva, 1205 Geneva, Switzerland
{pierrette.bouillon,johanna.gerlach,raphael.rubino}@unige.ch

Abstract

The aim of the study presented in this paper is to investigate whether Large Language Models can be leveraged to translate French content from existing websites into their B1-level simplified versions and to integrate them into an accessible HTML structure. We design a CMS agnostic approach to webpage accessibility improvement based on prompt engineering and apply it to Geneva University webpages. We conduct several automatic and manual evaluations to measure the accessibility improvement reached by several LLMs with various prompts in a zero-shot setting. Results show that LLMs are not all suitable for the task, while a large disparity is observed among results reached by different prompts. Manual evaluation carried out by a dyslexic crowd shows that some LLMs could produce more accessible websites and improve access to information.

1 Introduction

According to the Federal Statistical Office, the number of students accessing higher education in Switzerland has doubled since 2000, while the number of students with disabilities has decreased and remains the lowest compared to other groups, such as people of foreign origin[1]. This low penetration rate could be explained, among other reasons, by the difficulty of accessing information (Yerlikaya and Onay Durdu, 2017).

Since 2004, information accessibility has been a legal requirement in Switzerland for all areas of life, with the adoption of the Federal Act on the Elimination of Discrimination against People with Disabilities (LHand), as well as Switzerland's ratification of the UN Convention on the Rights of Persons with Disabilities (UNCRPD) in 2014. The Uni-Access project[2], financed by swissuniversities[3], aims to understand the barriers faced by users of Geneva University websites. In line with the recommendations of the new version of the Swiss accessibility standard for websites eCH-0059[4], it proposes concrete solutions to integrate simplified language and sign language on university webpages, including corpora and tools.

The Uni-Access pipeline for creating accessible webpages, given original webpages that are not optimized for accessibility, consists in three main steps: 1) intra-linguistic translation of the original content by an Easy-to-Read (E2R) expert into a B1-level simplified version and validation of the result with the content creator and the different target groups, 2) translation of the simplified version into sign language videos by deaf translators at the level of sentence or paragraph, and 3) creation of the webpage with the institution's CMS[5] following WCAG2.2[6] web accessibility guidelines [7].

The aim of the study presented in this paper is to investigate whether LLMs (Large Language Model) can be leveraged to translate French content from existing websites into a B1-level simplified version and to integrate it into a highly accessible HTML structure. We design a CMS agnostic approach to webpage accessibility improvement based on prompt engineering and apply it to Geneva University webpages. To the best of our knowledge, this is a first attempt at leveraging LLMs for joint linguistic and technical accessibil-

[1]Please see the Federal Statistical Office https://www.bfs.admin.ch/bfs/fr/home/statistiques/situation-economique-sociale-population/egalite-personnes-handicapees/formation/niveau-formation.html

[2]https://www.unige.ch/uni-access

[3]https://www.swissuniversities.ch/en/

[4]eCH-0059 – Accessibility Standard 3.0. Retrieved from https://www.ech.ch/fr/ech/ech-0059/3.0

[5]for Geneva University: Concrete CMS version 8.5.17

[6]https://www.w3.org/TR/WCAG22/

[7]Examples of web pages can be found on the Uni-Access project webiste: https://www.unige.ch/uni-access/demos

Proceedings of the 1st Workshop on Artificial Intelligence and Easy and Plain Language in Institutional Contexts (AI & EL/PL), pages 1–13, June 23, 2025

ity improvement. The main contributions of this work are: 1) the comparison of various prompts and open-weights pre-trained LLMs to jointly transform existing webpages into their simplified versions and 2) a two-step evaluation process relying on automatic metrics and manual evaluation through crowdsourcing.

The remainder of this paper is organized as follows. In Section 2, we present previous work on LLMs applied to web accessibility. Section 3 describes our methodology, including the models used, our prompting method and evaluation protocol. Finally, the results are detailed in Section 4 followed by a conclusion in Section 5.

2 LLM for Web Accessibility

Creating websites following the `Uni-Access` pipeline is time consuming and labor intensive, which limits its positive impact. In Switzerland, for example, the presence of simplified and sign language has been reported to still be anecdotal in the web ecosystem (David et al., 2023; Rodríguez Vázquez et al., 2022). Recently, LLMs have been studied as a means to create more accessible content (Freyer et al., 2024), and enhance linguistic and technical web accessibility.

Linguistic accessibility Different studies explore the potential of ChatGPT for content adaptation to simplified language (Easy to read – E2R – or Plain language), for example (Madina et al., 2024; Deilen et al., 2024). Common findings are that generated texts are easier than originals, but do not meet specific criteria (Madina et al., 2024). They also contain a lot of content related mistakes (Deilen et al., 2024), and fail to perform logical reordering at the text level (Madina et al., 2024) and to give explanations (Saggion, 2024).

Technical accessibility Previous studies explored LLMs' ability to assist in creating specific accessible content for web applications and examined ChatGPT's ability to fix web accessibility issues, but no previous study seems to have investigated the ability of LLM to adapt a source website into the corresponding accessible B1 version (López-Gil and Pereira, 2024; Aljedaani et al., 2024).

3 Methodology

We describe the methodology employed, including the automatic accessibility improvement approach using LLMs, the dataset used in our experiments, the pre-trained models and prompts selection, as well as the user evaluation.

3.1 Automatic Accessibility Improvement

Given an existing website without improved accessibility, our goal is to prompt a LLM in a zero-shot fashion to obtain a highly accessible website following pre-defined rules (presented in Appendix A), with a valid HTML structure and B1-level French content. We hand-crafted various prompts, written in English or French, and selected the best performing one. The exact prompt and its variants used in our experiments are presented in Appendix C. The input of each LLM tested in our study is composed of a hand-crafted prompt followed by the HTML content to be processed for accessibility improvement. Due to the recent publication of the WCAG2.2 guidelines, and based on the publication dates of the LLMs tested, we specify an earlier WCAG version in the prompt, assuming that LLMs training data might contain an earlier version of the guidelines.

3.2 Dataset

Our dataset consists in two pages from the Geneva University website, manually simplified following the `Uni-Access` pipeline. Original and simplified pages are presented in Appendix D. Both pages describe complex administrative procedures – one about the library book lending service (noted *Biblio*) and the other about the conditions for accessing a specific educational program (noted *Horizon*). The original pages achieve various levels of linguistic and technical accessibility. In particular, both pages contain a lot of jargon. The second page also features a HTML table that does not comply with accessibility guidelines.

3.3 Model Selection

Improving Web accessibility involves transforming the linguistic content and HTML structure of existing websites. Thus, an ideal LLM for the `Uni-Access` pipeline would be trained on various levels of French language (eg. A1, B2, etc.) and on web-related languages (eg. HTML, Javascript, etc.). However, due to the prohibitive costs of training LLMs on large amounts of data, we selected pre-trained models amongst popular open-weights LLMs, trained in a multilingual fashion with both natural and programming languages.

Preliminary accessibility experiments conducted in-house on various prompts and LLMs allowed us to select the best performing models for the task. From an initial pool of 9 pre-trained models (see Appendix B), 4 were selected for the automatic and manual evaluation, before selecting the best performing model, which was used for the crowd-based evaluation. The selection of 4 models from the initial pool relied on a two-step evaluation process:

i) automatic evaluation using publicly available metrics[8], namely:

- WAVE, identifying WCAG related errors on webpages[9]
- AMesure, focusing on text difficulty for French. It provides a global readability score for the text, that is computed by a readability formula. The output score ranges from 1 (for very easy texts) to 5 (for very complex texts) and is yielded by a support vector machine classifier combining 10 linguistic features of the text (François et al., 2014; François et al., 2020).[10]
- CEFRLex, performing token-level classification according to French levels (A1 to C2) based on existing dictionaries (François et al., 2014; Pintard and François, 2020).[11]
- W3C Validator, assessing the validity of a webpage HTML code[12]

ii) manual evaluation to verify for textual content omission caused by the LLM during the translation into French B1 language. For the manual evaluation, we asked a member of Geneva University administrative staff with expert knowledge of university policies and procedures to define ten questions for each webpage to be processed. We then checked if the LLM outputs contained the answers to all questions.

3.4 User evaluation

To assess whether the transformation of the pages improves their understandability, and thereby their usefulness for end-users seeking information, we carried out a reading comprehension test with users (Scarton and Specia, 2016). We included in this evaluation all three versions of the two webpages: the original, the manually simplified and the LLM output that achieved the highest score during model selection. We measure the user's ability to answer questions about the page content, the time required to find the answers in the page, and we collect the user's subjective opinion of the page's readability. Participants were recruited on the Prolific platform[13]. We used the platform's screeners to select participants with fluent French and to create two groups: dyslexic and non-dyslexic. For this study, we chose a between-subjects design in order to avoid learning effects. Each of the 6 pages was submitted to 10 participants. On each page, participants had to 1) sequentially answer three questions related to the page content (one yes/no question, two short answer questions), and 2) rate the page's readability on a six-point scale. Timestamps for page loading and response submission were collected through the page. All participants were paid a fixed amount for the task according to estimated completion time and Prolific's payment principles.

4 Results

This section presents the results obtained with automatic and manual evaluation during the model selection process, as well as the results obtained with the crowd-based manual evaluation.

4.1 Model Selection

As mentioned, the model selection follows a two-step process based on LLMs outputs: automatic evaluation for linguistic and technical accessibility, and manual verification of information omission.

Automatic evaluation results are presented in Table 1 for the *Biblio* and *Horizon* webpages. We evaluated the original webpages, their manually improved versions, as well as their automatically processed versions produced by LLMs. The AMesure metric indicates that LLMs do not reach the readability level of the manually produced *Biblio* page, although they do improve the original textual content. The token-level classification done by the CEFRLex metric shows a strong disparity among LLMs and prompts, especially for the A1 level. Especially, for the *Biblio* webpage, the model #7 with the first prompt reaches a higher ratio of A1 classified tokens compared to the manually processed page. However, LLMs tend to produce outputs with fewer tokens compared to *original* and *manual*, which motivates our manual evaluation to verify for information omission, because shorter

[8]All metrics were accessed online in March 2025.
[9]`https://wave.webaim.org/`
[10]`https://cental.uclouvain.be/amesure/`
[11]`https://cental.uclouvain.be/cefrlex/analyse/`
[12]`https://validator.w3.org`
[13]`https://www.prolific.com/`

prompt	model	tokens	AMesure	CEFRLex (% tokens)								W3C	WAVE	
				A1	A2	B1	B2	C1	C2	unk.	ign.		err.	contr.
				Webpage: Biblio										
–	original	792	3	57.1	3.2	8.6	6.4	0.5	0.6	4.5	19.1	13	2	2
–	manual	748	1	59.6	4.9	5.5	2.9	0.1	0.3	4.5	22.1	2	2	2
1	2	758	2	59.5	3.3	8.0	5.9	0.5	0.7	3.2	18.9	26	2	2
	5	862	2	52.7	3.4	7.8	5.9	0.5	0.6	5.1	24.1	8	2	0
	7	592	2	60.1	2.5	7.8	6.6	0.7	0.2	2.7	19.4	6	2	0
	9	442	2	47.7	3.2	6.6	5.2	0.0	1.1	5.9	30.3	7	2	0
2	2	179	2	55.3	3.9	8.4	5.0	1.1	0.0	3.9	22.3	15	2	0
	5	853	2	52.3	3.4	7.9	6.0	0.5	0.6	5.2	24.3	6	2	0
	7	728	3	59.6	3.0	8.4	6.5	0.5	0.7	3.2	18.1	6	2	0
	9	533	3	43.0	3.0	6.2	6.6	0.0	0.8	5.1	35.5	9	2	0
3	2	660	2	59.2	3.5	7.4	5.5	0.3	0.6	3.3	20.2	15	2	2
	5	851	2	52.3	3.4	7.9	6.0	0.5	0.6	5.2	24.2	6	2	0
	7	676	2	59.8	3.1	8.4	6.7	0.6	0.7	2.7	18.0	7	2	0
	9	534	2	47.9	3.2	6.0	6.9	0.2	0.7	5.1	30.0	10	2	0
				Webpage: Horizon										
–	original	698	3	52.0	4.6	9.6	8.6	1.9	0.1	3.7	19.5	17	3	1
–	manual	938	2	60.6	5.0	5.5	5.1	0.3	0.1	2.5	20.9	14	3	0
1	2	242	2	54.1	4.1	10.3	5.8	1.2	0.0	5.8	18.6	12	2	0
	5	833	2	54.4	4.3	8.8	7.1	1.2	0.0	3.0	21.2	7	2	0
	7	590	3	58.0	3.9	7.6	6.3	1.0	0.7	2.4	20.2	6	2	0
	9	391	3	48.3	3.3	6.9	9.5	1.0	0.0	2.3	28.6	6	2	0
2	2	249	3	49.8	4.4	8.4	9.2	1.2	0.0	7.6	19.3	12	2	0
	5	672	2	54.6	4.0	8.8	7.3	1.8	0.0	3.3	20.2	9	3	0
	7	433	2	59.1	4.6	7.2	6.2	0.9	0.0	2.8	19.2	7	2	0
	9	451	3	45.2	3.3	10.4	7.5	1.8	0.2	2.0	29.5	7	2	0
3	2	415	2	46.5	3.9	8.4	9.2	2.2	0.0	9.9	20.0	6	2	0
	5	731	2	54.6	4.2	8.3	7.1	1.5	0.0	3.0	21.2	11	3	0
	7	479	3	58.7	4.6	7.1	6.3	0.6	0.2	1.9	20.7	6	2	0
	9	524	3	51.7	4.2	8.6	8.2	1.0	0.0	3.2	23.1	7	2	0

Table 1: Comparison between four pre-trained LLMs and three prompt variants for the automatic accessibility improvement of the webpages *Biblio* (top) and *Horizon* (bottom) according to automatic metrics measuring linguistic and technical accessibility. The *unk.* and *ign.* columns indicate the unknown and ignored tokens of the CEFRLex metric, respectively. The *err.* and *contr.* columns denote the global and contrast errors of the WAVE metric, respectively. For model and prompt IDs, please refer to Appendix B and to Appendix C. Bold values are prompts and models selected for crowd-based evaluation.

webpages could lack mandatory information included in the *original* and *manual* versions.

Manual verification for information omission is based on a set of 10 questions drafted by a domain expert. For each question, we check if the LLM outputs contain the answer and annotate them accordingly in a binary fashion. The average scores per prompt variant and model, for the two webpages of our study, are presented in Table 2. These results highlight the importance of careful prompt crafting, for instance with model #5 reaching 0.9pts (max. 1.0) with the first prompt and 0.1 with the second prompt on the *Biblio* webpage. The same model does not perform well on the *Horizon* webpage, while model #2 shows less variability on this page among the prompt variants.

Based on the automatic and manual evaluation results, the final prompts are #1 and #3 for the webpages *Horizon* and *Biblio* respectively. The best model for both pages is *Qwen2.5-Coder-32B-Instruct* (Hui et al., 2024).[14]

4.2 User Evaluation

The crowd-based user evaluation was carried out on 6 webpages (2 original webpages, their manually improved version and the best LLM outputs). We collected 10 responses for each of the 6 pages. Table 3 shows the number of correct responses by page and question. Some participants responded in languages other than French, or with full sen-

[14] https://huggingface.co/Qwen/Qwen2.5-Coder-32B-Instruct

prompt	model	*Biblio*	*Horizon*
1	2	0.8	0.8
	5	0.9	0.1
	7	0.8	**0.8**
	9	0.6	0.7
2	2	0.8	0.8
	5	0.1	0.2
	7	0.9	0.5
	9	0.7	0.6
3	2	0.3	0.8
	5	0.9	0.2
	7	**0.9**	0.7
	9	0.9	0.8

Table 2: Manual verification of information omission for three prompts and four pre-trained models on two webpages, *Biblio* and *Horizon*, for the automatic accessibility improvement task. Scores are averaged binary labels indicating if the answer of a specific question is present in the LLM output. For model and prompt IDs, refer to Appendix B and to Appendix C, respectively. Bold values are prompts and models selected for crowd-based evaluation.

	question 1		question 2		question 3	
	d	nd	d	nd	d	nd
			Webpage: Biblio			
original	4	5	4	10	3	4
manual	2	3	7	9	2	3
LLM	4	4	8	8	3	4
			Webpage: Horizon			
original	8	9	6	2	7	9
manual	9	9	2	5	10	9
LLM	9	10	2	4	10	7

Table 3: User evaluation of original pages, their manually improved accessibility version and the LLM output, in terms of correct responses by webpage and participant group (*d* and *nd* denote the dyslexic and the non-dyslexic group of evaluators, respectively).

	N	dyslexic	N	non-dyslexic
		Webpage: Biblio		
original	5	5.20 (0.84)	10	4.70 (1.06)
manual	8	5.88 (0.35)	10	5.10 (1.29)
LLM	8	5.50 (0.76)	8	5.88 (0.35)
		Webpage: Horizon		
original	9	4.89 (1.36)	10	5.50 (0.97)
manual	10	5.70 (0.48)	10	5.60 (0.70)
LLM	10	5.50 (0.97)	10	5.30 (1.06)

Table 4: Mean readability scores and standard deviations (in brackets) by webpage and participant group when manually evaluating original pages, their manually accessibility improved version and the LLM output.

tences instead of the expected short answer. Some responses also led us to believe that participants used LLMs to obtain answers to the questions. Nevertheless, we considered as correct all responses containing the required information.

Multiple causes can lead to an incorrect response in a crowdsourcing context: participants not understanding the page and/or question, careless participants, difficult questions, etc. In order to exclude participants who had not followed the instructions and provided random or irrelevant responses from further analysis, we removed from the dataset the responses where none of the three questions had been answered correctly.

We first calculated the **average readability scores** for this dataset, based on the readability ratings given by participants on a 6-point scale after completing the questions. Table 4 gives the average scores by page and group. Overall the manually simplified versions were rated higher than the original pages. In all cases, with the exception of the non-dyslexic group when evaluating the *Biblio* webpage, the LLM versions are halfway between the original and the manually simplified versions, suggesting the changes made by the models improve perceived readability.

Using this dataset, we also calculated the **time in seconds** for the task. It was measured over all three questions, from page load until the submission of the answer to the third question. Due to the uncontrolled conditions in which participants completed the tasks, the measured times could have been affected by activities unrelated to the task. Outliers were therefore identified and 7 were removed from the dataset using the Interquartile Range (IQR) method with a threshold of $\pm 1.5 \times$IQR.

Table 5 shows the median response times for the remaining data. We observe that for the original and manually simplified pages, participants from the dyslexic group spent more time on the task than the non-dyslexic participants. For both LLM versions, the median times are very close for both groups, suggesting that the simplified version might improve access to information for the dyslexic group. Figure 1 shows the median times

	N	dyslexic	N	non-dyslexic
		Webpage: Biblio		
original	4	435	9	129
manual	7	316	10	191
LLM	8	237	8	236
		Webpage: Horizon		
original	8	193	10	166
manual	9	209	8	158
LLM	10	173	10	171

Table 5: Median response time in seconds by webpage and participant group (outliers removed), when manually evaluating original pages, their manually accessibility improved version and the LLM output.

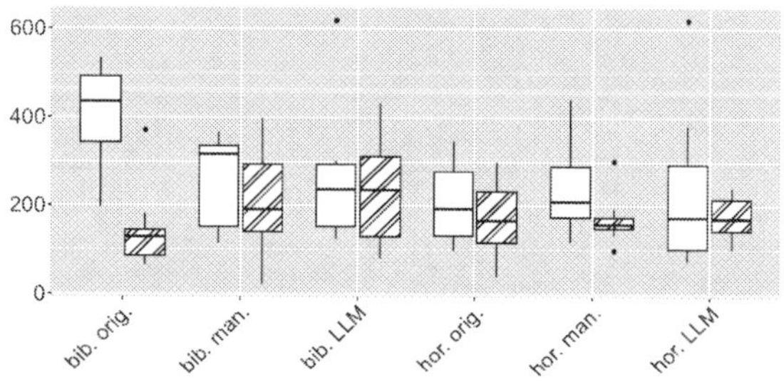

Figure 1: Response time in seconds by webpage (*bib* and *hor* denote the *Biblio* and *Horizon* webpages, respectively) and participant group (dyslexic in white, non-dyslexic striped) for each page (outliers removed) by page and group.

5 Conclusion and limitations

The main aim of this paper was to investigate whether LLMs could be used to transform academic websites into more accessible versions. We confirmed that LLMs could produce more accessible versions than their originals and improve access to information for dyslexic users. However, 1) not all LLMs are equally suitable for the task, notably regarding omissions and 2) the combination prompt/model leads to unstable performances for both linguistic and technical accessibility, as shown by the automatic metrics and manual verification.

Crowdsourcing had many advantages and enabled us to carry out a user study with different groups such as people with dyslexia. However, during the analysis of these results, incorrect answers were difficult to interpret due to the uncontrolled crowd-based evaluation conditions. Furthermore, it is possible that evaluators used other means of finding answers to the questions, such as publicly available LLMs, rather than consulting the presented page.

The number of participants could be increased further for future studies, but more comparisons are necessary to validate the experimental approach used, in particular the inclusion of multiple questions per page and the between-subjects design.

Despite all the ethical concerns, notably regarding the content-related issues, our conclusion is that a LLM, associated with a careful preselection and evaluation process, could contribute to level inequalities.

Acknowledgments

This work is part of the `Uni-Access` project funded by swissuniversities. We thank all the participants to the project, in particular Bastien David, Rebeka Mali, Lucia Morado, Irene Strasly and Silvia Rodriguez Vazquez.

References

Wajdi Aljedaani, Abdulrahman Habib, Ahmed Aljohani, Marcelo Eler, and Yunhe Feng. 2024. Does chatgpt generate accessible code? investigating accessibility challenges in llm-generated source code. In *Proceedings of the 21st International Web for All Conference*, W4A '24, page 165–176, New York, NY, USA. Association for Computing Machinery.

Bastien David, Lucía Morado Vázquez, and Elisa Casalegno. 2023. The inclusion of sign language on the swiss web ecosystem. *Journal of accessibility and design for all: JACCES*, 13(1):1–42.

Silvana Deilen, Ekaterina Lapshinova-Koltunski, Sergio Hernández Garrido, Christiane Maaß, Julian Hörner, Vanessa Theel, and Sophie Ziemer. 2024. Towards AI-supported health communication in plain language: Evaluating intralingual machine translation of medical texts. In *Proceedings of the First Workshop on Patient-Oriented Language Processing (CL4Health) @ LREC-COLING 2024*, pages 44–53, Torino, Italia. ELRA and ICCL.

Thomas François, Núria Gala, Patrick Watrin, and Cédrick Fairon. 2014. Flelex: a graded lexical resource for french foreign learners. In *International conference on Language Resources and Evaluation (LREC 2014)*.

Thomas François, Adeline Müller, Eva Rolin, and Magali Norré. 2020. AMesure: A web platform to assist the clear writing of administrative texts. In *Proceedings of the 1st Conference of the Asia-Pacific Chapter of the Association for Computational Linguistics and the 10th International Joint Conference on Natural Language Processing: System Demonstrations*, pages 1–7, Suzhou, China. Association for Computational Linguistics.

Thomas François, Laetitia Brouwers, Hubert Naets, and Cédrick Fairon. 2014. Amesure: a readability formula for administrative texts (amesure: une plateforme de lisibilité pour les textes administratifs) [in french]. In *JEP/TALN/RECITAL*.

Nils Freyer, Hendrik Kempt, and Lars Klöser. 2024. Easy-read and large language models: on the ethical dimensions of llm-based text simplification. *Ethics and Information Technology*, 26(3):50.

Binyuan Hui, Jian Yang, Zeyu Cui, Jiaxi Yang, Dayiheng Liu, Lei Zhang, Tianyu Liu, Jiajun Zhang, Bowen Yu, Kai Dang, et al. 2024. Qwen2. 5-coder technical report. *arXiv preprint arXiv:2409.12186*.

Juan-Miguel López-Gil and Juanan Pereira. 2024. Turning manual web accessibility success criteria into automatic: an llm-based approach. *Universal Access in the Information Society*.

Margot Madina, Itziar Gonzalez-Dios, and Melanie Siegel. 2024. A preliminary study of ChatGPT for Spanish E2R text adaptation. In *Proceedings of the 2024 Joint International Conference on Computational Linguistics, Language Resources and Evaluation (LREC-COLING 2024)*, pages 1422–1434, Torino, Italia. ELRA and ICCL.

Alice Pintard and Thomas François. 2020. Combining expert knowledge with frequency information to infer cefr levels for words. In *Proceedings of the 1st Workshop on Tools and Resources to Empower People with REAding DIfficulties (READI)*, pages 85–92.

Silvia Rodríguez Vázquez, Jesús Torres del Rey, Lucía Morado Vázquez, et al. 2022. Easy language content on the web: a multilingual perspective. *Investigaciones recientes en traducción y accesibilidad digital*.

Horacio Saggion. 2024. Artificial intelligence and natural language processing for easy-to-read texts. *Revista de Llengua i Dret*, pages 84–103.

Carolina Scarton and Lucia Specia. 2016. A reading comprehension corpus for machine translation evaluation. In *Proceedings of the Tenth International Conference on Language Resources and Evaluation (LREC'16)*, pages 3652–3658, Portorož, Slovenia. European Language Resources Association (ELRA).

Zehra Yerlikaya and Pınar Onay Durdu. 2017. Usability of university websites: A systematic review. In *Universal Access in Human–Computer Interaction. Design and Development Approaches and Methods: 11th International Conference, UAHCI*, pages 277–287. Springer.

A Rules for Manual Accessibility Improvement

A list of rules for manual improvement of existing Geneva University webpages were derived from the accessibility improved pages produced by domain and accessibility experts. These rules are grouped in two categories, linguistic and technical accessibility.

Linguistic accessibility

- Text CEFR B1 level
- Make short sentences
- One idea per sentence
- Use frequent words
- Avoid passives
- Address the person directly
- Follow a logical order of information
- Reinforce coherence
- Don't use undefined abbreviations or terms/jargon
- Replace conditions with questions, for example:
  - If you live abroad, you have to pay fees.
  - Do you live abroad? You pay fees.

Technical accessibility

- Make bulleted lists to describe steps
- 1.5 line spacing
- Go to line after periods
- Non-breaking space before punctuation marks with a space
- Bold for important information, such as dates
- No images and description of images in text

B Models

We compare several models in a zero-shot setting using various prompts. The list of all pre-trained LLMs involved in our study is presented in Table 6 (All models have open weights and are available on the Hugging Face Hub[15]). From this initial list of models, we select a subset of four best performing models according to a brief manual check of the LLMs outputs. We removed models with non-HTML outputs, as well as outputs in other languages than French, and unmodified outputs compared to input webpages. The four models selected for automatic and manual evaluation are marked with * in Table 6.

C Prompts

Several hand-crafted prompts were tested in our experiments and the best performing variants are presented in Figure 2.

D Uni-Access Simplified Pages

[15]https://huggingface.co/

id	Model name	#params.
1	nvidia/Llama-3_1-Nemotron-51B-Instruct	51B
2	meta-llama/Llama-3.3-70B-Instruct⋆	70B
3	nvidia/Llama-3.1-Nemotron-70B-Instruct	70B
4	mistralai/Mistral-Nemo-Instruct-2407	12B
5	mistralai/Mistral-Small-24B-Instruct-2501⋆	24B
6	allenai/Llama-3.1-Tulu-3-70B	70B
7	Qwen/Qwen2.5-Coder-32B-Instruct⋆	32B
8	Qwen/Qwen2.5-72B-Instruct	72B
9	Qwen/QwQ-32B⋆	32B

Table 6: List of models used in our experiments. Model names match Hugging Face Hub identifiers. Number of parameters are in billions (noted *B*). Models kept for the automatic and manual evaluations are marked with ⋆.

Prompt #1

The task involves rewriting a fragment of HTML content to produce an HTML fragment following the WCAG 2.1 guidelines and the W3C validator. The output must comply with the following rules: For the text, rewrite in French for a CEFR B1 level, write short sentences, follow a logical order of information, only one idea per sentence, avoid the passive form, address the person directly, use frequent words, don't use undefined abbreviations, do not use terms or jargon, reinforce the coherence of the textual content, replace conditions with questions (for example, "Si vous habitez à l'étranger, vous devez payer des frais.", "Vous habitez à l'étranger ? Vous payez des frais."). The output format must be HTML and must respect the following rules: Follow WCAG 2.1 and W3C guidelines, use bulleted lists to describe steps, 1.5 line spacing, line breaks after periods, insert a non-breaking space before punctuation marks with a space, bold important information such as dates and places, do not include images but instead describe input images in the output HTML content. Output a full and well-formed HTML page in a single <main> tag without header nor footer.

Prompt #2

Given an HTML snippet, your task is to transform it and output an HTML snippet which must follow the WCAG 2.1 and W3C guidelines, as well as the following mandatory rules: For the text, rewrite in French for a CEFR B1 level, write short sentences, follow a logical order of information, write only one idea per sentence, avoid the passive form, address the person directly, use frequent words, do not use abbreviations, terms or jargon, reinforce the coherence of the textual content, replace conditions with questions (for example, "Si vous habitez à l'étranger, vous devez payer des frais.", "Vous habitez à l'étranger ? Vous payez des frais."). Rules for the HTML: Follow WCAG 2.1 and W3C guidelines, use bulleted lists to describe steps, use 1.5 line spacing with CSS, use line breaks after periods, insert a non-breaking space before punctuation marks with a space, highlight and bold important information such as dates and places, do not include images but instead describe them in the content. Output a full and well-formed HTML page in a single <main> tag without header nor footer, no comments nor notes.

Prompt #3

Given an HTML snippet, your task is to transform it and output an HTML snippet without removing any information from the input. The output must follow the WCAG 2.1 and W3C guidelines, and the following rules: For the text, rewrite in French for a CEFR B1 level, write short sentences, follow a logical order of information, write only one idea per sentence, avoid the passive form, address the person directly, use frequent words, do not use abbreviations, terms or jargon, reinforce the coherence of the textual content, replace conditions with questions (for example, "Si vous habitez à l'étranger, vous devez payer des frais.", "Vous habitez à l'étranger ? Vous payez des frais."). Rules for the HTML: Follow WCAG 2.1 and W3C guidelines, use bulleted lists to describe steps, use 1.5 line spacing with CSS, use line breaks after periods, insert a non-breaking space before punctuation marks with a space, highlight and bold important information such as dates and places, do not include images but instead describe them in the content. Output a full and well-formed HTML page in a single <main> tag without header nor footer, no comments nor notes.

Figure 2: Variants of the best performing hand-crafted prompt used in our experiments.

Figure 3: Original *Biblio* webpage

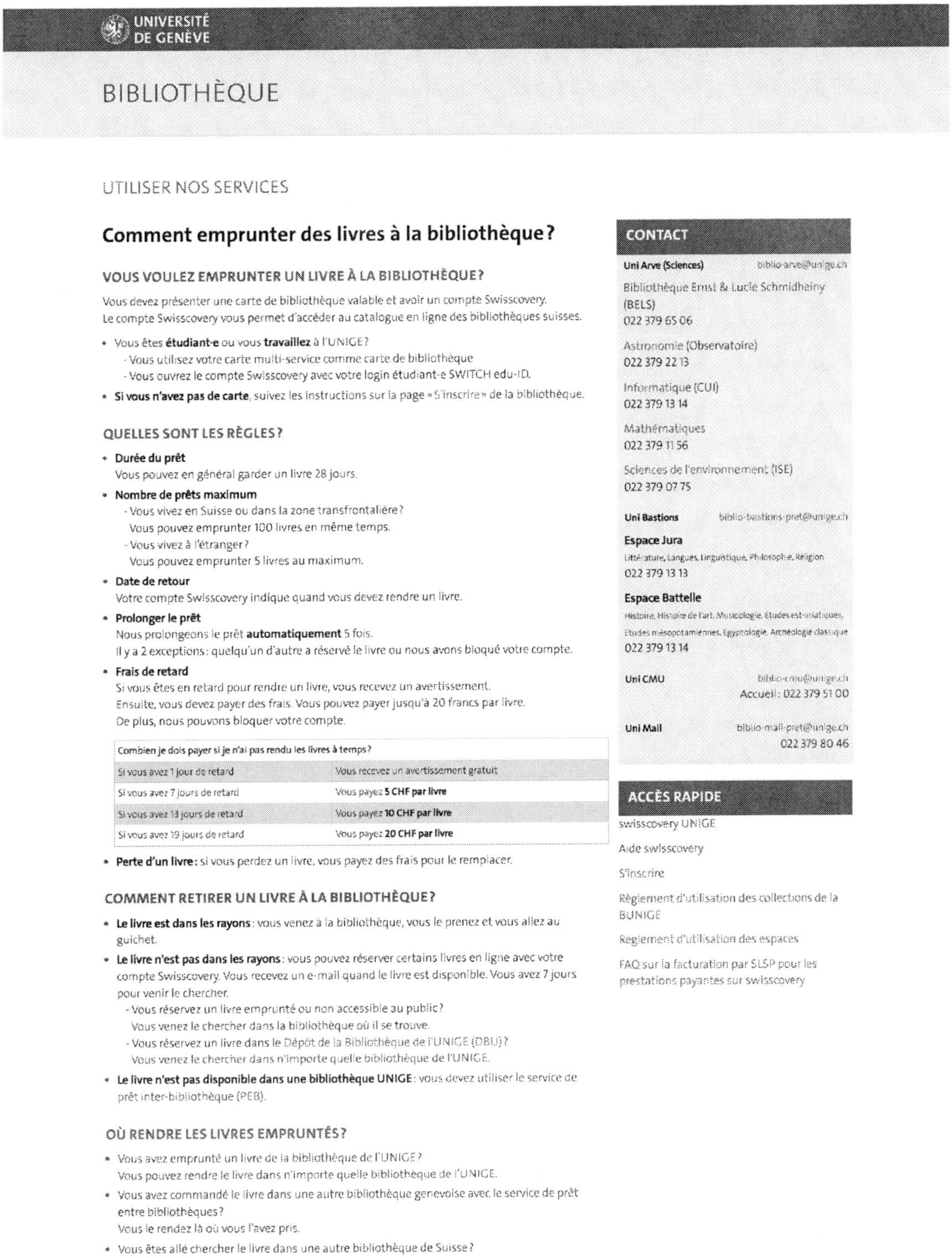

UNIVERSITÉ DE GENÈVE

BIBLIOTHÈQUE

UTILISER NOS SERVICES

Comment emprunter des livres à la bibliothèque?

VOUS VOULEZ EMPRUNTER UN LIVRE À LA BIBLIOTHÈQUE?

Vous devez présenter une carte de bibliothèque valable et avoir un compte Swisscovery.
Le compte Swisscovery vous permet d'accéder au catalogue en ligne des bibliothèques suisses.

- Vous êtes **étudiant-e** ou vous **travaillez** à l'UNIGE?
  - Vous utilisez votre carte multi-service comme carte de bibliothèque
  - Vous ouvrez le compte Swisscovery avec votre login étudiant-e SWITCH edu-ID.
- **Si vous n'avez pas de carte**, suivez les instructions sur la page « S'inscrire » de la bibliothèque.

QUELLES SONT LES RÈGLES?

- **Durée du prêt**
  Vous pouvez en général garder un livre 28 jours.
- **Nombre de prêts maximum**
  - Vous vivez en Suisse ou dans la zone transfrontalière?
    Vous pouvez emprunter 100 livres en même temps.
  - Vous vivez à l'étranger?
    Vous pouvez emprunter 5 livres au maximum.
- **Date de retour**
  Votre compte Swisscovery indique quand vous devez rendre un livre.
- **Prolonger le prêt**
  Nous prolongeons le prêt **automatiquement** 5 fois.
  Il y a 2 exceptions: quelqu'un d'autre a réservé le livre ou nous avons bloqué votre compte.
- **Frais de retard**
  Si vous êtes en retard pour rendre un livre, vous recevez un avertissement.
  Ensuite, vous devez payer des frais. Vous pouvez payer jusqu'à 20 francs par livre.
  De plus, nous pouvons bloquer votre compte.

Combien je dois payer si je n'ai pas rendu les livres à temps?	
Si vous avez 1 jour de retard	Vous recevez un avertissement gratuit
Si vous avez 7 jours de retard	Vous payez **5 CHF par livre**
Si vous avez 13 jours de retard	Vous payez **10 CHF par livre**
Si vous avez 19 jours de retard	Vous payez **20 CHF par livre**

- **Perte d'un livre:** si vous perdez un livre, vous payez des frais pour le remplacer.

COMMENT RETIRER UN LIVRE À LA BIBLIOTHÈQUE?

- **Le livre est dans les rayons**: vous venez à la bibliothèque, vous le prenez et vous allez au guichet.
- **Le livre n'est pas dans les rayons**: vous pouvez réserver certains livres en ligne avec votre compte Swisscovery. Vous recevez un e-mail quand le livre est disponible. Vous avez 7 jours pour venir le chercher.
  - Vous réservez un livre emprunté ou non accessible au public?
    Vous venez le chercher dans la bibliothèque où il se trouve.
  - Vous réservez un livre dans le Dépôt de la Bibliothèque de l'UNIGE (DBU)?
    Vous venez le chercher dans n'importe quelle bibliothèque de l'UNIGE.
- **Le livre n'est pas disponible dans une bibliothèque UNIGE**: vous devez utiliser le service de prêt inter-bibliothèque (PEB).

OÙ RENDRE LES LIVRES EMPRUNTÉS?

- Vous avez emprunté un livre de la bibliothèque de l'UNIGE?
  Vous pouvez rendre le livre dans n'importe quelle bibliothèque de l'UNIGE.
- Vous avez commandé le livre dans une autre bibliothèque genevoise avec le service de prêt entre bibliothèques?
  Vous le rendez là où vous l'avez pris.
- Vous êtes allé chercher le livre dans une autre bibliothèque de Suisse?

CONTACT

Uni Arve (Sciences) biblio-arve@unige.ch
Bibliothèque Ernst & Lucie Schmidheiny (BELS)
022 379 65 06
Astronomie (Observatoire)
022 379 22 13
Informatique (CUI)
022 379 13 14
Mathématiques
022 379 11 56
Sciences de l'environnement (ISE)
022 379 07 75

Uni Bastions biblio-bastions-pret@unige.ch
Espace Jura
Littérature, Langues, Linguistique, Philosophie, Religion
022 379 13 13
Espace Battelle
Histoire, Histoire de l'art, Musicologie, Etudes est-asiatiques, Etudes mésopotamiennes, Egyptologie, Archéologie classique
022 379 13 14

Uni CMU biblio-cmu@unige.ch
Accueil : 022 379 51 00

Uni Mail biblio-mail-pret@unige.ch
022 379 80 46

ACCÈS RAPIDE

swisscovery UNIGE
Aide swisscovery
S'inscrire
Règlement d'utilisation des collections de la BUNIGE
Reglement d'utilisation des espaces
FAQ sur la facturation par SLSP pour les prestations payantes sur swisscovery

Figure 4: Manually simplified *Biblio* webpage

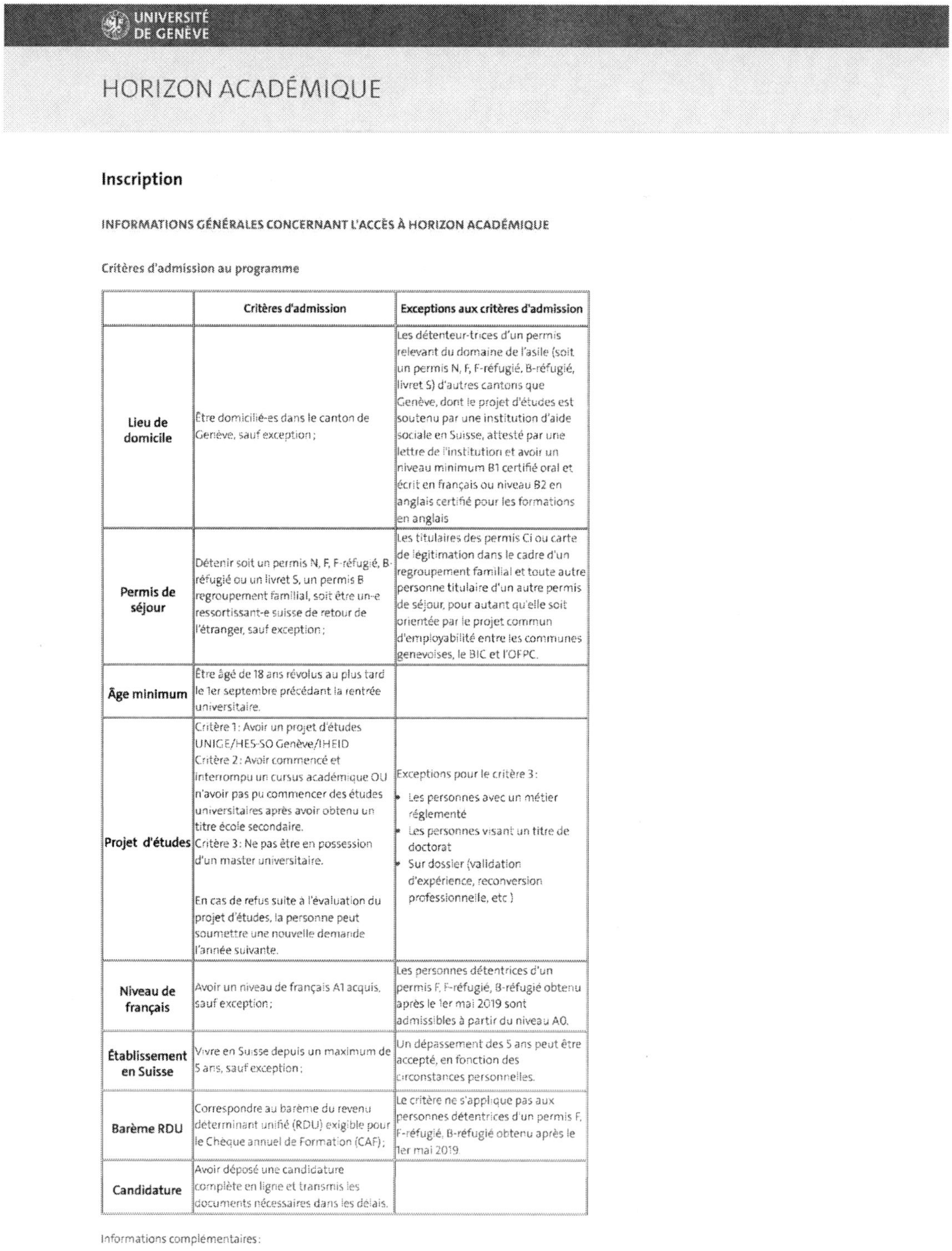

UNIVERSITÉ DE GENÈVE

HORIZON ACADÉMIQUE

Inscription

INFORMATIONS GÉNÉRALES CONCERNANT L'ACCÈS À HORIZON ACADÉMIQUE

Critères d'admission au programme

	Critères d'admission	Exceptions aux critères d'admission
Lieu de domicile	Être domicilié-es dans le canton de Genève, sauf exception ;	Les détenteur-trices d'un permis relevant du domaine de l'asile (soit un permis N, F, F-réfugié, B-réfugié, livret S) d'autres cantons que Genève, dont le projet d'études est soutenu par une institution d'aide sociale en Suisse, attesté par une lettre de l'institution et avoir un niveau minimum B1 certifié oral et écrit en français ou niveau B2 en anglais certifié pour les formations en anglais
Permis de séjour	Détenir soit un permis N, F, F-réfugié, B-réfugié ou un livret S, un permis B regroupement familial, soit être un-e ressortissant-e suisse de retour de l'étranger, sauf exception ;	Les titulaires des permis Ci ou carte de légitimation dans le cadre d'un regroupement familial et toute autre personne titulaire d'un autre permis de séjour, pour autant qu'elle soit orientée par le projet commun d'employabilité entre les communes genevoises, le BIC et l'OFPC.
Âge minimum	Être âgé de 18 ans révolus au plus tard le 1er septembre précédant la rentrée universitaire.	
Projet d'études	Critère 1: Avoir un projet d'études UNIGE/HES-SO Genève/IHEID Critère 2 : Avoir commencé et interrompu un cursus académique OU n'avoir pas pu commencer des études universitaires après avoir obtenu un titre école secondaire. Critère 3 : Ne pas être en possession d'un master universitaire. En cas de refus suite à l'évaluation du projet d'études, la personne peut soumettre une nouvelle demande l'année suivante.	Exceptions pour le critère 3 : • Les personnes avec un métier réglementé • Les personnes visant un titre de doctorat • Sur dossier (validation d'expérience, reconversion professionnelle, etc)
Niveau de français	Avoir un niveau de français A1 acquis, sauf exception ;	Les personnes détentrices d'un permis F, F-réfugié, B-réfugié obtenu après le 1er mai 2019 sont admissibles à partir du niveau A0.
Établissement en Suisse	Vivre en Suisse depuis un maximum de 5 ans, sauf exception ;	Un dépassement des 5 ans peut être accepté, en fonction des circonstances personnelles.
Barème RDU	Correspondre au barème du revenu déterminant unifié (RDU) exigible pour le Chèque annuel de Formation (CAF) ;	Le critère ne s'applique pas aux personnes détentrices d'un permis F, F-réfugié, B-réfugié obtenu après le 1er mai 2019.
Candidature	Avoir déposé une candidature complète en ligne et transmis les documents nécessaires dans les délais.	

Informations complémentaires :

Figure 5: Original *Horizon* webpage

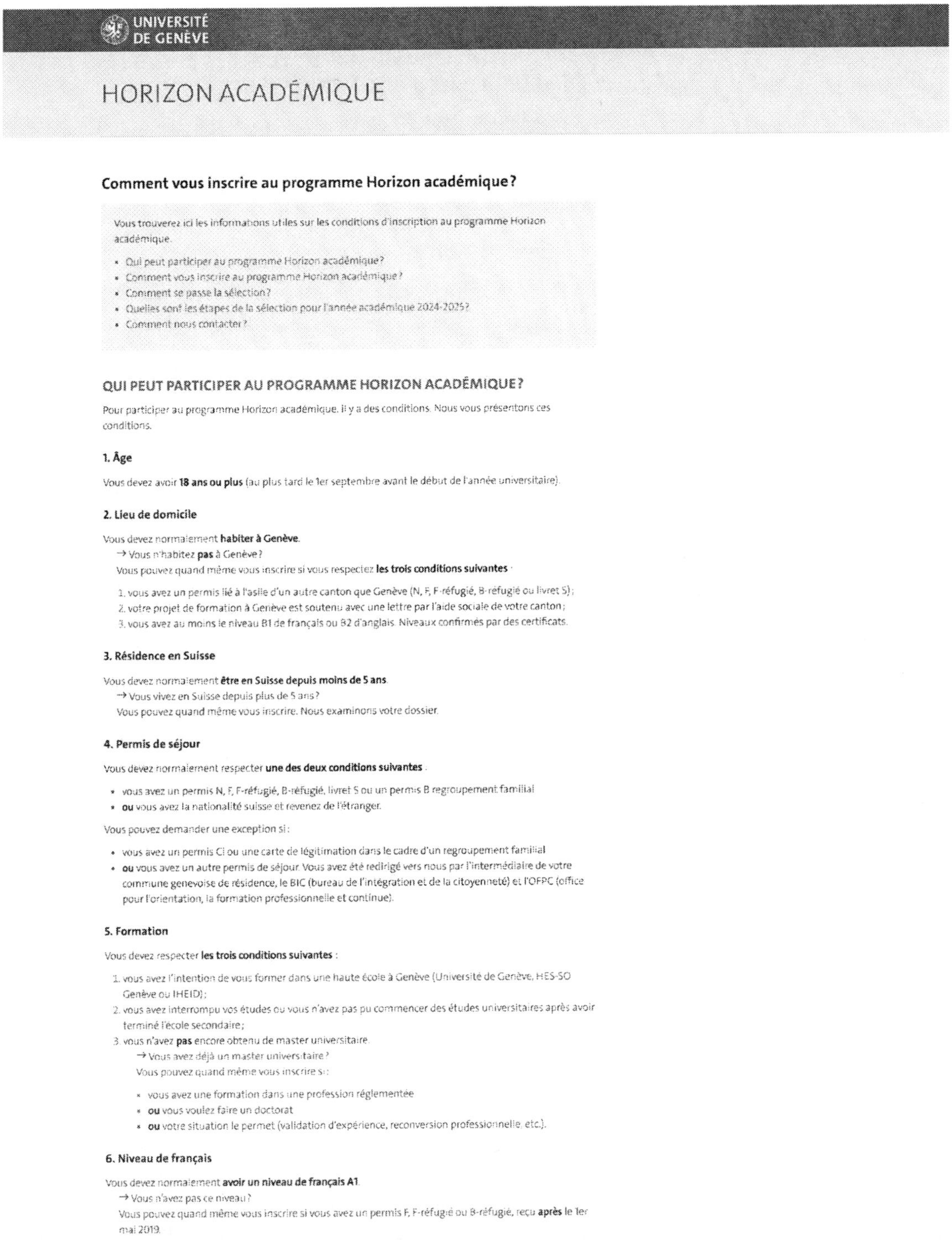

UNIVERSITÉ
DE GENÈVE

HORIZON ACADÉMIQUE

Comment vous inscrire au programme Horizon académique?

Vous trouverez ici les informations utiles sur les conditions d'inscription au programme Horizon académique.

- Qui peut participer au programme Horizon académique?
- Comment vous inscrire au programme Horizon académique?
- Comment se passe la sélection?
- Quelles sont les étapes de la sélection pour l'année académique 2024-2025?
- Comment nous contacter?

QUI PEUT PARTICIPER AU PROGRAMME HORIZON ACADÉMIQUE?

Pour participer au programme Horizon académique, il y a des conditions. Nous vous présentons ces conditions.

1. Âge

Vous devez avoir **18 ans ou plus** (au plus tard le 1er septembre avant le début de l'année universitaire).

2. Lieu de domicile

Vous devez normalement **habiter à Genève**.
→ Vous n'habitez **pas** à Genève?
Vous pouvez quand même vous inscrire si vous respectez **les trois conditions suivantes** :

1. vous avez un permis lié à l'asile d'un autre canton que Genève (N, F, F-réfugié, B-réfugié ou livret S);
2. votre projet de formation à Genève est soutenu avec une lettre par l'aide sociale de votre canton;
3. vous avez au moins le niveau B1 de français ou B2 d'anglais. Niveaux confirmés par des certificats.

3. Résidence en Suisse

Vous devez normalement **être en Suisse depuis moins de 5 ans**.
→ Vous vivez en Suisse depuis plus de 5 ans?
Vous pouvez quand même vous inscrire. Nous examinons votre dossier.

4. Permis de séjour

Vous devez normalement respecter **une des deux conditions suivantes** :

- vous avez un permis N, F, F-réfugié, B-réfugié, livret S ou un permis B regroupement familial
- **ou** vous avez la nationalité suisse et revenez de l'étranger.

Vous pouvez demander une exception si :

- vous avez un permis Ci ou une carte de légitimation dans le cadre d'un regroupement familial
- **ou** vous avez un autre permis de séjour. Vous avez été redirigé vers nous par l'intermédiaire de votre commune genevoise de résidence, le BIC (bureau de l'intégration et de la citoyenneté) et l'OFPC (office pour l'orientation, la formation professionnelle et continue).

5. Formation

Vous devez respecter **les trois conditions suivantes** :

1. vous avez l'intention de vous former dans une haute école à Genève (Université de Genève, HES-SO Genève ou IHEID);
2. vous avez interrompu vos études ou vous n'avez pas pu commencer des études universitaires après avoir terminé l'école secondaire;
3. vous n'avez **pas** encore obtenu de master universitaire.
   → Vous avez déjà un master universitaire?
   Vous pouvez quand même vous inscrire si :
   - vous avez une formation dans une profession réglementée
   - **ou** vous voulez faire un doctorat
   - **ou** votre situation le permet (validation d'expérience, reconversion professionnelle, etc.).

6. Niveau de français

Vous devez normalement **avoir un niveau de français A1**.
→ Vous n'avez pas ce niveau?
Vous pouvez quand même vous inscrire si vous avez un permis F, F-réfugié ou B-réfugié, reçu **après** le 1er mai 2019.

Figure 6: Manually simplified *Horizon* webpage

How Artificial Intelligence can help in the Easy-to-Read Adaptation of Numerical Expressions in Spanish

Mari Carmen Suárez-Figueroa and **Alejandro Muñoz-Navarro** and **Isam Diab**
Ontoloy Engineering Group (OEG)
Universidad Politécnica de Madrid
Madrid, Spain
mcsuarez@fi.upm.es, alejandro.mnavarro@upm.es, isam.diab@upm.es

Abstract

Numerical expressions, specifically the use of fractions and percentages in texts, may pose a difficulty in the reading comprehension process for different groups of the population, including persons with cognitive disabilities. As an element that facilitates reading comprehension, the Easy-to-Read (E2R) methodology, created to achieve the cognitive accessibility, recommends avoiding the use of fractions and percentages. If it is necessary to include them, their equivalence or explanation should be described. In order to help people who have difficulties in reading comprehension when they have to deal with fractions and percentages, we have developed an initial method for adapting numerical expressions in an automatic way in Spanish. This method is based on (a) Artificial Intelligence (AI) methods and techniques and (b) the E2R guidelines and recommendations. In addition, the method has been implemented as a web application. With the goal of having our research in the context of the responsible AI, we followed the human-centred design approach called participatory design. In this regard, we involved people with cognitive disabilities in order to (a) reinforce the adaptations provided by E2R experts and included in our method, and (b) evaluate our application to automatically adapt numerical expressions following an E2R approach. Moreover, this method can be integrated into institutional procedures, such as those of university administrations and public organisations, to enhance the accessibility of official documents and educational materials.

1 Introduction

Numerical expressions are defined as expressions that denote quantities, optionally accompanied by a numerical modifier, such as *more than a quarter* or *almost 97 %*, where *more than* and *almost* take the role of numerical modifiers (Bautista et al., 2017). Different groups of the population, including people with cognitive or intellectual disabilities, experience some difficulties regarding the reading comprehension process of such numerical expressions. For such a reason, the Easy-to-Read (E2R) methodology (Inclusion Europe, 2009; Nomura et al., 2010; AENOR, 2018) recommends avoiding the use of fractions and percentages in text materials. The goal of this methodology is to present clear and easily understood content by providing a collection of guidelines concerning both the content of texts and their design and layout. This methodology was created with the aim of improving the cognitive accessibility of those groups of the population who present reading comprehension difficulties.

When a particular document needs to be adapted to Easy-to-Read, the E2R methodology is applied in a manual fashion following three key activities: E2R analysis, E2R adaptation and E2R validation (AENOR, 2018). This manual process is labour-intensive and costly, and it would benefit from having technological support. In this context, our research is focused on applying different Artificial Intelligence (AI) methods and techniques[1] to (semi)-automatically perform both the analysis and the adaptation of documents to obtain easy-to-read versions of original documents. Furthermore, it should be mentioned that our general intention is to conduct research and develop applications in the context of the responsible AI (Akata et al., 2020). Specifically, we understand responsible AI as inclusiveness and explainability. In this paper, we present our approach for including people with cognitive disabilities in our research; while explainability is out of the scope of this paper.

In this paper, we present an initial proposal for

[1]We are investigating symbolic (such as knowledge representation) and subsymbolic (such as machine learning) approaches in AI as well as the combination of both.

Proceedings of the 1st Workshop on Artificial Intelligence and Easy and Plain Language in Institutional Contexts (AI & EL/PL), pages 14–24, June 23, 2025

adapting numerical expressions in an automatic way in texts written in Spanish, in particular expressions that contain fractions and percentages. This adaptation proposal follows the Easy-to-Read (E2R) methodology and is aligned with the preferences expressed by E2R experts in a previous study (Suárez-Figueroa et al., 2022), in which they identified the adaptation of numerical expressions as one of the guidelines they would like to see automated. Based on this feedback, we developed the support tool described in that study.

There are other studies that performed a quite similar process, which is the automatic simplification[2] of numerical expressions in various languages such as English (Bautista et al., 2011; Power and Williams, 2011), German (Suter et al., 2016) and Spanish (Bautista et al., 2013; Bautista and Saggion, 2014b,a; Bautista et al., 2017) using different methods and techniques that are explained in Section 2. Nevertheless, such attempts do not involve target groups with cognitive disabilities in the development of the system. Our approach therefore focusses on covering this gap by involving both E2R experts and people with cognitive disabilities in our work.

Additionally, our development is designed to be used in institutional contexts where accessibility is a priority. For example, the Language Centre[3] of the Universidad Politécnica de Madrid could integrate our system to enhance the accessibility of its learning materials, ensuring that numerical expressions do not become a barrier for students with cognitive disabilities or non-native speakers. Likewise, institutional bodies such as the Rectorate of the Universidad Politécnica de Madrid could leverage this system to adapt official documents, making them more accessible to all members of the university community, including faculty, staff, and students who may face difficulties with complex numerical representations. By applying our approach in such institutional environments, we aim to contribute to fostering inclusiveness and accessibility in academic and administrative communications.

The rest of the paper is organised as follows: Section 2 is devoted to the state-of-the-art on (a) the difficulties that numerical expressions raise regarding cognitive accessibility, and (b) the automatic approaches for identifying and adapting this type of structures in different languages. In Section 3 we present our proposal for performing an automatic E2R adaptation of fractions and percentages. Section 4 summarises the participatory design approach we followed to include people with cognitive disabilities in our AI-based development; this section also shows the results we obtained from this inclusive strategy. Section 5 describes our web application for automatically adapting numerical expressions and shows the results obtained in a preliminar user-based evaluation. Finally, we present some conclusions and future work.

2 State of the Art

Since our work focusses on developing an initial automatic adaptation of numerical expressions (specially fractions and percentages) in text written in Spanish following the E2R guidelines, in this section we address (a) the problematic these structures pose, and (b) the automatic approaches that have been developed to date for the identification and transformation of numerical expressions in different languages.

2.1 Numerical Expressions and Cognitive Accessibility

Disciplines such as experimental psychology and cognitive neuropsychology have dealt with the study of number processing and calculation over the last decades, since mathematical reasoning helps people develop, as it comes from a basic human need to communicate and describe things like quantities and measurements (Piaget and Inhelder, 1969). However, there are groups of people who present some difficulties when reading numerical expressions, i.e. expressions that denote quantities, optionally accompanied by a numerical modifier.

A specific difficulty that involves learning or understanding numeracy in general and numerical expressions in particular is dyscalculia, which includes difficulties in understanding numbers, manipulating, learning math facts, and a number of other symptoms related to counting money, understanding prices or remembering dates (Landerl et al., 2004; Butterworth, 2010). Such a difficulty (also referred to as a cognitive disability) affects the daily life of people with reading comprehension impairments, since everything around us contains numerical information (e.g. daily news or public information). Moreover, it has been evidenced in

[2]Text adaptation always aims to transform texts to meet the needs of a specific audience, while text simplification tends to reduce the complexity of texts and does not always take the final user into account (Saggion, 2022).

[3]https://www.lenguas.upm.es/

some studies (Rello et al., 2013) that the presence of numerical information in a text impacts negatively on its readability and understandability for people with dyslexia.

For these reasons, technological aids can greatly benefit the adaptation of numerical expressions into E2R versions to facilitate cognitive accessibility.

2.2 Automatic Approaches for Adapting Numerical Expressions

In the context of text simplification and E2R adaptation of texts, few works have addressed the automatic adaptation of numerical expressions in different languages. Power and Williams (Power and Williams, 2011) studied how authors present numerical information in English news articles, focusing on variations in mathematical forms (such as fractions and percentages) and in the level of precision used to express the same quantity. They developed a rule-based system to adapt original proportions and evaluated its effectiveness by comparing the model's predictions with the values suggested by survey participants.

Also in English, Bautista and colleagues (Bautista et al., 2011) studied preferences for rounding numerical expressions to common values, as well as different simplification strategies depending on the original proportion. The system they developed was designed specifically for English and was not intended for any particular group of readers. The authors conducted a survey in which experts in numeracy were asked to simplify a range of proportion expressions with three different readerships in mind. The responses were consistent with their intuitions about how common values are considered simpler and how the value of the original expression influences the chosen simplification.

With respect to languages other than English, in the system developed by Suter and colleagues (Suter et al., 2016) for adapting German texts, numbers written as words and special characters are replaced by digits and appropriate word substitutions using manually created dictionaries.

As regards Spanish (the language we are dealing with in our research), Bautista and colleagues have been working on different approaches (Bautista et al., 2013; Bautista and Saggion, 2014b,a; Bautista et al., 2017) to simplify numerical expressions using parallel corpora of original and manually simplified texts. The numerical simplification was implemented by a rule-based system that included a numerical simplification prototype and a syntactic simplification module to preserve simplicity and meaning.

However, none of the aforementioned efforts has been based on responsible AI, as they have not included groups of people with cognitive disabilities in the development of numerical expression simplification systems. Such a gap is indeed an open issue in the text simplification task literature, since such systems are designed without considering the user, which can lead to underestimating the reader's capabilities (Saggion, 2018). For this reason, in this paper we focus on the adaptation of numerical expressions in Spanish, including both E2R experts and people with cognitive disabilities in our research and development processes.

3 Initial Method for an E2R Adaptation of Fractions and Percentages

The final aim of the proposed method is (a) to detect fractions and percentages in texts written in standard Spanish, and (b) to replace such structures by the most appropriate paraphrasing formula with the goal of being E2R compliant. This method is based both on symbolic AI (e.g. production rules and syntactic patterns) [4] and subsymbolic AI (e.g. machine learning-based Natural Language Processing) methods and techniques (Norvig and Russell, 2021).

This initial method consists of the following high-level activities: (1) Natural Language Processing (NLP), which includes a cleanup of the text using regular expressions and a tokenization step, (2) Fractions and Percentages Identification, and (3) Fractions and Percentages Adaptation. Figure 1 shows the low-level steps of our initial method.

The first activity in our proposed method is text preprocessing. The original text is prepared by separating the paragraphs, looking for line breaks, replacing the words *por ciento* ('per cent') with the symbol %, and establishing a space between the number and the symbol[5] to facilitate the tokenization task (e.g. *10 %*). By the same token, double spaces are removed, spaces are included before and

[4] Using symbolic AI makes it relatively straightforward to provide explanations about what has happened and why. Since symbolic systems are based on explicit rules and representations, they allow for transparent reasoning processes. This means that each step taken by the system can be traced and understood, making it easier to explain both the outcomes and the underlying logic that led to them.

[5] Decision based on the rules for writing percentages presented by the Spanish linguistic foundation Fundéu (`https://www.fundeu.es/recomendacion/porcentajes-claves-de-redaccion/`).

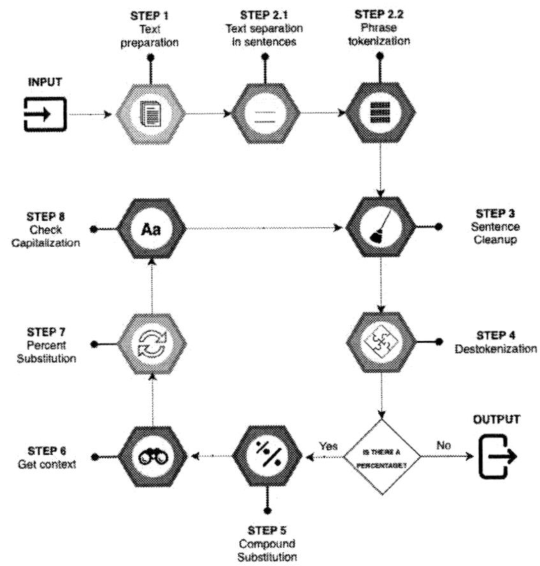

Figure 1: Method Workflow.

after hyphens (e.g. *Madrid-Málaga* to *Madrid - Málaga*) and contractions in Spanish are extended (*al* to *a el* and *del* to *de el*). Figure 1 shows this first activity in Steps 1, 2.1 and 2.2. In addition, a clean-up task is also performed to remove unusual symbols such as parentheses (Step 3 in Figure 1). We decided to use the solution proposed by Drndarevic and colleagues (Drndarevic et al., 2013), thus eliminating both the parentheses and their content; although we are aware of the risk of this action with respect to information loss.

On the other hand, since fractions and percentages are just different ways of showing the same value, we decided to replace fractions whose numerator is less than the denominator with a percentage (e.g. *1/2* is replaced by *50 %*). This action is performed in order to use only one single approach for both situations (fractions and percentages); that is, we generalise the way of treating those numerical structures. After the text preprocessing activity, the identification of fractions and percentages is simplified to detokenize the sentence and look for the symbol % (Step 4 in Figure 1).

The activity of adapting fractions and percentages is based on what is mentioned in the E2R methodology (García Muñoz, 2012; AENOR, 2018), that is, the most appropriate way to adapt fractions or percentages is to use paraphrasing words that preserve the same meaning as the numerical structure. In order to select the most suitable set of words we contacted E2R experts to discuss with them the best options without adding complexity to the text and keeping the original meaning. The result of the discussion with the experts is summarised in Table 1 and Table 2[6]. Such tables show that the percentages were organised by ranges and context, and for each percentage range a set of words is suggested. In addition, during this process, we identified two different structures in sentences with percentages: (a) simple structures, which contain just one percentage (e.g. *un 20 %*) (equivalent to 'just 20 %'); and compound structures, which contain a list of percentages (e.g. *Entre un 10 y un 20 %* ('Between 10 and 20 %'), *Subió desde un 20 a un 50 %* ('It went up from 20 to 50 %'). One way to reduce the complexity of the latter case is to remove the word *entre* or *desde* and replace the two numbers by the mean or the subtraction (e.g. *Un 15 %, Subió un 30 %*) (Step 5 in Figure 1). Once substitution is performed, the sentences present a simple structure that can be adapted as a simple percentage (Step 6 in Figure 1).

Table 1: Adaptation proposals (written in Spanish) organised by different established ranges.

Ranges (%)	**Adaptation Proposal**
0	No + nada / Ninguno / Ninguna
1–9	Muy poco / Muy poca / Muy pocos / Muy pocas
10–24	Un poco / Poca / Pocos / Pocas
25	La minoría
26–40	1 de cada 3
41–49	Casi la mitad
50	La mitad
51–74	Más de la mitad
75	La mayoría
76–90	Mucho / Mucha / Muchos / Muchas
91–99	Casi todo / Casi toda / Casi todos / Casi todas / Casi muy / Casi el total
100	Todo / Toda / Todos / Todas / Muy / El total
101–154	Más del total
155–254	El doble
255–354	El triple
+355	N veces el total

In the following subsections, we explain the details of the proposed E2R suggestions for adapting

[6]Adaptation proposals are written in Spanish. English versions of those proposals are available at: `https://zenodo.org/records/15213107`.

Table 2: Adaptation proposals (written in Spanish) organised by different established ranges for cases related to units of measurement (e.g. Kg, L, among others).

Ranges (%)	Adaptation Proposal
0	No + nada
1−24	Casi nada
25−49	Menos de la mitad de 1
50	La mitad de 1
51−74	Más de la mitad de 1
75−90	Casi 1
100	1

fractions and percentages in each of the ranges presented in Table 1 and Table 2.

3.1 General Proposal

This proposal is based on the ranges presented in Table 1 to adapt phrases regardless of their context.

Concerning the first case referred to the 0 % interval, it is worth mentioning that in Spanish, double negations occur, that is, a particular scheme of negation in which two negative elements appear (e.g. *no + nada* or *ninguno/ninguna*[7] *('no + nothing or none))*. Double negation does not change the negative meaning of the sentence, but is not always needed. If the verb takes precedence over the percentage, it is necessary to use the adverb *no* in preceding it; otherwise it is not necessary to be denied. In addition, in some cases we have observed that the sentence contained the word *con* ('with') referring to the percentage. In this case it is replaced by *sin* ('without'). To carry out this substitution there are two different paraphrasing suggestions: *nada* or *ninguno/a*. In cases where the percentage is followed by a word in the masculine gender (i.e. *de los*) we use *ninguno*, and for feminine cases (i.e. *de las*) we use *ninguna*. In any other case, we use the word *nada* ('nothing').

For the intervals 1-9 %, 10-24 %, and 76-90 %, our adaptation follows a similar method to the previous scenario. Typically, based on the specific range, we use terms such as *muy poco/muy poca/muy pocos/muy pocas* ('somewhat') for the interval 1-9 %; *un poco/poca/pocos/pocas* ('a little'/'few'), for the interval 10-24 %; and *mucho/mucha/muchos/muchas* ('many') for the interval 76-90 % in the paraphrased adaptations. When the percentage is followed by the preposition *de* ('of'), we examine the subsequent token. If this token is one of *el/la/los/las* ('the'), the percentage is directly substituted by a word matching its number and gender (e.g. *Un 10 % de los libros* ('10 % of the books') to *Pocos de los libros* ('Few of the books'). Otherwise, we use a natural language processor to determine the token's number and gender, and then perform the appropriate percentage substitution. Furthermore, we omit the preposition *de* when the word that follows is not a determiner (e.g. *Un 10 % de estudiantes* ('10 % of the students') to *Pocos estudiantes* ('Few students')), with the exception of masculine singular terms (e.g. *Un 10 % de azúcar* ('10 % of sugar') to *Un poco de azúcar* ('A bit of sugar')). Additionally, when we use the terms *un poca/pocos/pocas* in the substitution, if a preposition precedes the percentage, we replace *poca* by *poco* and introduce a determiner (*un/unos/unas* ('a/an/some/a little/a few')) agreeing in gender and number with the rest of elements of the sentence. For instance, *Con un 10 % de sal* ('With 10 % of salt') is adapted as *Con un poco de sal* ('With a little salt').

As for the ranges from 25 % to 75 % we replace the percentage by the adaptation proposal shown in Table 1. However, in those cases where our new paraphrasing words contain *casi* ('almost') or *más de* ('more than'), we ignore these same words from our original sentence in order not to repeat them (e.g. *Casi un 49 % de los participantes* ('Almost 49 % of the participants') to *Casi la mitad de los participantes* ('Almost half of the participants')).

Additionally, for the range from 26 % to 40 %, we also change the noun to its plural form and the adjectives and verbs referring to the percentage to its singular form (e.g. *El 25 % de los alumnos ha aprobado el examen* ('25 % of the students passed the exam') to *La minoría de los estudiantes ha aprobado el examen* ('The minority of students has passed')). For the rest of the cases, we only replace the adjectives and verbs with their singular feminine form (e.g. *Un 50 % de los estudiantes han sido muy estudiosos* ('50 % of the students have been very studious') to *La mitad de los estudiantes ha sido muy estudiosa* ('Half of the students have been very studious')).

For the 91-100 % range, the procedure remains consistent with the previous intervals. By default, we opt for *casi todo* ('most of it') or *todo* ('all'), depending on the exact percentage. However, if the percentage is succeeded by the preposition *de*, we employ the Part of Speech (PoS) tags provided by spaCy of the subsequent words, simi-

[7]Note that in Spanish we use the slash symbol (/) to indicate gender and number variations of the same word.

lar to the approach for other ranges (e.g. *casi todo/a/os/as* or *todo/a/os/as*). If there is no determiner (*el/la/los/las*) after the preposition (*de*), we add the determiner that agrees in gender and number with the rest of the elements of the sentence (e.g. From *Un 95 % de estudiantes* ('95 % of students') to *Casi todos los estudiantes* ('Almost all students')). Furthermore, if a preposition other than *de* follows the percentage, we revert to the default method (e.g. *Un 95 % en agosto* ('95 % in August') to *Casi todo en agosto* ('Almost all in August')). In the presence of an adjective succeeding the percentage, the structures *casi muy* ('almost totally') or *muy* ('very') replace the percentage (e.g. *Un 95 % rebajado* ('95 % reduced') to *Casi muy rebajado* ('Almost totally discounted')). When a verb precedes the percentage and a punctuation mark follows, we use *casi el total* ('almost the total') or *el total* ('the total') (e.g. *Subió un 95 %* ('It went up by 95 %') to *Subió casi el total* ('It went up almost the total')); otherwise, we use *casi muy* or *muy*. In all other scenarios, the default approach is applied.

For percentages exceeding 100 %, we implement a rounding strategy. If the value is close to 100, we substitute it with *más del total* ('more than the total'). If it approaches 200, we opt for *el doble* ('double'); and for values nearing 300, *el triple* ('triple") is used. For all other cases, the percentage is replaced by the structure *N veces el total* ('N times the total'), where N represents the nearest rounded number divided by 100.

To conclude, it could be possible that we added new words at the beginning of the adapted sentences, and because of these changes, we have to check the capital letters of our text (Step 8 in Figure 1).

3.2 Specific Proposal for Percentages with Units of Measurement

In instances where the percentage is 0 %, we follow the *nada* ('nothing') word adaptation using the double negative *no* + *nada* when a verb precedes the preposition. Additionally, we omit the preposition and the unit of measure (i.e. Kg, L, etc.), as in *El paquete pesa un 0 % de kilo* ('The package weighs 0 % of a kilo'), adapted as *El paquete no pesa nada* ('The package weighs nothing').

For percentages within the range of 1 to 24 %, we use *casi nada* ('almost nothing'), also eliminating the preposition and the unit. For example, *El paquete pesa un 5 % de kilo* ('The package weighs 5 % of a kilo') is adapted as *El paquete pesa casi nada* ('The package weighs almost nothing').

As for the range 25-49 % we use the structure *menos de la mitad de 1* ('less than half of 1'), also removing the preposition before the unit of measurement, if present, and transforming the unit of measurement to singular, e.g. *El paquete pesa 1/4 de kilo* ('The package weighs 1/4 kilo'), is adapted as *El paquete pesa menos de la mitad de 1 kilo* ('The package weighs less than half of 1 kilo').

In the case of 50 % we use *la mitad de 1*, following the same method as above. For instance, *El paquete pesa 1/2 kilo* ('The package weighs 1/2 kilo') is adapted as *El paquete pesa la mitad de 1 kilo* ('The package weighs half of 1 kilo').

For the percentages within the range from 51 to 74 %, we use *más de la mitad de 1* ('more than half of 1'), following the same algorithm as in the previous cases, as we observe in *Usamos 60 % litros de agua* ('We use 60 % litres of water'), adapted as *Usamos más de la mitad de 1 litro de agua* ('We use more than half of 1 litre of water').

With respect to the percentages within 75-99 %, we use *casi 1* ('almost 1') following the same algorithm as in the previous cases. For example, *Usamos 3/4 litros de agua* ('We use 3/4 litres of water') is adapted as *Usamos casi 1 litro de agua* ('We used almost 1 litre of water').

Finally, in instances where the percentages are exactly 100 %, we use *1*, considering the same algorithm as in the previous cases. As an illustration, *Usamos 100 % litros de agua* ('We use 100 % litres of water') is adapted as *Usamos 1 litro de agua* ('We use 1 litre of water').

4 Inclusive AI: Involving People with Cognitive Disabilities

As mentioned in Section 1, our intention is to develop applications in the context of the responsible AI. In this paper we focus on the inclusiveness dimension by means of involving people with cognitive disabilities in the development team. Specifically, their involvement was performed through a human-centred design (Trewin et al., 2019). There are three potential approaches for integrating people with cognitive disabilities in the development processes (Trewin et al., 2019): Inclusive Design, Participatory Design, and Value-Sensitive Design. In our research we would like to design for and with people with cognitive disabilities, so we decided to use the inclusive design approach. As a first attempt, we used a survey method that allows us to gather feedback about which different ways to express fractions and percentages are closer to E2R structures.

In order to reinforce the collection of linguistic structures for adapting fractions and percentages given by the E2R experts (see Section 3), we decided to use a participatory design approach for gathering feedback about the easier way to express the aforementioned numerical structures from people with cognitive disabilities. For this purpose we conducted a 20-minutes on-line anonymous survey[8]. In this survey[9] we requested (a) opinions of people with cognitive impairments on the use of different ways to express fractions and percentages and (b) several demographic data. We recruited participants by emailing autonomic federations and associations of people with cognitive disabilities in Spain in February 2022.

After analysing the survey responses[10], findings indicate that, overall, participants consider simpler those sentences in which the typical ways of expressing percentages have been adapted, with an E2R approach in mind, by using synonym formulas. In fact, these data confirm the different options proposed by E2R experts (see Table 1).

In more specific detail, data reveal that participants' preferences can be classified into the following scenarios considering the adaptation proposals for each range posed in Table 1:

Scenario A. In this scenario, sentences in which the range of the numerical expression (both percentages and fractions) is between 1 and 49 are considered. In this case, the synonymous adapted option *un(os) poco(s)* ('(a) few') is the most chosen option among the participants in opposition to the most typical ways to represent numerical structures whose meaning is a percentage or a fraction (that is, *30%*, *twenty-five percent*, and *one fifth*).

Scenario B. Likewise, in this scenario sentences in which the numerical expression ranges from 51 to 100 are treated. As a result, participants preferred the adapted version *más de la mitad* ('more than a half') against the rest of non-adapted options (e.g. *60%*, *seventy-five percent*, and *three quarters*).

Scenario C. Finally, this scenario addresses numerical expressions relating to the middle range. Participants similarly chose the synonymous adapted formulas *mitad* and *medio/a* (both have the meaning of 'half').

5 Web Application for Adapting Numerical Expressions

As a proof of concept, we have developed a web application to detect fractions and percentages in texts written in Spanish, and adapt them following the most appropriate E2R translation guidelines. This application is based on the E2R method described in Section 3 and on the feedback gathered about the easier way to express numerical expressions described in Section 4. This application requires a sentence written in Spanish as an input and provides a simpler version of the original sentence as an output. Our application was designed with two options for text input: (a) manual writing or (b) file upload. Furthermore, following the E2R methodology, we adapted the interface of our web application: we limited the number of characters per line (60 characters) and we aligned the text to the left; we used a font size of 14 points or higher, with a line spacing of 1.5 greater than the default; we used font in black with a white background for easy reading; and the different navigation buttons have a yellow background and dark blue lettering to draw the user's attention away from the other elements on the same page. Figure 2 shows a screenshot of the web application in which an example of a text, written in Spanish, with six sentences containing fractions or percentages, is used as input text and the easy-to-read version is the output text.

Our web application has been implemented in Python 3.10, using the Django framework (version 4.0.1). We used the NLTK library[11] for phrase-level tokenization and the spaCy library[12] for word-level tokenization. It is worth mentioning that in Spanish, since words have different forms depending on gender and number, we used spaCy PoS tags to replace the percentage to preserve the consistency of the whole sentence.

Regarding the evaluation carried out with the application, it is worth mentioning that the functional evaluation (Section 5.1) focusses on testing the functionalities and an initial user-based evaluation (Section 5.2) centres on knowing whether the

[8]The questionnaire is implemented as a Google Form and it is available at: https://zenodo.org/records/15213107

[9]Survey design and demographic information about participants are available at: https://zenodo.org/records/15213107.

[10]Responses are available at: https://zenodo.org/records/15213107.

[11]https://www.nltk.org/

[12]https://spacy.io/

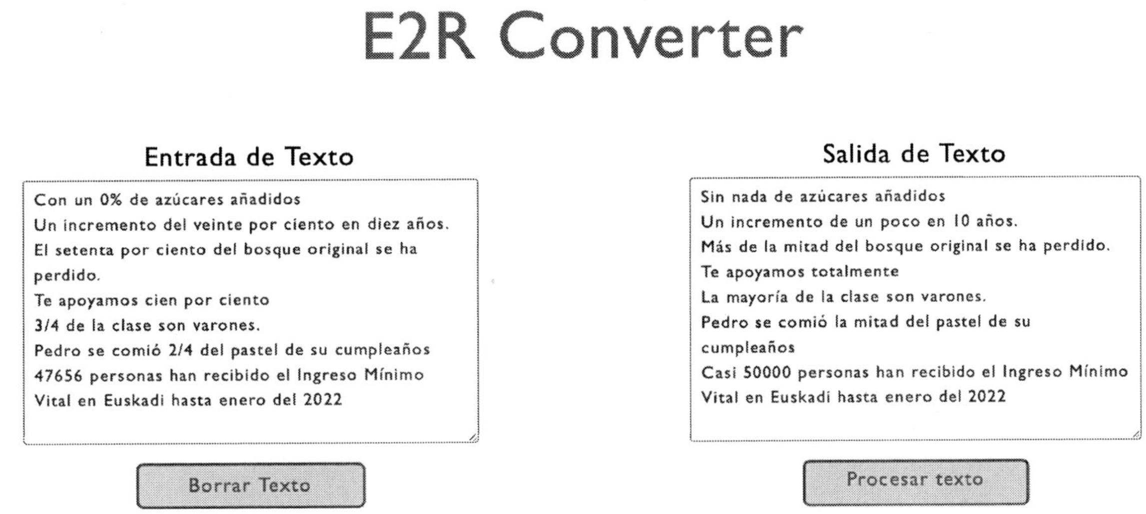

Figure 2: Screenshot of the proof of concept.

E2R adaptations provided by our application are comprehensible for people with cognitive disabilities.

5.1 Functional Evaluation

We tested the identification and adaptation functionalities of our proof of concept with a collection of 360 texts written in Spanish[13]: 180 sentences extracted from a Spanish corpus[14] by searching for the word sequences *por ciento* ('per cent'), *dos quintos* ('two fifths') or *un tercio* ('one third'), and 180 phrases that are quotes attributed to famous people such as Albert Einstein or Leonardo da Vinci among many others, which do not need any substitution. The results have been manually classified into true positives (TP) or true negatives (TN) based on accurate identification and, in the case of TP, on accurate adaptation. In contrast, they were labelled false negatives (FN) if the adaptation was incorrect or false positives (FP) if the adaptation was unwarranted and the original sentence was altered. To measure the effectiveness of our web application, we have tracked two of the metrics used to evaluate classification systems. On the one hand, the so-called sensitivity, which in our context represents the probability of correctly identifying a sentence that needs to be adapted. On the other hand, the metric of specificity, which represents the probability of correctly identifying a sentence that does not need adaptation. Currently, our application has a sensitivity of 91.81% compared to a specificity of 95.23 %. Thus, we could say that it is more specific than sensitive. This is the situation that we are aiming for, as our goal is to avoid false positives.

5.2 Preliminary User-Based Evaluation

This evaluation was carried out using an on-line questionnaire. The questionnaire[15] was divided into two main parts: (1) one part with questions related to participants' demographics, background and experience in E2R validation; and (2) the other part that includes 15 single-answer multiple choice questions to capture participants' opinions about how easy is the adaptation provided by our web application. The format of these 15 questions is always the same. Each question has 2 sentences (one is an original sentence and the other one is the sentence adapted by our service). After reading with calm each question, participants should choose one option among the following ones: (a) Sentence 1 is the one you understand best; (b) Sentence 2 is the one you understand best; (c) I understand both sentences well; and (d) I do not understand either of the two sentences. The questionnaire was validated by an E2R expert.

21 participants responded to the questionnaire, 11 males and 10 females, all from Madrid. 5 of them had a high level of reading comprehension, 13 a medium level, 1 a medium-high level and 2 a low level[16]. Their distribution by age is 4, 12 and 5

[13]The collection of texts is available at: https://zenodo.org/records/15213107.

[14]https://www.wordandphrase.info/span/

[15]The questionnaire is implemented as a Google Form and it is available at: https://zenodo.org/records/15213107.

[16]This information was provided by the support professionals of the organisations.

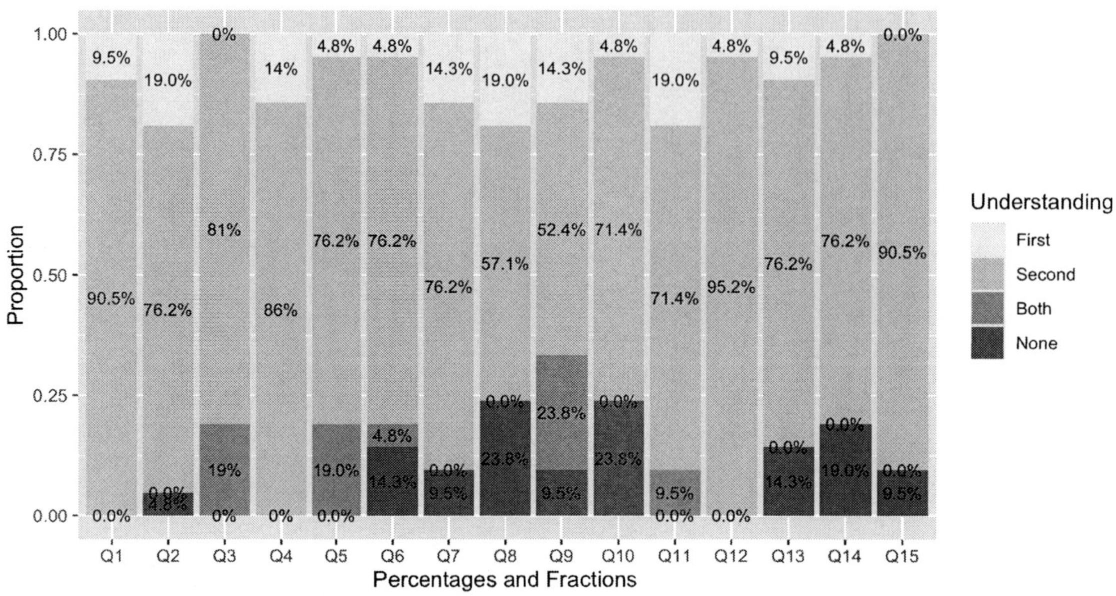

Figure 3: Summary of percentages in the user-based evaluation.

participants in the ranges 18-30, 31-45 and 46-60 respectively. Regarding the impairments, 17 had an intellectual disability, two people had intellectual plus physical disability, one other had intellectual plus mental disability and the last one declared to have a rare disease. As for their occupation, 10 were E2R validators, 7 were users of occupational centres, and the remaining were two retired people, a kit man, and an unemployed.

Figure 3 shows the percentages of responses for each available option and question when assessing the usefulness of the wording our web application gives with respect to percentages and fractions in the text. *First* refers to the original sentence and *Second* refers to the adaptation made by our application. *Both* indicates the participant understands well both sentences and *None* is chosen by a participant who understands neither of them. Through the 15 questions, the proportion of times the second sentence was chosen as the preferred option by the participants is overwhelming. Although there were different levels of understanding throughout the questions, even for the most difficult ones (the ones showing non-zero percentages in the option *None*) the simplification made by our application outnumbers the rest.

6 Conclusions and Future Work

This paper presents an initial method, based on AI, for detecting fractions and percentages in texts written in Spanish, and adapting such numerical structures into easy-to-read versions. A crucial task in the development of this method has been the selection of the most appropriate E2R paraphrasing formulas for such numerical structures. To perform this task we follow a mixed approach: on the one hand, we contacted E2R experts in order to discuss with them the most appropriate adaptation of fractions and percentages; on the other hand, we complement the proposals obtained by the experts with feedback gathered from people with cognitive disabilities. Feedback has been obtained by applying an inclusive design approach. The involvement of people with cognitive disabilities was materialised by participating in one on-line survey. In such a survey, participants were asked about their preferences with respect to the simplicity of parapharsing formulas to express fractions and percentages. Data gathered in this survey reinforced the set of synonym formulas used in our method for adapting fractions and percentages to an E2R version.

This straightforward declarative method has been implemented in a simple-to-use web application; in which the design of the user interface has been developed based on the E2R methodology. Elements such as the number of characters per line, text alignment, font size, line spacing, and colour contrast, among others, have been taken into account. This web application has initially been evaluated by people with cognitive disabilities. This user-based evaluation has been performed using online questionnaires. This is a first approximation to a deeper evaluation of the web application, since the sample size was not large, but prospects are optimistic. Thus, currently, we could say that adaptations provided by our application seem to be easier than original texts including fractions and percentages written in a standard way.

In addition to its relevance for individual users, our proposal may also be of great value in institutional environments where accessibility is a fundamental requirement. University administrations, government agencies and public institutions frequently produce documents that include numerical expressions, which can pose comprehension problems for some readers. By integrating this method into institutional procedures, organisations such as the Rectorate of the Universidad Politécnica de Madrid or the Language Centre could ensure that official communications, policies and teaching materials are more accessible.

As further research, we are going to analyse in more depth the data gathered in our inclusive co-design process for selecting the most appropriate E2R adaptations for fractions and percentages. In addition, we have planned to design an evaluation activity involving both E2R experts and people with cognitive disabilities. Our plan here is to have a larger sample size of participants. Finally, we would like to explore different ways to explain both the process and the outcomes in our method and application. In this regard, our aim is to cover the explainability dimension in the context of responsible AI.

Acknowledgments

This research has been carried out in the context of the project "Artificial Intelligence for Easy Reading - Cognitive Accessibility (AI&LF)" (Reference: APOYO-JOVENES-21-8AV1UF-119-OEUU22). This research Project has been funded by the Comunidad de Madrid through the call Research Grants for Young Investigators from Universidad Politécnica de Madrid. In addition, the research presented in this paper has been partially financed by Asociación Inserta Innovación (part of Grupo Social Once) through Prosvasi Ciencia y Tecnología Para La Inclusión, A.I.E., within the project ACCESSJOBS. We would like to thank Plena Inclusión España for its help in organising the participatory design involving people with cognitive disabilities, as well as the Federations of Organisations of People with Intellectual or Developmental Disabilities in Madrid, Comunidad Valenciana, and Andalucía for their participation in the study. We would like to thank Isa Cano and María José Sánchez for their help in organising the user-based evaluation of our web application. In addition, we really appreciate the collaboration provided by (a) ACCEDES (Entornos y Servicios Accesibles SL.) and its cognitive accessibility validation team, made up of people with intellectual disabilities, from the "Así Mejor" Program of workshops and activities of the Tres Cantos City Council (Madrid) and (b) the users of the CO-FOIL "cuarentainueve" of the Association Somos Diferencia (AMP). Finally, we would like to express thanks to Arminda Moreno for her help in the analysis of the data gathered in the user-based evaluation.

References

AENOR. 2018. *Easy-to-Read. Guidelines and recommendations for the production of documents (UNE 153101:2018 EX).* Asociación Española de Normalización.

Zeynep Akata, Dan Balliet, Maarten Rijke, Frank Dignum, Virginia Dignum, Guszti Eiben, Antske Fokkens, Davide Grossi, Koen Hindriks, Holger Hoos, Hayley Hung, Catholijn Jonker, Christof Monz, Mark Neerincx, Frans Oliehoek, Henry Prakken, Stefan Schlobach, Linda Gaag, Frank Harmelen, and Max Welling. 2020. A research agenda for hybrid intelligence: Augmenting human intellect with collaborative, adaptive, responsible, and explainable artificial intelligence. *Computer*, 53:18–28.

Susana Bautista, Raquel Hervás, Pablo Gervás, and Javier Rojo. 2017. An approach to treat numerical information in the text simplification process. *Universal Access in Information Society*, 16(1):85–102.

Susana Bautista, Raquel Hervás, Pablo Gervás, Richard Power, and Sandra Williams. 2011. How to make numerical information accessible: Experimental identification of simplification strategies. In *INTERACT 2011. Lecture Notes in Computer Science*, pages 57–64.

Susana Bautista, Raquel Hervás, Pablo Gervás, Richard Power, and Sandra Williams. 2013. A system for the simplification of numerical expressions at different levels of understandability. In *Natural Language Processing for Improving Textual Accessibility (NLP4ITA 2013)*, pages 10–19.

Susana Bautista and Horacio Saggion. 2014a. Can numerical expressions be simpler? implementation and demostration of a numerical simplification system for Spanish. In *Proceedings of the Ninth International*

Conference on Language Resources and Evaluation (LREC'14), pages 956–962, Reykjavik, Iceland. European Language Resources Association (ELRA).

Susana Bautista and Horacio Saggion. 2014b. Making numerical information more accessible: The implementation of a numerical expression simplification system for spanish. *ITL - International Journal of Applied Linguistics*, 165:299–323.

Brian Butterworth. 2010. Foundational numerical capacities and the origins of dyscalculia. *Trends in Cognitive Sciences*, 14(12):534–541. Special Issue: Space, Time and Number.

Biljana Drndarevic, Sanja Štajner, Stefan Bott, Susana Smith Bautista, and Horacio Saggion. 2013. Automatic text simplification in spanish: A comparative evaluation of complementing modules. In *Conference on Intelligent Text Processing and Computational Linguistics*, pages 488–500.

Óscar García Muñoz. 2012. *Lectura fácil: Métodos de redacción y evaluación.* Real Patronato sobre Discapacidad.

Inclusion Europe. 2009. *Information for All. European standards for making information easy to read and understand.* Inclusion Europe.

Karin Landerl, Anna Bevan, and Brian Butterworth. 2004. Developmental dyscalculia and basic numerical capacities: A study of 8-9-year-old students. *Cognition*, 93(2):99–125.

M. Nomura, G. S. Nielsen, International Federation of Library Associations and Institutions, and Library Services to People with Special Needs Section. 2010. *Guidelines for easy-to-read materials.* IFLA Headquarters, The Hague.

Peter Norvig and Stuart J. Russell. 2021. *Artificial Intelligence: A modern approach (4th Edition).* Pearson Global Editions.

Jean Piaget and Barbel Inhelder. 1969. *Psicología del niño.* Ediciones Morata S.L.

Richard Power and Sandra Williams. 2011. Generating Numerical Approximations. *Computational Linguistics*, 38(1):113–134.

Luz Rello, Susana Bautista, Ricardo Baeza-Yates, Pablo Gervás, Raquel Hervás, and Horacio Saggion. 2013. One half or 50%? an eye-tracking study of number representation readability. In *IFIP Conference on Human-Computer Interaction*, volume 8120, pages 229–245.

Horacio Saggion. 2018. Text Simplification. In *The Oxford Handbook of Computational Linguistics.* Oxford University Press.

Horacio Saggion. 2022. 1114text simplification. In *The Oxford Handbook of Computational Linguistics.* Oxford University Press.

Julia Suter, Sarah Ebling, and Martin Volk. 2016. Rule-based automatic text simplification for german. In *Proceedings of the 13th Conference on Natural Language Processing (KONVENS 2016)*, pages 279–287.

Mari Carmen Suárez-Figueroa, Isam Diab, Edna Ruckhaus, and Isabel Cano. 2022. First steps in the development of a support application for easy-to-read adaptation. *Universal Access in the Information Society*, 23(1):365–377.

Shari Trewin, Sara Basson, Michael Muller, Stacy Branham, Jutta Treviranus, Daniel Gruen, Daniel Hebert, Natalia Lyckowski, and Erich Manser. 2019. Considerations for ai fairness for people with disabilities. *AI Matters*, 5(3):40–63.

Large Language Models Applied to *Controlled Natural Languages* in Communicating Diabetes Therapies

Federica Vezzani*, Sara Vecchiato, Elena Frattolin*****
* Centro studi in Terminologia Computazionale, DISLL, U. of Padua, Italy
** Laboratorio di redattologia e traduttologia, DILL, U. of Udine, Italy
*** DPIA, U. of Udine, Italy
federica.vezzani@unipd.it ; sara.vecchiato@uniud.it ; elena.frattolin@uniud.it

Abstract

The aim of this exploratory study is to test the possibility of enhancing the quality of institutional communication related to diabetes self-treatment by switching from manual to prompt-based writing. The study proposes an investigation into the use of prompts applied to controlled natural language, particularly in Italian, French and English. Starting from a corpus of three comparable texts concerning the so-called *Rule of 15*, a reformulation is undertaken in accordance with the principles of controlled natural languages. Feedback will be gathered through a Likert scale questionnaire and a comprehension test administered to anonymous volunteers.

1 Introduction

This study lies at the crossroads of Terminology and Writing Studies, as fields aimed at delivering clear and accessible information (Cleary 2021; Schubert 2012; Giles 1990; Clerc 2022). It focuses on controlled natural languages, or CNLs (Ryan 2009) as an alternative to plain language for communicating very specialised content that requires terminological precision, such as instructions for administering drugs. Examples of CNLs include Simplified Technical English (STE), Italiano Tecnico Semplificato (ITS), and Français rationalisé (FR) (ASD 2021; COM&TEC 2024; GIFAS 1998). This research has two closely related objectives. First, it evaluates the applicability of CNLs in the medical field, with a focus on texts related to diabetes management. Second, it investigates the effectiveness of using Large Language Models (LLMs) for automatic text simplification through CNL-based prompts. In doing so, the study also compares the quality of automated simplifications with those produced by human editors, assessing their respective strengths and limitations. It also highlights the benefits of terminological standardization and proposes updates to the simplification rules and glossary of FR. For each language, we started with a single prompt with instructions, which was then followed by some adjustments. In particular, the instruction concerning the number of words per sentence had to be rechecked and corrected.

2 Research Context

2.1. Medical instructional texts

The study is set against the backdrop of Type 1 Diabetes (T1D) and the necessity of clear informational materials for self-management, particularly in cases of hypoglycaemia. In diabetes, hypoglycaemia presents immediate risks, such as seizures, unconsciousness, and coma, as well as long-term complications, including cardiovascular diseases and neuropathy (Cryer & Arbeláez 2017). Effective written communication is crucial to ensure that individuals with diabetes can understand and apply self-care guidelines correctly (Beck & al. 2017; Aprile 2007). A specific focus is placed on the *Rule of 15*, [1] a protocol for managing mild to moderate hypoglycaemia. Using a corpus of institutional texts from diabetology, this research aims to assess the applicability of the technical guidelines provided by STE, FR and ITS in prompt engineering.

2.1 Controlled Natural Languages vs Plain Language vs Easy Language

CNLs differ from plain and easy languages in a number of characteristics. As Kittredge (2003)

[1] https://www.pharmacists.ca/cpha-ca/assets/File/diabetes/Infographic_Hypoglycemia.pdf

Proceedings of the 1st Workshop on Artificial Intelligence and Easy and Plain Language in Institutional Contexts (AI & EL/PL), pages 25–29, June 23, 2025

pointed out, plain language is based on universal principles applicable to all languages, whereas CNLs are tailored to the specific morphological, syntactic, and lexical characteristics of each language. On the other hand, Vecchiato & al. (forth.), suggested describing CNLs by considering the lexical level separately from syntax in contrast to easy languages, which work with a basic vocabulary and morphosyntax. For this reason, CNLs lend themselves well to communication with an audience that is familiar with the disciplinary content in question.

2.2 FR vs STE vs ITS

FR differs from STE and ITS in its development. While STE and ITS are regularly updated by their respective organizations, FR has not seen the same progress. Introduced in the 1990s, the project was eventually abandoned in favour of English (Emorine 1995). Unlike STE and ITS, which are continuously refined, the French guidelines (FR) have not undergone significant updates since their original development. This lack of modernization affects FR across all domains, not just in the medical field. As a result, FR faces challenges in meeting contemporary readability standards and user needs. Nevertheless, the principles outlined in FR remain relevant, particularly in specialised domains where French is still used as a language of communication. One such domain is aeronautics, as discussed by Condamines (2018a; 2018b).

3 Method

3.1 Corpus selection

A reference corpus was established, consisting of three texts, each written in one of the three languages considered. The three texts selected for analysis provide essential information on hypoglycaemia and the *Rule of 15*. They were written by scientific societies or local and national associations of diabetes specialists, who guide patients in the self-management of the disease. Therefore, they share a similar communication framework, including the client (patient), writer, and reader (Clerc 2022). They are also characterised by a similar use of images, the presence of complementary information, the use of scientific terminology, and a more or less complex syntax. Furthermore, the texts belong to the so-called explanatory and procedural text types (Adam 2017), but depending on the texts, one type prevails over the other. The French and English text are translations of each other and show a slight discrepancy in word count, which can be linked to a more general tendency of the French language to use more words than English (Liberman 2022): in fact, the English documents has 488 words, the French text contains 558, and the Italian 316 words. An initial assessment of the text difficulty was obtained using software based on readability formulas. The French text has an overall difficulty rating of 2 out of 5 according to the AMesure test (François & al. 2018). The English text scored 53.49 ("fairly difficult") on the Flesch Reading Ease scale. The Italian text received a score of 47 on the Gulpease index, indicating that it may be challenging for readers with lower secondary education, but accessible for those with upper secondary education (Lucisano, & CORRIGE 2024).

3.2 Rewriting in CNL using prompt engineering

As it is well known, the guidelines of CNLs organise the text on several levels. Firstly, the content is required to be carefully planned, according to a logical sequence. In addition, it is required to use only terms selected from a pre-established glossary, and to use them in a redundant manner, i.e., avoiding the use of hypernyms or other elements that might create doubts about the referent. Finally, the syntax is extremely simplified, with the indication, for example, to express one concept per period, to always use affirmative sentences where possible, and to use only certain verb tenses and modes. A separate section deals with the use of punctuation, in particular exclamation marks and cautionary words (ASD 2021; COM&TEC 2024; GIFAS 1998).

The three original texts underwent reformulations to CNLs. An initial reformulation was conducted by humans using STE, ITS and FR guidelines; the resulting texts were then compared with the originals, highlighting differences in terminology, sentence structure, and readability (Vecchiato & al. forth.). A second reformulation was carried out on the same texts, this time using a large language model (chatGPT-4). In order to do this, prompts were written in alignment with the STE, ITS and FR guidelines. This second draft was compared with the original and the first reformulation in CNL.

3.3 Feedback

In order to evaluate the improvement of the effectiveness (Beaudet 2001) of reformulated texts, a comprehension questionnaire modelled on previous work on plain language is being developed (Vecchiato & al 2022). A first part of the questionnaire consists of questions aimed at finding out the respondents' attitudes towards the text (Joshi & al. 2015; Likert 1932). A second part of the questionnaire consists of a text comprehension test, with questions intended to test the effectiveness of the reformulation with regard to some particularly complex and difficult to understand/implement points of the *Rule of 15*. In particular, the comprehension of the terms indicating substances that can be used as well as the actions to be performed with these substances will be tested.

This aspect highlights the crucial balance between terminological precision and accessibility in medical texts (Vecchiato 2022). In line with Gabriele Pallotti's (2015: 118) approach, we identify three types of complexity: *structural complexity, cognitive complexity*, and *developmental complexity*. While technical accuracy ensures that health guidelines are correctly interpreted and applied, excessive structural complexity (i.e., specialised terms) can lead to excessive cognitive complexity, and hinder comprehension for non-specialist readers. CNLs provide a structured approach to addressing this challenge by enforcing controlled vocabularies and standardised sentence structures, allowing for greater clarity without compromising essential medical information.

For example, instead of *"Ingest 15 grams of a rapid-acting carbohydrate"*, a CNL-based reformulation could specify: *"Eat one tablespoon of sugar or drink half a glass of fruit juice."* Similarly, *"Administer an appropriate dose of glucagon"* might become: *"If unconscious, inject one dose of glucagon as instructed on the package."* These adjustments make critical information more applicable and easier to understand.

Indeed, the impact of such simplifications on medical comprehension is especially relevant in diabetes management, where clear and applicable instructions are vital. By comparing human and AI-assisted text reformulations, this study aims to evaluate whether CNL-based simplifications enhance understanding while preserving medical accuracy. The findings will contribute to refining CNL guidelines for healthcare communication, ensuring that essential information remains both precise and accessible.

The questionnaire will be submitted to three groups of anonymous volunteers who have been diagnosed with type 1 diabetes. The first group will respond on the original text, the second group on the text modified by a human, and the third group on the text modified via prompt. The respondents will be chosen from among people from different countries through cooperation with diabetes associations. The selected participants will be over 18 years of age. In an initial anonymous questionnaire, they will be asked some information that is considered predictive of a certain approach. In particular, they will be asked to specify how long ago they received their diagnosis, whether and how they regularly inform themselves about diabetes (e.g., from newspapers, social networks or through participation in an association, *see* Dietz & al. 2023), and to give indications about their level of literacy (Sikora & al. 2019).

4 Discussion

The use of CNLs in medical communication presents both advantages and risks. Particular attention is given to the benefits of text simplification, which may enhance comprehension for a broader audience, including individuals living with the disease. At the same time, potential risks associated with overgeneralisation of specialised information will be considered to ensure accurate and effective communication for all stakeholders. Simplification improves readability and accessibility, making vital health information comprehensible to a broader audience. However, excessive simplification can lead to loss of critical medical nuances, increasing the risk of misinterpretation. For this reason, the use of CNLs can be a reasonable compromise between syntactic simplification and terminological precision.

5 Conclusion and Perspectives

In this exploratory study, the question was raised as to the effectiveness of medical texts offered to people with diabetes for the self-management of hypoglycaemia. The three chosen texts (Italian,

French, and English) are representative of those used for patient education. These texts were reformulated according to the guidelines of CNLs, first by humans and then using prompt engineering. In order to evaluate the effectiveness of the two reformulations, a questionnaire will be submitted to three groups of anonymous volunteers.

The answers to the questionnaire will allow us to assess the extent to which CNLs can improve the communication of the *Rule of 15*, and whether there is a gap in effectiveness between manual and automated editing. Furthermore, the presence of three languages may provide additional data regarding this margin for improvement, due to the fact that these three languages do not have the same tradition of clear writing (Sabatini 2002; Meschonnic 1997; Schriver 2017; Cutts 2020). Finally, this survey also offers the advantage of proposing an update of FR, to bring it into line with the current medical lexicon.

Declaration on the use of Generative AI and Machine Translation

During the preparation of this work, the authors used X-GPT-4 in order to: Grammar and spelling check, formulation of examples in section 3.3. Part of this text was written in English, while part of it was written in Italian and translated into English with DeepL.com. After using these tools, the authors reviewed and edited the content as needed and take full responsibility for the publication's content.

References

Adam, J.-M. (2017). Les Textes : Types et prototypes (4e éd.). Paris : Armand Colin.

Aprile, V. & al. (2007). Risultati nazionali dello studio QUADRI (QUalità dell'Assistenza alle persone Diabetiche nelle Regioni Italiane). ISS. https://www.epicentro.iss.it/igea/pdf/istisan_quadri.pdf

ASD Security and Defence Industries Association of Europe. (2021). ASD-STE100 Simplified Technical English (STE) (EUROPEAN UNION Patent 017966390). https://www.asd-ste100.org/

Barthe, K., Juaneda, C., Leseigneur, D., Loquet, J.-C., Morin, C., Escande, J., & Vayrette, A. (1999). GIFAS Rationalized French: A Controlled Language for Aerospace Documentation in French. Technical Communication, 46(2), 220–229.

Beaudet, C. (2001). Clarté, lisibilité, intelligibilité des textes : Un état de la question et une proposition pédagogique. *Recherches En Rédaction Professionnelle*, *1*(1), 1–19.

Beck, J., Greenwood, D. A., Blanton, L., Bollinger, S. T., Butcher, M. K., Condon, J. E., Cypress, M., Faulkner, P., Fischl, A. H., Francis, T., Kolb, L. E., Lavin-Tompkins, J. M., MacLeod, J., Maryniuk, M., Mensing, C., Orzeck, E. A., Pope, D. D., Pulizzi, J. L., Reed, A. A., Wang, J. (2018). 2017 National Standards for Diabetes Self-Management Education and Support. *The Diabetes Educator*, *44*(1), 35–50. https://doi.org/10.1177/0145721718754797

Centre de traitement automatique du langage (CENTAL), & Service de la langue française. (2025). *Amesure*. AMESURE. https://cental.uclouvain.be/amesure/

Cleary, Y. (2021). The Profession and Practice of Technical Communication, London: Routledge. https://doi.org/10.4324/9781003095255

Clerc, I. (2022). Introduction. In I. Clerc (Éd.), Communication écrite État-citoyens. Défis numériques, perspectives rédactologiques, Québec : Les Presses de l'Université Laval, 5-18. https://www.pulaval.com/livres/communication-ecrite-etat-citoyens-defis-numeriques-perspectives-redactologiques

COM&TEC Associazione Italiana per la Comunicazione Tecnica (2024). Cos'è l'ITS?, https://www.italianotecnicosemplificato.it/cose-its/

Condamines, A. (2018a). Pour le développement d'une linguistique ergonomique : l'exemple des langues contrôlées. *Le travail humain*. 81(3), 205-226. https://doi.org/10.3917/th.813.0205.

Condamines, A. (2018b). La linguistique appliquée en entreprise : une linguistique ergonomique à l'intersection de la linguistique de corpus, de la psycholinguistique et de l'ergonomie. *Éla. Études de linguistique appliquée,* 190(2), 205-216. https://doi.org/10.3917/ela.190.0205.

Cryer, P. E., & Arbeláez, A. M. (2017). Hypoglycemia in Diabetes. In Textbook of Diabetes (pp. 513–533). John Wiley & Sons, Ltd. https://doi.org/10.1002/9781118924853.ch35.

Cutts, M. (2020). Oxford Guide to Plain English (Fifth Edition), Oxford: Oxford University Press.

Dietz, C. J., Sherrill, W. W., Ankomah, S., Rennert, L., Parisi, M., & Stancil, M. (2023). Impact of a Community-based Diabetes Self-management

Support Program on Adult Self-care Behaviors. *Health Education Research*, 38(1), 1–12. https://doi.org/10.1093/her/cyac034

Emorine, M. (1995). Lexique contrôlé : modélisation et implémentation, *Terminology. International Journal of Theoretical and Applied Issues in Specialized Communication*, 2.2: 293-323. https://doi.org/10.1075/term.2.2.07emo

Feng, L., Jansche, M., Huenerfauth, M., & Elhadad, N. (2010). A Comparison of Features for Automatic Readability Assessment. *Proceedings of the 23rd International Conference on Computational Linguistics*: Posters, 276–284.

François, T., Müller, A., Degryse, B., & Fairon, C. (2018). AMesure : Une plateforme web d'assistance à la rédaction simple de textes administratifs. *Repères DoRiF, 16, Littératie et intelligibilité*. https://www.dorif.it/reperes/thomas-francois-adeline-muller-baptiste-degryse-cedrick-fairon-amesure-une-plateforme-web-dassistance-a-la-redaction-simple-de-textes-administratifs/

GIFAS (1998). Guide du Français Rationalisé, Paris.

Giles, T. D. (1990). The Readability Controversy: A Technical Writing Review. *Journal of Technical Writing and Communication*, 20.2: 131-138. https://doi.org/10.2190/U4FF-0L5Q-FPD4-2DCJ

Joshi, A., Kale, S., Chandel, S., & Pal, D. (2015). Likert Scale: Explored and Explained. *British Journal of Applied Science & Technology*, 7(4), 396–403. https://doi.org/10.9734/BJAST/2015/14975

Kittredge, R. I. (2003). Sublanguages and Controlled Languages. In Ruslan Mitkov, (Ed.), The Oxford Handbook of Computational Linguistics, Oxford: Oxford University Press, 430–447. https://doi.org/10.1093/oxfordhb/9780199276349.013.0023

Kuhn, T. (2014). A Survey and Classification of Controlled Natural Languages. *Computational linguistics*, 40.1: 121-170. https://doi.org/10.1162/COLI_a_00168.

Liberman, M. (2022, May 28). Comparing phrase lengths in French and English. *Language Log*. https://languagelog.ldc.upenn.edu/nll/?p=54806

Likert R. (1932). A Technique for the Measurement of Attitudes. *Archives of Psychology*, 22, 5-55.

Lucisano, P. Piemontese, M.E. (1988). GULPEASE: una formula per la predizione della difficoltà dei testi in lingua italiana, Scuola e città, 3, 110-124. https://hdl.handle.net/11573/450554

Lucisano, P., & Corrige. (2024). L'indice Gulpease | pro.corrige.it. Retrieved 11 January 2024, from https://pro.corrige.it/ortografia/lindice-gulpease/

Meschonnic, H. (1997). De la langue française: Essai sur une clarté obscure, Paris: Hachette.

Pallotti, G. (2015). A Simple View of Linguistic Complexity. *Second Language Research*, 31(1), 117–134. https://doi.org/10.1177/0267658314536435

Ryan, R. (2009). Les langues contrôlées, une valeur ajoutée pour le traducteur. *Traduire*, 220, https://doi.org/10.4000/traduire/389.

Sabatini, F. (2003). L'italiano lingua utilitaria. In L. Schena & L. T. Soliman (Eds.), L'italiano lingua utilitaria. XI Incontro del Centro Linguistico Università Bocconi, 23 novembre 2002, Milan: EGEA, 17–22.

Schriver, K. A. (2017). Plain Language in the US Gains Momentum: 1940–2015. *IEEE Transactions on Professional Communication*, 60(4), 343–383. https://doi.org/10.1109/TPC.2017.2765118.

Schubert, K. (2012). Technical Communication and Translation. Communication on and Via Technology. Berlin/Boston: Mouton De Gruyter, 111-128. https://doi.org/10.1515/9783110260274.111

Security and Defence Industries Association of Europe (2021). ASD-STE100 Simplified Technical English (STE), EUROPEAN UNION Brevet 017966390, https://www.asd-ste100.org/

Sikora, J., Evans, M. D. R., & Kelley, J. (2019). Scholarly culture: How books in Adolescence Enhance Adult Literacy, Numeracy and Technology Skills in 31 Societies. *Social Science Research*, 77, 1-15. https://doi.org/10.1016/j.ssresearch.2018.10.003.

Vecchiato, S., Vezzani, F., Frattolin, E. (*forthcoming*). Revisiter le Français Rationalisé : enjeux terminologiques, *LTT 2024*.

Vecchiato, S. (2022). Clear, Easy, Plain, and Simple as Keywords for Text Simplification. *Frontiers in Artificial Intelligence*, 5. https://doi.org/10.3389/frai.2022.1042258.

Vecchiato, S., Gerolimich, S., & Casini, M. (2022). « Écrire sur les antibiotiques, c'est pas automatique ! » Enquête italien-français pour une modélisation de la médiation ergonomique dans l'éducation à la santé. In I. Clerc (Ed.), Communication écrite État-citoyens. Défis numériques, perspectives rédactologiques, Québec : Les Presses de l'Université Laval, 83-98. https://www.pulaval.com/livres/communication-ecrite-etat-citoyens-defis-numeriques-perspectives-redactologiques

Simplifying Lithuanian texts into Easy-to-Read language using large language models

Simona Kuoraitė
Vilnius University
Faculty of Mathematics and Informatics
Institute of Informatics
Vilnius, Lithuania
simona.kuoraite@mif.stud.vu.lt

dr. Valentas Gružauskas
Vilnius University
Faculty of Mathematics and Informatics
Institute of Informatics
Vilnius, Lithuania
valentas.gruzauskas@mif.vu.lt

Abstract

This paper explores the task of simplifying Lithuanian texts into Easy-to-Read language. Easy-to-Read is a form of language written in short, clear sentences and simple words, adapted for people with intellectual disabilities or limited language skills. The aim of this work is to investigate how the large language model Lt-Llama-2-7b-hf, pre-trained on Lithuanian language data, can be adapted to the task of simplifying Lithuanian texts into Easy-to-Read language. To achieve this goal, specialized datasets were developed to fine-tune the model, and experiments were carried out. The model was tested by comparing texts in their original language and texts with a prompt adapted to the task. The results were evaluated using the SARI metric for assessing the quality of simplified texts and a qualitative evaluation of the large language model. The results show that the fine-tuned model sometimes simplifies text better than a model that was not fine-tuned, but that a larger and more extensive dataset would be needed to achieve significant results, and that more research should be carried out on fine-tuning the model for this task.

1 Introduction

In recent years, there has been increasing attention on accessibility for all individuals. According to the World Health Organization, more than a billion people in the world, around 16% of the global population, have a disability (Glo, 2022). Among them, some individuals have cognitive disabilities, learning difficulties, or limited language proficiency, which makes accessing information challenging (Miesenberger and Petz, 2014). Easy to Read (ETR) language is a form of language designed to improve information accessibility by simplifying texts using short, clear sentences and simple words, adapting them for people who struggle with understanding standard texts. While ETR guidelines exist, the process of manually adapting texts remains time-consuming and resource-intensive. In Lithuania, ETR language has only recently gained recognition, and the availability of accessible content in the Lithuanian language remains limited. One of the main challenges is the lack of professionals or volunteer organizations capable of translating texts into ETR language. Without automated tools to assist in simplifying texts, the process is slow. The introduction of transformer-based architectures has significantly improved natural language processing (NLP) (Lauriola et al., 2022), enabling large language models (LLMs) like BERT (Devlin et al., 2019), GPT (Brown et al., 2020), T5 (Raffel et al., 2023) and others to generate text quicker and with higher quality (Vaswani et al., 2017). These advancements have also made it possible to adapt pre-trained models for specific tasks, such as simplifying texts to ETR. Transformers utilize a self-attention mechanism, which allows them to focus on relationships between different parts of a text sequence, understanding the importance of each word in the context. This makes them more effective than Recurrent Neural Networks (RNNs) (Karita et al., 2019). Until recently, NLP technologies for the Lithuanian language lagged behind, limiting progress in this field. However, the recent development of LLMs such as Lt-Llama-2 presents new opportunities for text simplification in Lithuanian (Nakvosas et al., 2024). This study explores how Lt-Llama-2 can be adapted for the text simplification task by fine-tuning the pre-trained Lt-Llama-2-7b-hf model for simplifying Lithuanian text into ETR.

Proceedings of the 1st Workshop on Artificial Intelligence and Easy and Plain Language in Institutional Contexts (AI & EL/PL), pages 30–37, June 23, 2025

2 Methodology

2.1 Datasets

Some Lithuanian texts are already being simplified into ETR by specialists. These texts can be found online, often as PDF files, with the original texts also being publicly available. These documents were used as the main source for fine-tuning and testing the model for the task of simplifying Lithuanian text.

For the experiments, we focused on ETR content of the 2nd level, which is the middle level of simplification, aimed at people with cognitive challenges (e.g. people with mild intellectual disabilities). These texts are also useful for people who are not native speakers of Lithuanian, but have already acquired a basic knowledge of the language. (Bružaitė-Liseckienė et al., 2021). The simplified texts were compared to the original counterparts, and datasets were created of simplified and original text pairs. While creating the dataset, the main challenge was ensuring that each record in the dataset had both the original and the corresponding simplified text, removing any texts where the simplified version added or omitted context compared to the original.

The final dataset consisted of 125 records, each containing at least one sentence. Overall, the original texts contained 2287 words, while the simplified texts contained 1974 words. The distribution of original and simplified texts, as well as their sources, is displayed in Table 1.

2.2 Text simplification

For the text simplification to ETR task, we chose the transformer based model Lt-Llama-2-7b-hf (Nakvosas et al., 2024), pre-trained on a large amount of Lithuanian data by Neurotechnology. This model was chosen because of the lack of strong LLMs pre-trained on the Lithuanian language. To evaluate whether fine-tuning the model would improve its ability to simplify texts, we conducted experiments with both the pre-trained model and the fine-tuned model. The results from both models were compared.

Additionally, we tested the effects of providing a prompt to both models during the text simplification task and compared those results as well. In the context of prompt engineering, several techniques were used to enhance the performance of the models. One common and effective method is "Think Step By Step" (Chain-of-Thought, CoT) (Kojima et al., 2023). This approach involves adding the phrase "think step by step" at the end of the prompt, guiding the model to break down complex tasks into more simple steps. Another widely used technique is "few-shot" prompting (Sivarajkumar et al., 2024). Using this technique, the provided prompt had a few examples of original and simplified texts so the model would understand the expected outcome better. In total, as shown in Table 2, 4 experiments were conducted.

2.3 Optimization algorithm

The Paged AdamW algorithm (Loshchilov and Hutter, 2019) was used for the optimization, adapted for 8-bit precision computing. This optimizer helped to significantly reduce memory usage and increase training efficiency, which was particularly important when working with a large language model and limited resources.

2.4 Learning Rate Configuration

For the model fine-tuning process, a learning rate of 3×10^{-5} was chosen to ensure a stable and balanced learning process. To further enhance adaptation, a warm-up phase was incorporated. During the first 30 steps, the learning rate was gradually increased from a very low value to the fixed value of 3×10^{-5}. This gradual increase helped prevent abrupt weight updates at the start of the training when the model was not yet sufficiently adapted to the text simplification task (Popel and Bojar, 2018).

Additional studies, such as (Smith et al., 2018), emphasize the importance of not only selecting an appropriate learning rate but also adjusting the batch size to ensure faster and more efficient model training. In line with these findings, we used a batch size of 8, expecting improved model performance and reduced fine-tuning time.

2.5 Evaluation of simplified texts

For the evaluation of simplified texts, 10% of the dataset was chosen. The texts were evaluated using both automatic metrics and by using an LLM as a judge. While LLM-based evaluation can provide a scalable alternative to human judgment (Gu et al., 2025), it may not always align with human perception and could exhibit biases or inconsistencies (Ferrer et al., 2021), in some cases, providing overly high or low scores. Therefore, incorporating human evaluation in future research would be advisable to ensure a more comprehensive understanding of the quality of the simplified texts.

Text source	Number of records	Number of words in the original text	Number of words in the simplified text
Annual report of the President of the Republic of Lithuania	31	1002	767
A guide to housekeeping and building a social circle	16	284	205
Ministry of Defence Guidelines on Emergency and Preparing for Wartime	61	766	758
A guide to the fight for women's rights	17	253	244

Table 1: Distribution of original and simplified texts in the dataset

Experiment No.	Experiment description
EXP1	Only pre-trained model
EXP2	Pre-trained model tested using prompt
EXP3	Fine-tuned model
EXP4	Fine-tuned model tested using prompt

Table 2: Experiments with the Lt-Llama-2-7b-hf model

2.5.1 Simplified text evaluation using SARI metric

To evaluate the quality of the simplified texts automatically, we used the System Output Against Reference Sentences for Text Simplification (SARI) metric (Xu et al., 2016). SARI is a widely used metric for evaluating simplified texts. It measures the quality of simplified text by assessing three key operations: addition, keeping, and deletion of words in the simplified sentence. The metric provides a mean score based on these operations.

$$\text{SARI} = d_1 F_{\text{add}} + d_2 F_{\text{keep}} + d_3 P_{\text{del}} \quad (1)$$

where

$$d_1 = d_2 = d_3 = \frac{1}{3} \quad (2)$$

$$P_{\text{operation}} = \frac{1}{k} \sum_{n=1}^{k} p_{\text{operation}}(n) \quad (3)$$

$$R_{\text{operation}} = \frac{1}{k} \sum_{n=1}^{k} r_{\text{operation}}(n) \quad (4)$$

$$F_{\text{operation}} = \frac{2 \times P_{\text{operation}} \times R_{\text{operation}}}{P_{\text{operation}} + R_{\text{operation}}} \quad (5)$$

operation $\in \{\text{del}, \text{keep}, \text{add}\}$ and k where k is the highest n-gram order.

2.5.2 Simplified text evaluation using LLM as a judge

To assess the quality of the simplified texts, we also used an LLM, specifically OpenAI's GPT-4o-mini. The model was asked to evaluate simplified texts using three criteria: clarity, context retention and simplicity. The simplified texts were assessed on a scale of 0 to 10 for each criterion, as well as an overall score. The evaluation was conducted in Google Colab by calling the API with a carefully crafted prompt, which included the original text, the professionally simplified text, and the model-generated simplified text from the experiments. The criteria for evaluation, specified in the prompt, were:

- Clarity: To assess how easily the text can be understood by people with intellectual disabilities or limited reading skills.
- Context: To assess whether the simplified text retains the meaning of the original text and whether important details have been lost.
- Simplicity: To assess whether the text is written in clear, short sentences and simple words.

3 Results

3.1 Fine-tuning Lt-Llama-2-7b-hf

Before conducting the experiments, we fine-tuned the pre-trained Lt-Llama-2-7b-hf model with 90% of the data from the created dataset. Figure 1 displays how Cross-Entropy Loss changes in the process of fine-tuning the model for both training and validation datasets which were split into 80% and 10% of the original dataset size respectively.

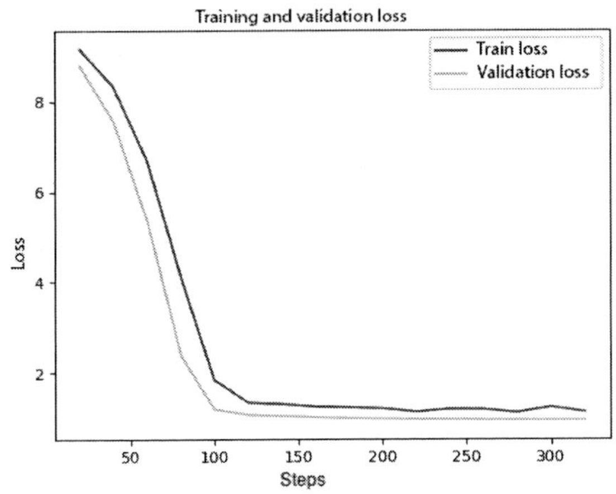

Figure 1: Variation of model learning loss for training and validation datasets over learning time

The X axis displays the number of iterations, which are computed as follows:

$$\text{Total training steps} = \frac{N}{B \times G} \times E \quad (6)$$

where:

- N is the number of examples in the dataset,
- B is the batch size,
- G is the gradient accumulation steps,
- E is the number of epochs.

While the Y axis displays the value of the loss. In the graph, we could observe that at the start of the fine-tuning process, the loss is high for both training and validation data. However, the loss decreases rapidly subsequently, indicating that the model quickly learns to discriminate between a large number of text features and then the learning process slows down. Although in the further iterations, the loss is decreasing very slowly, it decreases for both datasets equally, which lets us assume that even though the dataset is small, the model is not memorizing text features and overfitting.

3.2 Evaluation of simplified texts

After fine-tuning the model for the text simplification task, the model was given data from the test dataset to simplify. A preliminary analysis of the simplified texts for all 4 experiments shows that regardless of fine-tuning, the results were sometimes aleatory with completely unrelated texts like not-simplified, just paraphrased texts or rewriting the prompt. That could happen because of the small training dataset or the inability of the model to adapt for this specific task. On the other hand, in some of the generated texts, it was noticeable that sentences were a slightly shorter or some more simple words were used.

Experiment No.	SARI result mean
EXP1	52.063
EXP2	44.233
EXP3	52.435
EXP4	55.648

Table 3: The mean of SARI results for test dataset for different experiments

3.3 Evaluation using SARI

Table 3 displays SARI evaluations for all 4 experiments. The results for SARI are expressed between 0 and 100, and as the table shows, they remain relatively low. Nevertheless, it is noticeable that the fine-tuned model performs slightly better than the pre-trained LLM, pointing towards potential benefits from fine-tuning. Similarly, the results where higher when including a prompt for simplifying text, indicating that using a prompt can enhance the results of the text simplification task.

3.4 Evaluation using GPT-4o-mini as a judge

After evaluating the model using the SARI metric, a more subjective assessment was performed using GPT-4o-mini as an evaluator to gain further insights into the quality of the simplified texts. The results, presented in Table 4, show ratings on a scale from 1 to 10, assigned by GPT-4o-mini for two samples created using the four different techniques.

The evaluations indicate that the results of the different experiments vary from average (e.g., 4/10 for EXP1, Sample 1) to very high (e.g., 9/10 for EXP2, Sample 2). The lowest ratings were given to the results of EXP1 and EXP3, particularly for Sample 1, which was poorly rated across all criteria, with context being the most negatively impacted. This might seem like a reasonable evaluation, as the original text contained important information on where to seek help in case of emergency, which was missing in the simplified version.

On the other hand, the highest overall ratings for simplified texts were given to the results of EXP2 and EXP4 with Sample 2. These results highlight a critical insight: large language models like GPT-4o-mini, while powerful, may not always be fully reliable as evaluators. The results for these experiment and sample pairs were actually just rewrites of the original prompt instead of simplified sentences, but the model evaluated them as successfully simplified.

4 Discussion

During the fine-tuning of the Lt-Llama-2-7b-hf model, the loss values showed a gradual decrease, demonstrating that the model effectively learned to adapt to both training and validation data. As the number of iterations increased, the loss decreased quickly at first, but began to slow down, indicating that the model was learning the features necessary for simplification tasks.

When testing the fine-tuned model on the text simplification task, the results indicated that the model was not yet fully adapted to simplify texts efficiently. While some outputs were simplified to shorter sentences with simpler words, other results were unclear or consisted of paraphrased text or the provided prompt, deviating from the expected simplification. Both the SARI metric and GPT-4o-mini evaluations confirmed that the fine-tuned and non-fine-tuned models produced similar results, with relatively low scores across all experiments. The best results were obtained for the EXP4 experiment with an average SARI value on 55.648. This shows that the adapted model balanced word addition, keeping, and deletion better than the non-adapted model, but achieved only the average possible SARI score. For the GPT-4o-mini model evaluation, EXP2 and EXP4 performed best overall, particularly for Sample2, which consistently received higher ratings (up to 9/10 for clarity and simplicity). In contrast, Sample1 results across all experiments remained noticeably weaker, indicating that model performance varied significantly depending on input content rather than experimental configuration alone.

In terms of model fine-tuning, in this study, we focused on fine-tuning the Lt-Llama-2 model for the text simplification task using the Paged AdamW optimizer and a gradual learning rate warm-up to ensure memory efficiency and stable training on a relatively small dataset. While this approach is widely used and effective for similar tasks, it's worth noting that alternative fine-tuning strategies, such as weight freezing or layer-wise learning rate adjustment, could also be explored. These techniques can help optimize model performance and further reduce memory consumption, particularly when working with larger datasets. For instance, freezing certain layers during fine-tuning (or "salting" the weights) could enable more efficient transfer learning by focusing on specific aspects of the model's knowledge while avoiding unnecessary updates. This is especially beneficial when training on smaller datasets, as it prevents overfitting and ensures faster convergence.

Moreover, there are additional methods worth considering for improving fine-tuning an LLM for the text simplification task, such as transfer learning and progressive document-level simplification. Transfer learning allows fine-tuning a pre-trained model to a new task by leveraging knowledge from larger, more diverse datasets, which could be explored in future work. Similarly, progressive simplification, as discussed in studies like (Fang et al., 2025), emphasizes simplifying text at different levels of complexity, potentially improving model accuracy and usability, especially for challenging linguistic tasks.

By integrating these approaches, we could not only improve model performance for simplifying Lithuanian texts, but also expand its applicability to a broader range of texts and simplification levels. As suggested by (Parthasarathy et al., 2024), incorporating these methods into a fine-tuning pipeline could help mitigate challenges and lead to breakthroughs in text simplification tasks, making the model more robust and adaptable to various types of input.

As part of our future research, we are preparing a proposal to extend this work by incorporating Human Feedback Reinforcement Learning (HF-RL). This approach would allow us to fine-tune the model using direct human feedback, improving its ability to generate more accurate and useful simplifications. Additionally, we plan to explore multi-stage fine-tuning, where we will combine open-source datasets with our own domain-specific data. This will help us create a more comprehensive fine-tuning process, potentially improving model performance in text simplification tasks.

4.1 Comparison to other research

In comparison to similar research, while text simplification in the Lithuanian language remains limited, a notable study focused on the simplification of administrative texts into plain language rather than

Experiment No.	Example No.	Clarity	Context	Simplicity	General Rating
EXP1	Sample1	4/10	3/10	5/10	4/10
EXP1	Sample2	7/10	5/10	8/10	6/10
EXP2	Sample1	6/10	5/10	7/10	6/10
EXP2	Sample2	9/10	7/10	9/10	8.5/10
EXP3	Sample1	4/10	3/10	5/10	4/10
EXP3	Sample2	8/10	7/10	9/10	8/10
EXP4	Sample1	4/10	5/10	6/10	5/10
EXP4	Sample2	8/10	7/10	9/10	8/10

Table 4: Example results evaluation by GPT-4o-mini

Study	Language	Model	Dataset Size
(Mandravickaitė et al., 2025)	Lithuanian	T5, mBART, Lt-Llama-2	~2142 pairs
(Martínez et al., 2024)	Spanish	LLaMA-2	~2081 pairs
(Barbu et al., 2025)	Estonian	LLaMA 3.1, OpenNMT	~50,416 pairs

Table 5: Overview of fine-tuning datasets used in related studies

ETR (Mandravickaitė et al., 2025). Their approach involved fine-tuning transformer-based models, including T5, mBART, and Lt-Llama-2—the only non-multilingual model in the task - on a dataset of complex and simplified administrative texts. The results indicated that "in many cases, instead of simplifying the provided sentences, the fine-tuned model simply expanded them by adding information that was not present in the original complex sentences". While T5 and mBART showed better results, with SARI scores ranging from 54.12 to 72.98, the fine-tuned Lt-Llama-2 underperformed. The study emphasized the importance of high-quality training data and task-specific fine-tuning challenges, also highlighted in our research.

In addition to the Lithuanian-focused study, two significant studies in other languages provide valuable comparisons for our work. The first study (Martínez et al., 2024) investigated simplifying Spanish texts into ETR using the Llama-2 model. Their approach involved fine-tuning the Llama-2 model on complex and simplified Spanish sentences, including a translation approach, where complex Spanish text was translated to English, simplified, and translated back to Spanish. The results showed improvements in readability and accessibility, with qualitative evaluations confirming the model's ability to simplify content while preserving its meaning.

In comparison, while our study focuses on the Lithuanian language, the successful application of Llama-2 for text simplification to ETR in Spanish suggests the model's flexibility. Although the datasets and languages differ, the findings imply that with adequate fine-tuning and dataset preparation, Llama-2 could potentially be applied to Lithuanian text simplification tasks as well, as well as opening the possibility of simplifying text using a translation technique.

Another relevant study (Barbu et al., 2025) investigated Estonian text simplification using LLMs. This research is relevant since the Estonian language, like Lithuanian, is a less-resourced language with limited LLM tools. The study involved fine-tuning Llama on a custom dataset, combining both translated data and GPT-4-generated simplifications, and comparing it to other LLMs such as DRESS, OpenNMT, and T5. A comparison of Llama 3.1 and OpenNMT models revealed that while OpenNMT achieved a slightly higher BLEU score (30.05 vs. 27.04), indicating better alignment with reference texts, Llama 3.1 outperformed OpenNMT on the SARI metric (49.72 vs. 47.43), suggesting more effective text simplification. Additionally, Llama 3.1 had a slightly lower FKGL score (8.71 vs. 9.02), indicating slightly easier readability. Despite these similarities in automatic metric performance, manual evaluations by three native Estonian speakers rated Llama 3.1 significantly higher (3.03 vs. 1.6 on a 4-point scale), demonstrating its superior ability to simplify texts to ETR standards in terms of grammar, readability, meaning preservation, and simplification.

As summarized in Table 5, our dataset was considerably smaller compared to other studies in the field. While (Mandravickaitė et al., 2025) used administrative texts and (Martínez et al., 2024) leveraged both real and translated data, our study was limited to a smaller corpus of ETR-specific texts. This difference in dataset size and diversity may partially explain the lower performance of our fine-tuned model, especially since effective LLM adaptation often requires tens of thousands of training examples to generalize well.

5 Conclusion

In conclusion, even though large language models such as Lt-Llama-2-7b-hf have significant potential for text simplification tasks, the results showed that these models, even when fine-tuned, require further refinement to perform well in text simplification tasks. While fine-tuning loss results indicated that the model was adapting to the text simplification task and the fine-tuned model achieved better results than the non-fine-tuned one, the overall performance was still moderate, with the highest SARI score of 55.648 for the EXP4 experiment. To improve the model's performance, further experiments should focus on optimizing the fine-tuning parameters and increasing the dataset size. This would allow the model to adapt to a wider range of text simplification tasks.

References

2022. *Global Report on Health Equity for Persons with Disabilities*, 1st ed edition. World Health Organization, Geneva.

Eduard Barbu, Meeri-Ly Muru, and Sten Marcus Malva. 2025. Improving Estonian Text Simplification through Pretrained Language Models and Custom Datasets. *arXiv preprint*. Citation-key: simplifying-estonian-text arXiv:2501.15624 [cs].

Tom B. Brown, Benjamin Mann, Nick Ryder, Melanie Subbiah, Jared Kaplan, Prafulla Dhariwal, Arvind Neelakantan, Pranav Shyam, Girish Sastry, Amanda Askell, Sandhini Agarwal, Ariel Herbert-Voss, Gretchen Krueger, Tom Henighan, Rewon Child, Aditya Ramesh, Daniel M. Ziegler, Jeffrey Wu, Clemens Winter, Christopher Hesse, Mark Chen, Eric Sigler, Mateusz Litwin, Scott Gray, Benjamin Chess, Jack Clark, Christopher Berner, Sam McCandlish, Alec Radford, Ilya Sutskever, and Dario Amodei. 2020. Language Models are Few-Shot Learners. *arXiv preprint*. ArXiv:2005.14165 [cs].

Justina Bružaitė-Liseckienė, Inga Daraškienė, and Laura Vilkaitė-Lozdienė. 2021. Teksto lengvai suprantama kalba rengimo gairės.

Jacob Devlin, Ming-Wei Chang, Kenton Lee, and Kristina Toutanova. 2019. BERT: Pre-training of Deep Bidirectional Transformers for Language Understanding. *arXiv preprint*. ArXiv:1810.04805 [cs].

Dengzhao Fang, Jipeng Qiang, Yi Zhu, Yunhao Yuan, Wei Li, and Yan Liu. 2025. Progressive Document-level Text Simplification via Large Language Models. *arXiv preprint*. ArXiv:2501.03857 [cs].

Xavier Ferrer, Tom van Nuenen, Jose M. Such, Mark Coté, and Natalia Criado. 2021. Bias and Discrimination in AI: a cross-disciplinary perspective. *IEEE Technology and Society Magazine*, 40(2):72–80. ArXiv:2008.07309 [cs].

Jiawei Gu, Xuhui Jiang, Zhichao Shi, Hexiang Tan, Xuehao Zhai, Chengjin Xu, Wei Li, Yinghan Shen, Shengjie Ma, Honghao Liu, Saizhuo Wang, Kun Zhang, Yuanzhuo Wang, Wen Gao, Lionel Ni, and Jian Guo. 2025. A Survey on LLM-as-a-Judge. *arXiv preprint*. ArXiv:2411.15594 [cs].

Shigeki Karita, Nanxin Chen, Tomoki Hayashi, Takaaki Hori, Hirofumi Inaguma, Ziyan Jiang, Masao Someki, Nelson Enrique Yalta Soplin, Ryuichi Yamamoto, Xiaofei Wang, Shinji Watanabe, Takenori Yoshimura, and Wangyou Zhang. 2019. A Comparative Study on Transformer vs RNN in Speech Applications. In *2019 IEEE Automatic Speech Recognition and Understanding Workshop (ASRU)*, pages 449–456, SG, Singapore. IEEE.

Takeshi Kojima, Shixiang Shane Gu, Machel Reid, Yutaka Matsuo, and Yusuke Iwasawa. 2023. Large Language Models are Zero-Shot Reasoners. *arXiv preprint*. ArXiv:2205.11916 [cs].

Ivano Lauriola, Alberto Lavelli, and Fabio Aiolli. 2022. An introduction to Deep Learning in Natural Language Processing: Models, techniques, and tools. *Neurocomputing*, 470:443–456.

Ilya Loshchilov and Frank Hutter. 2019. Decoupled Weight Decay Regularization. *arXiv preprint*. ArXiv:1711.05101 [cs].

Justina Mandravickaitė, Eglė Rimkienė, Danguolė Kotryna Kapkan, Danguolė Kalinauskaitė, Antanas Čenys, and Tomas Krilavičius. 2025. Automatic Text Simplification for Lithuanian: Transforming Administrative Texts into Plain Language. *Mathematics*, 13(3):465. Citation-key: text-simplification-in-Lithuanian.

Paloma Martínez, Alberto Ramos, and Lourdes Moreno. 2024. Exploring Large Language Models to generate Easy to Read content. *Frontiers in Computer Science*, 6:1394705. Citation-key: simplifying-in-spanish.

Klaus Miesenberger and Andrea Petz. 2014. Easy to Read on the Web – State of the Art and Research Directions. *Procedia Computer Science*, 27:318–326.

Artūras Nakvosas, Povilas Daniušis, and Vytas Mulevičius. 2024. Open Llama2 Model for the Lithuanian Language. *arXiv preprint*. ArXiv:2408.12963 [cs].

Venkatesh Balavadhani Parthasarathy, Ahtsham Zafar, Aafaq Khan, and Arsalan Shahid. 2024. The Ultimate Guide to Fine-Tuning LLMs from Basics to Breakthroughs: An Exhaustive Review of Technologies, Research, Best Practices, Applied Research Challenges and Opportunities. *arXiv preprint*. ArXiv:2408.13296 [cs].

Martin Popel and Ondřej Bojar. 2018. Training Tips for the Transformer Model. *The Prague Bulletin of Mathematical Linguistics*, 110(1):43–70. ArXiv:1804.00247 [cs].

Colin Raffel, Noam Shazeer, Adam Roberts, Katherine Lee, Sharan Narang, Michael Matena, Yanqi Zhou, Wei Li, and Peter J. Liu. 2023. Exploring the Limits of Transfer Learning with a Unified Text-to-Text Transformer. *arXiv preprint*. ArXiv:1910.10683 [cs].

Sonish Sivarajkumar, Mark Kelley, Alyssa Samolyk-Mazzanti, Shyam Visweswaran, and Yanshan Wang. 2024. An Empirical Evaluation of Prompting Strategies for Large Language Models in Zero-Shot Clinical Natural Language Processing: Algorithm Development and Validation Study. *JMIR Medical Informatics*, 12:e55318.

Samuel L. Smith, Pieter-Jan Kindermans, Chris Ying, and Quoc V. Le. 2018. Don't Decay the Learning Rate, Increase the Batch Size. *arXiv preprint*. ArXiv:1711.00489 [cs].

Ashish Vaswani, Noam Shazeer, Niki Parmar, Jakob Uszkoreit, Llion Jones, Aidan N Gomez, Łukasz Kaiser, and Illia Polosukhin. 2017. Attention is all you need. In *Advances in neural information processing systems*, volume 30. Curran Associates, Inc.

Wei Xu, Courtney Napoles, Ellie Pavlick, Quanze Chen, and Chris Callison-Burch. 2016. Optimizing Statistical Machine Translation for Text Simplification. *Transactions of the Association for Computational Linguistics*, 4:401–415.

ChatGPT and Mistral as a tool for intralingual translation into Easy French

Julia Degenhardt
Université Bourgogne Europe / Maison de l'Université, Esp. Erasme, 21078 Dijon
Julia.Degenhardt@ube.fr

Abstract

FALC is a simplified variety of French designed to enhance text comprehensibility and accessibility. Despite its societal benefits, the availability of FALC texts remains limited due to the costly human translation process. This study explores the potential of LLMs, specifically ChatGPT and Le Chat, as a tool for automatic intralingual translations. The AI-generated translations of standard French texts on sexual health are compared to human-translated versions. The corpus-based study combines qualitative and quantitative approaches to evaluate content accuracy, readability and syntactic complexity.

1 Introduction

Like other Easy languages FALC (français facile à lire et à comprendre) is a complexity reduced variety of French, that follows guidelines to enhance text comprehensibility and accessibility (Lindholm & Vanhatalo, 2021). The French government promotes its use to improve societal inclusion of people with disabilities. In 2021 a charter on the accessibility of the communication between government and citizens was published, including recommendations to produce texts in FALC (Charte d'accessibilité, 2022). Despite, these efforts the number of texts available in FALC is rather small, the main reasons being high costs and difficulties to translate into FALC (Chehab et al., 2019).

Using generative AI to optimize the translation process could increase the text volume. Although scepticism and negative attitudes towards ChatGPT and other large language models do exist in the translation industry, the European Language Industry Study 2024 (ELIS) reveals that their use is growing. In 2024, 21% of the Language Service Companies had already implemented a LLM into their workflow (ELIS, 2024). In the study by Rivas Ginel and Moorkens (2024) 40% of the translators claimed they used ChatGPT regularly or occasionally, which further underlines the growing impact of LLMs in interlingual translation. This trend is backed up, by recent studies evaluating the proficiency of LLMs for the task. Although proficiency differs across models and languages, the results are promising and show potential (Jiao et al., 2023; Zhang et al., 2023; Zhu et al., 2024). LLMs have also been successfully tested on simplification tasks (Kew et al., 2023). Producing Easy Language texts is a form of intralingual translation and closely linked to text simplification. Yet, the potential of LLMs for this task remains largely unexplored. Deilen et al. (2023) explored the use of ChatGPT as a CAT tool for translations into Easy German. The authors obtained promising results, yet comparable studies for Easy French do not exist.

The present pilot study tries to address this research gap. The main question is how well ChatGPT and Mistral's LLM Le Chat can simplify a source text into FALC and whether they can be a useful tool especially for translators, but also for end-users. The analysis is a mix of qualitative and quantitative methods and focusses on content, readability and syntactic complexity. For this purpose, AI-generated translations – standard French into FALC – are compared to human-translated versions. The corpus contains 15 source texts in standard French on sexual health topics and their respective translation in three versions: human translator vs. ChatGPT vs. Le Chat.

The remainder of this paper is structured as follows: Section 2 reviews the current usage as well as the social and legal framework of FALC in France. Section 3 presents related work on Automatic Text Simplification in French and the

Proceedings of the 1st Workshop on Artificial Intelligence and Easy and Plain Language in Institutional Contexts (AI & EL/PL), pages 38–54, June 23, 2025

usage of LLMs for simplification and translation. Data and methodology are described in Section 4 and the results follow in section 5. To conclude, the main findings are summarised, and an outlook is given.

2 Easy Language

2.1 FALC – Easy French

Easy Language is an umbrella term for different simplified language varieties that aim at making information – mainly but not exclusively written texts – more accessible to different target groups with diverse communicative needs. The main target audiences addressed by Easy Languages are people with cognitive impairments or learning disabilities, aphasia, dementia, deaf or hard of hearing, functionally illiterate adults and foreign language learners (Lindholm & Vanhatalo, 2021b; Maaß, 2020). Easy Languages reduce the complexity on different linguistic levels (lexical, syntactical, discourse) in order to enhance comprehensibility and readability and to reduce the cognitive processing costs (Hansen-Schirra, Bisang, et al., 2020; Hansen-Schirra & Maaß, 2020). Producing Easy Language texts has been defined as a form of intralingual translation, which requires translational competences (Maaß, 2020).

Access to information is pivotal for inclusion and active participation in society, hence Easy Languages fall within the scope of accessible communication. Different texts can represent different communication barriers that hinder comprehension. That is for example the case if the text is not perceivable due to sensory impairments, if the language of the text in unknown to the reader or if the complexity of the content exceeds their cognitive processing capacities (Rink, 2019). Easy Language translation seeks to overcome these communication barriers in order to produce texts that are retrievable, perceptible, comprehensible, linkable, acceptable and action-enabling (Maaß, 2020). In France, Easy Language is known under the acronym FALC, which stands for "Français Facile à Lire et à Comprendre" and is commonly used in France, Belgium and Switzerland. Other terms referring to the same linguistic variety are "Français facile" or "Facile à Lire" (Canut et al., 2020; Vandeghinste et al., 2021).

2.2 Societal and legal framework

In 2005 the law (Loi n° 2005-102, 2005) on the rights of people with disabilities was passed by the French parliament. It is the most important legal text to date in France concerning equal rights, opportunities and participation. Article 47 of the law states that public authorities are obliged to make their online communication services accessible, however the text does not specify the means by which this aim is to be achieved. French Sign Language is the only form of accessible communication that is explicitly mentioned in the legal text (Loi n° 2005-102, 2005). Consequently, there is no legal framework regarding texts in FALC in France, as it is the case in Germany. This might be one of the reasons why providing simplified versions is still rather an exception than the rule.

Nonetheless, awareness of accessible communication has grown in recent years. In 2021 the French government published the first version of the "Charte d'accessibilité de la communication de l'État", which recommends providing additional texts in FALC (Charte d'accessibilité, 2022). The charter specifically mentions electoral programs as one of the document types that should be made available in FALC. This was implemented by a great number of candidates during the election campaign in 2022. Furthermore, a campaign with the headline "*Imaginer un quotidien où rien n'est vraiment pensé pour vous*" (engl.: "Imagine a daily life where nothing is designed for you.") was launched in 2025. The aim is to raise awareness on accessibility amongst public agents in general, but also to enhance knowledge about specific measures for communicative inclusion like FALC (Ministère du Travail, de la Santé, des solidarités et des familles, 2025). Most of the texts currently available in FALC are informative, focusing on areas such as disability, inclusion, healthcare, political participation and cultural events, for example in the form exhibition guides for museums (Chehab et al., 2019).

2.3 Text production

Research activities on Easy Language varieties in France have also lagged behind those in other European countries, including Germany, Spain, Finland, where research activity but also the number of available texts has been increasing (for an overview see Lindholm & Vanhatalo, 2021a). Although the French guidelines for producing texts in FALC have available since 2009, a survey on its use amongst public and private organizations in 2019 revealed that producing FALC texts is seen as time-consuming and too difficult. The organisations surveyed are aware of the necessity, but they often do not know how to integrate FALC translation processes into their workflow (Chehab et al., 2019). In France the professionalisation of the field is in its early stages, professional translators are rare, but demand is growing. This situation suggests that there is a growing need to optimize the translation process, incorporating at least some degree of automation.

3 Related Work

3.1 Automatic Text Simplification in French

Text simplification can be generally defined "as the process of reducing the linguistic complexity of a text, while still retaining the original information content and meaning." (Siddharthan, 2014, p. 259). Automatic Text Simplification (ATS) has been researched for years, not only to produce readable texts for humans but also as a form of pre-processing for other NLP tasks. As there is a great need for simplified texts in order to enhance societal inclusion, provision has become increasingly important (Saggion, 2024).

Most of the early research on ATS was carried out in English and corpus data on other languages like French was scarce, which hindered the development of performant statistical, rather than less performant rule-based, tools for simplification in French. Seretan analyzed the simplification strategies adopted by human translators and derived a ruleset for syntactical simplification in French from the results (Seretan, 2012). Brouwers et al. described the main linguistic levels of transformation: lexical, discursive and syntactical and incorporated them into a rule-based system. This approach obtained good results, with about 80% of the generated sentences being correct (Brouwers et al., 2014).

In recent years, interest has shifted towards machine-learning approaches and much research has been dedicated to the construction of French parallel corpora to address the lack of data. Ormaechea & Tsourakis created the open-source Wikipedia Vividia Corpus (WIVICO 10) by extracting and aligning complex/simple sentence pairs from comparable corpora (Ormaechea & Tsourakis, 2023). They also addressed the problem that simplified sentences can still exhibit complex structures and that complexity evaluation does not always account for this. Most evaluation measures can only identify whether the generated sentence is simpler, but not to which degree. As 'simpler' does not immediately equal maximum simplicity and comprehension, this is problematic for the evaluation of ATS tools. To improve the assessment of sentence complexity, the authors fine-tuned a pre-trained BERT classification model. Results showed that their model is useful for automatic creation of simplified datasets as it provides a finer-grained assessment of simplification (Ormaechea & Tsourakis, 2024). Another available French corpus that has been used to evaluate ATS systems, is the ALECTOR corpus created by Gala et al. (2020). It contains literary and scientific texts conceived for elementary school children and their respective simplified versions. Simplified versions were created manually by applying simplification strategies on lexical, morphological and syntactical level. Although initially collected to assess reading errors and to improve reading skills in young children with dyslexia, it is also useful for ATS (Gala et al., 2020). ALECTOR served as the basis to develop the French ATS system HECTOR. This system combines a rule-based and an embedding-based approach to perform simplification at lexical, syntactical and discursive level. Given the focus of the corpus data, it has a strong focus on learner texts for young children. The researchers obtained good results for syntactical simplification, but the system was less powerful at lexical and discursive level (Todirascu et al., 2022). The CLEAR corpus, which comprises original and simplified texts in French from the medical domain, has also been used to address automatic sentence extraction and alignment (Cardon & Grabar, 2019; Grabar & Cardon, 2018). This small specialized corpus also provided data for a later study by Cardon & Grabar, where they showed that that high quality specialized data and translated corpora can be successfully used to train ATS models, even if performance will increase in line with the size of the data set (Cardon & Grabar, 2020). These findings were confirmed by Abdul Rauf et al. (2020), who used a synthetic corpus, consisting of the French translations of English source texts of the Newsela corpus, to train their simplification model. Although their results varied across the different levels of complexity, the authors' overall conclusion was that small data batches and translated corpora can result in acceptable simplifications (Abdul Rauf et al., 2020). While the previous mentioned ATS models explored simplification on various text levels, the *FrenLys* tool investigates lexical simplification. It generates, selects and ranks synonyms to replace complex words in a text. (Rolin et al., 2021).

3.2 LLMs for intralingual translation tasks and simplification

Easy Language translation is a form of intralingual translation. While research on the former is scarce, many studies have assessed the capabilities of LLMs for interlingual translation tasks. The results are heterogeneous but promising, showing that performance depends significantly on the model, the languages and the prompts used. Especially for high-resource languages, LLMs can produce qualitatively good and competitive outputs (Hendy et al., 2023; Jiao et al., 2023; Zhu et al., 2024). According to Vilar et al., who tested the MT capabilities of an LLM against state-of-the art MT systems, the LLM "matches the fluency but lags the accuracy of conventional NMT" (Vilar et al., 2022). Despite some weaknesses, the usefulness of LLM interlingual translation has been demonstrated, suggesting that such approaches may also produce useful results for intralingual tasks.

Besides interlingual MT, the simplification capacities of LLMs have also been assessed. Feng et al. performed sentence simplification using ChatGPT amongst others and concluded that "LLMs outperformed current state-of-the-art [sentence simplification] methods." (Feng et al., 2023). In regard to text simplification, Kew et al. also concluded that LLMs perform better than state-of-the art text simplification baseline models (2023). Furthermore, these findings are confirmed by Qiang et al. who claim that the GPT-4o model "not only simplifies text effectively but also produces output that is easier to read." (Qiang et al., 2025). Although text simplification and intralingual translation into Easy Languages are not the same (different target groups, specific rule set, etc.), reducing complexity is crucial for both operations. Thus, one can hypothesise that LLMs do not only perform well in ATS but also in Easy Language translation. Yet, their potential remains mostly unexplored. For Easy German, Anschütz et al. (2023) and Klöser et al. (2024) demonstrated that pre-training LLMs with Easy Language data combined with fine-tuning results in models that can produce satisfying Easy German texts. Deilen et al. (2023) examined the usability of ChatGPT as a CAT tool for intralingual translation of administrative texts into Easy German. The author's results were promising: ChatGPT produced texts that were simpler on some linguistic levels but also contained content errors. Hence, they concluded that ChatGPT can be useful but not without post-editing (Deilen et al., 2023). Arguably, using LLMs or other ATS tools for Easy Language text production is of great interest, because it might save time and money, two factors which are often named as major impediments for Easy Language translations (Chehab et al., 2019). Increasing the number of texts produced in Easy Language plays a crucial role in the efforts to make society more accessible. The social dimension of Easy Language translation is also a driver of research on the automatization of the process (Saggion, 2024). Although it comes with its challenges, the use of machine translation, terminology management, etc. has become increasingly important for intralingual as well as interlingual translators (Hansen-Schirra et al., 2020). LLMs hold a large potential as they are free and easy to use. However, for French this potential remains currently unexplored. This pilot study is a first approach to bridge this research gap and to initiate a discussion on using LLMs as a tool for producing texts in Easy French.

4 Methodology

4.1 Data Collection

The present study is based on a French monolingual corpus. It consists of original source texts (ST) in standard French and the translated target texts (TT) of these STs in FALC in three different versions. The different versions of these TTs are:

1. official TTs translated by human translators, that were published on the websites alongside the standard French STs. These texts were collected as part of the corpus.

2. TTs that were generated by the author using two different Large Language Models.

The LLMs chosen for this study are ChatGPT (version 4o mini) by OpenAI and Le Chat (version

Mistral Large) by Mistral AI. ChatGPT seems like an obvious choice due to its popularity, the user-friendly interface and free subscription. Furthermore, other studies in the field have already discussed ChatGPT's potential for intralingual (Deilen et al., 2023) and interlingual (Jiao et al., 2023) translation, and prompting strategies have also often been tested on ChatGPT (Campesato, 2024; Gao et al., 2024). Le Chat is very similar to ChatGPT: both are free, and the user interfaces hardly differ from each other as they are dialogue-based. Although it is certainly less popular on an international scale than other LLMs like Google's Gemini, Mistral AI is one of the most successful European AI companies. The French-based company signed a contract with Microsoft in 2024, which further increased its market value (Braune, 2024). Since public agents are amongst the groups for whom using an LLM for translations into FALC might be beneficial, the fact that France Travail (the French public employment service) already is one of Mistral AI's clients was another argument for choosing Le Chat (Mistral AI, n.d.).

The STs are informative texts from the medical domain [1]. Most texts concern sexual and reproductive health subjects and are targeted at young adults, while some texts aim to inform a broader audience about mental health or breast cancer. While the source texts include domain-specific language, they are written for lay people and not domain experts. All texts were originally published in France between 2019 and 2024 and are freely available online.

The main selection criterion for the texts was that a clear link between the target text in FALC and the source text in standard French could be established. As mentioned above, this is rarely the case in France – most FALC texts available online are not labelled as translations and cannot be traced back to a source text (Chehab et al., 2019). In that respect, it is also difficult to get information about the professional background of the translators. It is more likely that they are working in the disability field than as professional translators (ibid.). Some of the texts have been produced in cooperation with associations for people with disabilities. However, it remains unclear whether their role relates to consultation, translation or proofreading. Ideally, this information would be included within the corpus metadata, but it is not available. Furthermore, the target texts had to be comparable in terms of domain and subject. Thus, texts about other subjects than health were excluded from this study. Those criteria clearly limit the number of eligible texts. Considering that the number of texts in FALC is already small, some compromises in the collection process were necessary to increase the sample size (Chehab et al., 2019; Rodríguez Vázquez et al., 2022). On the one hand, this concerns the text length, which differs. On the other hand, this concerns the lack of metadata, especially regarding the professional background of the translators. However, restricting the selection to texts of similar length or to the availability of metadata would not have yielded a sufficiently large corpus.

To summarize, the corpus consists of 32214 words in total, distributed across four subcorpora. Each subcorpus contains 15 texts. ST_StFR contains the STs in Standard French. The TTs in FALC are categorized according to the translation process: human translators (TT-1_human) vs. LLM-generated versions (TT-2_ChatGPT and TT-3_LeChat). Table 1 shows the number of words in each subcorpus.

subcorpus	words
ST_StFR	10143
TT-1_human	9705
TT-2_ChatGPT	7490
TT-3_LeChat	4876
total	32214

Table 1: Corpus Statistics

4.2 Prompting Strategies

LLMs generate their output based on the prompt provided by the user. The quality and structure of the prompts plays a crucial role and affects the output. Different prompts will produce different responses, and the same prompt will not reproduce the same answer. The more precise and well-structured the prompt the more concise the output will be. Especially for complex tasks, well-designed prompts are pivotal. In general, instructional and guided prompts that give clear instructions and provide additional context produce

[1] Please see the appendix for a list of the source texts and the respective links.

more precise output than open-ended prompts (Campesato, 2024).

This holds also true for translation tasks. Here context helps the model to better resolve ambiguity and choose suitable equivalents based on the provided context (Campesato, 2024; Hui Jiao et al., 2024). The benefits of assigning a role to the model are well-known and again, clarity is key. For translation tasks, assigning the role of a translator instead of just an author yields better results (He, 2024). Other studies have shown that providing domain specific information, such as indicating the translation direction, the style and text type of the translated texts, the text function and the target audience, tends to improve the quality of the target texts (Gao et al., 2024; Hui Jiao et al., 2024; Yamada, 2023). All these findings were considered for the prompts used in this study. The initial prompt[2] includes the following key information:

- role: translator
- task: simplify according to the FALC rules; the basic principles, e.g. short sentences, active voice, explication of complex words, were introduced in the prompt to provide context to the task
- direction: intralingual, standard French to Français Facile à Lire et à Comprendre (FALC)
- target audience: people with reading difficulties
- domain & text type: informative, sexual health

In their study on ChatGPT as a CAT tool for Easy German, Deilen et al. (2023) compared two different prompts. One approach was to break down the simplification process into linguistic levels. Although this prompting strategy complies with the finding that step by step-instructions are beneficial (Hui Jiao et al., 2024), this technique was not adopted here, because it is more time-consuming and it did not outperform the holistic approach in each category (Deilen et al., 2023). As iterations are recommended (Campesato, 2024), ChatGPT and Le Chat were asked three times to simplify the text. The second and third prompt asked the models to further simplify the text they just produced by keeping the rules of FALC in mind. The third simplified version was integrated in the corpus and analysed.

4.3 Data analysis

4.4 Content

A qualitative analysis of five source texts and their respective target texts was done manually. The chosen texts are about abortion, menstruation, sexually transmitted diseases, contraceptives and breast cancer screening. The analysis focusses on information consistency, added explications and content errors. The concept of a faithful delivery of the original message and information consistency are often seen as ideals in the context of automatic text simplification (Siddharthan, 2014) and Easy Language translation (Maaß & Rink, 2020). However, there is a risk of informational overload for the target audiences of Easy Language when the text contains too much information and becomes too long. The translators need to cut out non-essential information in order not to exceed the cognitive processing capacities of the readers (Maaß & Rink, 2020). Consequently, omissions cannot be counted as content errors in general. Easy Language translation settings are often characterised by an asymmetry in knowledge and translators face the challenge of bridging this gap and building common ground between producer and reader. Thus, adding information is as necessary as reducing information. The challenge is to decide whether information is crucial or not. For that matter, knowledge about the target group is a necessary competence for the translators to make adequate decisions (Hansen-Schirra, Bisang, et al., 2020; Maaß, 2020). The question is, then, whether LLMs are also capable of making these choices or whether too much information is omitted. The resulting hypothesis is that LLMs omit more information than the human translator and that they produce more errors, due to hallucinations, as it was the case with ChatGPT for Easy German (Deilen et al. 2023).

4.5 Readability

The readability was assessed through different measurements. First, the Moving-Average Type-Token-Ratio (MATTR) was calculated for each text. A lower MATTR indicates less lexical diversity and consequently higher readability. In

[2] Please see the appendix for the entire prompt

contrast to the TTR, which highly depends on text length, the MATTR is insensitive to text lengths as it calculates the type-token ratio over a sliding window (Covington & McFall, 2010). It has been demonstrated that MATTR is a reliable index to measure lexical diversity (Bestgen, 2024; Kettunen, 2014). The window-size was set to 50 tokens[3]. Secondly, the lexical density (LD) was computed. It describes the proportion between content and grammatical words in a text. A lower LD is an indicator for higher readability (Baker, 1995). Lastly, the AMesure-score was used to assess the overall readability. AMesure is a readability measurement tool for French language, initially designed to assess administrative texts. It takes into account various parameters of readability (e.g. lexical density, type-token-ratio, sentence length, verbal forms) to evaluate a text on a scale from 1 to 5 – the lower the score the more readable (François et al., 2014; François et al., 2020).

4.6 Syntactical complexity

Syntactic simplicity contributes to the comprehensibility of a text (Christmann & Groeben, 2019). The FALC guidelines recommend short sentences that only express one idea. Subordinate clauses should be avoided (Inclusion Europe, 2009). A smaller amount of dependency relations indicates lower complexity (Deilen et al., 2023; Deilen et al., 2024). Consequently, the TTs are expected to contain fewer complex clauses than the STs.

To evaluate the syntactical complexity of the target texts, the dependency parser from the Stanza NLP Library was used (Qi et al., 2020). Stanza extracts dependency relations as described in the Universal Dependencies (UC) framework (Marneffe et al., 2021). Based on Deilen et al., 2023 the following dependency relations were selected for the analysis: acl (clausal modifier of noun), acl:recl (relative clause modifier), advcl (adverbial clause modifier), aux:pass (passive auxiliary), appos (appositional modifier), ccomp (clausal complement), xcomp (open clausal complement), nsubj:pass (passive nominal subject), parataxis.

[3] Covington & McFall, 2010 do not recommend a specific window-size, but Bestgen, 2024 found that 50 is common.

5 Results

5.1 Content

In the small selection of 15 target texts (human translator, ChatGPT, LeChat) no content error was detected. This finding is not consistent with the results by Deilen et al., who found at least one piece of incorrect information in over 60% of the ChatGPT texts (2023).

The qualitative content analysis did not confirm the hypothesis: human translators were not more consistent than the LLMs; on the contrary, the LLMs omitted less information units, as table 2 shows.

<table>
<tr><td></td><td colspan="4">Total counts of information units</td></tr>
<tr><td>Text</td><td>ST</td><td>TT-1</td><td>TT-2</td><td>TT-3</td></tr>
<tr><td>Menstruation</td><td>50</td><td>41</td><td>46</td><td>39</td></tr>
<tr><td>Abortion</td><td>44</td><td>43</td><td>39</td><td>24</td></tr>
<tr><td>Contra-ceptive</td><td>56</td><td>42</td><td>50</td><td>45</td></tr>
<tr><td>IST</td><td>83</td><td>48</td><td>71</td><td>65</td></tr>
<tr><td>Breast Cancer screening</td><td>119</td><td>36</td><td>83</td><td>56</td></tr>
<tr><td></td><td>352</td><td>210</td><td>289</td><td>229</td></tr>
</table>

Table 2: Number of information units

The most striking discrepancy concerns the brochure on breast cancer screening. If the information units in the ST are compared to those included in the human translation, 2/3 were omitted. These omissions are for example: symptoms for breast cancer are not explained, none of the statistics mentioned in the ST were cited in the TT, difference between benign cysts and cancers is not explained. Despite the fact that some of those information units could be classified as crucial, the TT does include much information about the screening procedure, which is not included in the ST. The focus of the texts shifted. While the ST is more general and gives some information about early symptoms and why and how to do a screening, the human TT is very specific about the screening but completely omits the symptoms. Such a shift in focus was only detected in this case, all the other analysed TTs kept the main subject.

As the numbers in Table 2 show, the simplified versions include less information than the ST. This is in line with the FALC requirements: omissions are necessary to not overstrain the processing capacities of the target audiences (Hansen-Schirra et al., 2020). The following examples [4] will illustrate some cases of omissions.

Example 1: The source text explains early signs of a pregnancy.

1. Le premier indicateur d'une grossesse est souvent un retard de règles. Tu peux aussi avoir d'autres signes : nausées, mal à la poitrine, ventre gonflé… [The first indicator of pregnancy is often a late period. You may also have other signs: nausea, chest pain, a swollen belly,…] – ST-StFR

Le Chat translated this part as follows:

2. Comment savoir si on est enceinte ? Faites un test de grossesse. [How to know if you are pregnant? Take a pregnancy test.] – TT-3_LeChat

Nothing is said about early symptoms, which is a complete omission. This kind of information loss is problematic, because the reader is not well informed. It also negatively affects the coherence of the text, as the link between cause (early pregnancy signs) and consequence (take a test) is not clearly established as it is the case in the ST. ChatGPT and the human translator on the other hand translate the cause-consequence relation consistently as:

3. Un retard des règles peut être un signe de grossesse. Tu peux aussi avoir : des nausées (mal au ventre), des douleurs dans la poitrine, un ventre gonflé. [A late period can be a sign for pregnancy. You may also have: nausea (belly ache), pain in your chest, a swollen belly.] – TT-2_ChatGPT

4. Pour savoir si tu es enceinte, il y a plusieurs signes: tes règles sont en retard, tu as la nausée, tu as mal à la poitrine, tu as le ventre gonflé… [There are several signs that you may be pregnant: your period is late, you feel nauseous, your chest hurts, your stomach is swollen...] – TT-1_human

Example 2: The ST on menstruation states the following:

1. Si tu as d'autres symptômes douloureux qui t'empêchent de faire tes activités habituelles (douleur jusqu'à vomir, évanouissements...), il se peut que tu souffres d'endométriose. N'hésite pas a consulter. [If you have other painful symptoms that prevent you from doing your usual activities (pain to the point of vomiting, fainting, etc.), you may be suffering from endometriosis. Don't hesitate to get a consultation.] – ST_StFR

The Le Chat (2) and the human TT (3) are both less specific, Le Chat does not even mention endometriosis. Only ChatGPT (4) omits no information:

2. Si tu as beaucoup de douleurs, parle à un médecin. [If you have a lot of pain, speak to a doctor.] – TT-3_LeChat

3. Si tu as vraiment très mal, tu peux aller voir un médecin. Tu as peut-être une maladie, qu'on appelle l'endométriose. [If you're in really bad pain, you can go and see a doctor. You may have a condition called endometriosis.] – TT-1_human

4. Si la douleur est très forte (par exemple, vomir ou s'évanouir), cela peut être un signe d'endométriose. Cela signifie qu'il faut consulter un médecin. [If the pain is severe (e.g. vomiting or fainting), this may be a sign of endometriosis. This means that a doctor should be consulted.] – TT-2_ChatGPT

Example 3: The source text explains that dropping hormone levels are what causes the body to evacuate the uterine lining at the end of each menstrual cycle if no egg is fertilized. While each target text explains that the body expels the uterine lining when fertilization has not occurred, none of

[4] Examples are originals taken from the corpus. However, the original layout of the FALC texts (one line, one sentence) was not maintained here.

them mentions that falling hormone levels are the cause.

1. Si l'ovule n'est pas fécondé, l'utérus se vide. [If the egg is not fertilized, the uterus empties.] – TT-2_ChatGPT

2. Si l'ovule n'est pas fécondé, l'utérus se débarasse de sa muqueuse. [If the egg is not fertilized, the uterus sheds its lining.] – TT-1_human

Example 4: The ST about sexually transmitted diseases explains that HP-viruses can be benign but some types might cause cancer. The LLM generated TTs do inform about the cancer risk, but not about benign forms. The human translator omits both information units.

1. Certains HPV peuvent causer des cancers. Un vaccin existe pour les éviter. [Some HPVs can cause cancers. A vaccine exists to prevent them.] – TT-3_LeChat

2. Les papillomavirus : Il existe un vaccin. [HPV: a vaccine exists.] – TT-1_human

Example 5: The ST about the morning-after pill explains the time frame for effective use, but the human translator omitted that information unit completely, in both LLM versions it is included:

1. Il faut prendre la contraception d'urgence. Tu peux la prendre jusqu'à 5 jours après le rapport. [You need to take emergency contraception. You can take it up to 5 days after intercourse.] – TT-2_ChatGPT

2. Prenez la pilule d'urgence dès que possible. Vous avez jusqu'à 5 jours pour la prendre. [Take the emergency pill as soon as possible. You have up to 5 days to take it.] – TT-3_LeChat

3. Il faut la prendre le plus tôt possible après un rapport à risque. [Take it as soon as possible after unprotected intercourse.] – TT-1_human

Example 6: The ST on sexually transmitted diseases explains three different types of screening, e.g. blood analysis. However, the human translator only lists two of the methods, while ChatGPT and Le Chat included all three.

1. Selon l'IST, le test peut être différent (sang, urine, auto-prélèvement). [Depending on the STI, the test may be different (blood, urine, self-sampling).] -TT-3_Le Chat

2. Tu peux aussi aller voir ton médecin, puis aller dans un laboratoire, où on testera ton sang, ou ton urine. [You can also see your doctor, then go to a laboratory, where your blood or urine will be tested.] – TT-1_human

These examples illustrate cases of complete omission. On the one hand, some can be rated as adequate omissions, e.g. example 3 and 6, on the other hand, in examples 4 and 5 crucial information is missing. Omissions always entail information loss, but these examples show that it is a gradable phenomenon. Reducing the amount of information is a common and necessary translation strategy (Hansen-Schirra et al., 2020; Maaß & Rink, 2020). Yet the decision often implies some degree of subjectivity, and the qualitative analysis shows that it is a problem for the translators and the LLMs.

Regarding the explanation of difficult concepts or words, the results are mixed. ChatGPT tends to add small explanations in brackets after a difficult word. While it is positive that the difficulty of a word was acknowledged, the format does not comply with the rules for FALC. More substantial explanations can be found in the texts translated by the human translator. For instance, in the text about the menstrual cycle, a whole paragraph was added, explaining what the period is: "Quand tu es une femme, ou une personne avec un utérus, tu peux avoir tes règles. L'utérus est un organe du corps humain. Quand tu as tes règles, du sang coule à l'extérieur de ton vagin. C'est naturel. Les règles font partie d'un cycle du corps, qu'on appelle le cycle menstruel." [When you are a woman, or a person with a uterus, you can have your periods. The uterus is an organ in the human body. When you have your period, blood flows out of your vagina. This is natural. Menstruation is part of a cycle in the body called the menstrual cycle.] – TT-1_human. Those kind of long explanations and additions have not been found in the TTs generated by the LLMs, although the prompt specified to add explanations if necessary.

5.2 Readability

Table 3 shows the Moving-Average Type-Token-Ratio and the lexical density for each subcorpus. As expected, the standard French STs have a higher mean MATTR than the TTs, indicating that the vocabulary used in the FALC texts is less diverse and, consequently, the texts are less complex. Amongst the TTs, the human versions have the lowest mean MATTR with 0.689 and ChatGPT produced the texts with the highest value.

These mean lexical density scores are interesting. One would expect a decrease from the STs to the TTs, but this only the case for the human translated TTs. Le Chat produced TTs that are denser than the STs and hence, presumably more complex.

Moving-Average Type-Token-Ratio (MATTR)			
subcorpus	mean value	highest value	lowest value
ST_StFR	0.757	0.797	0.69
TT-1_human	0.689	0.74	0.64
TT-2_ChatGPT	0.735	0.76	0.7
TT-3_Le Chat	0.702	0.741	0.615
Lexical Density			
ST_StFR	52%		
TT-1_human	48%		
TT-2_ChatGPT	52%		
TT-3_Le Chat	55%		

Table 3: MATTR and Lexical Density

The AMesure score was not as informative as expected, as all the STs scored 2 out of 5 (1 corresponds to the lowest complexity level), except for one text with a 3, indicating that the source texts already had a low level of complexity. The majority of the TT versions obtained the same score as the STs. All three TT versions of the text on violence in relationships, categorized as level 3, improved by one level. Most of the other TTs obtained the same score as the STs. This does not mean that the target texts have not been simplified at all, but rather that they have not been simplified sufficiently to change the overall score. As the AMesure score measures different parameters and weights them according to their impact on text complexity, it is probable that the simplifications made did not have enough weight to change the score (François et al., 2020).

5.3 Syntactical complexity

The analysis of the syntactic complexity shows that the source texts have the highest number of words per sentence with an average of 16. Le Chat produces the shortest sentences, with only 7 words/sentence on average. The source texts also have the smallest number of sentences in total, which is not surprising, as one important rule in FALC is to write short sentences and to split complex hypotactic sentences. As table 4 shows ChatGPT and LeChat are roughly similar in terms of total number of sentences, but not regarding the average sentence length. The corpus in the pilot study is too small to generalize but it seems that LLMs tend to produce shorter texts than human translators.

subcorpus	sentences in total	words/sentence
ST_StFR	633	16.02
TT-1_human	919	10.56
TT-2_ChatGPT	676	11.08
TT-3_Le Chat	667	7.31

Table 4: Sentence length

When comparing the relative frequencies of all examined dependency relations combined, complex clausal relations are most frequent in the STs. The TTs by ChatGPT, the human translators and Le Chat follow in descending order. Overall, the TTs contain less of the examined dependency relations, as Figure 1 illustrates. According to Deilen et al. (2023) decreasing frequencies of complex clausal relations indicate that the text is easier to understand.

The distribution of the different dependency relations over the subcorpora varies a lot. Even though the STs have higher counts in total, they do not exceed the TTs in every category. For instance, the human TTs include more clausal complements (ccomp) and more adverbial clause modifiers (advcl) than the STs. As subordinate clauses should be avoided according to the FALC rules, it is surprising that some of the clausal structures analysed are even more frequent in the TTs than in standard French. Open clausal complements (xcomp) are the most frequent dependency relation in the STs, the human TTs and the ChatGPT TTs. Xcomp-relations are core arguments of the verb, but without their own subject: as such, they often appear when modalities are expressed. Since the modal verb "pouvoir" (can) is either the second or

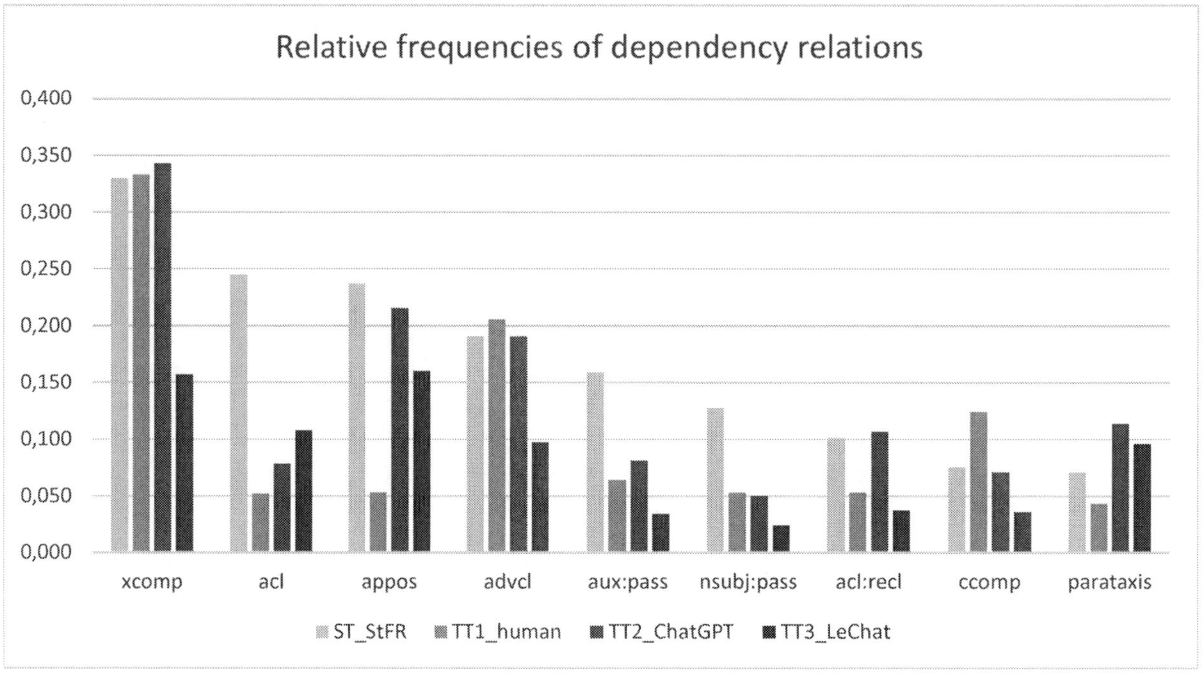

Figure 1: Relative frequencies of dependency relations

third most frequent verb in the subcorpora, the high number of xcomp-relations is not surprising. The following examples from the TT-2_ChatGPT subcorpus illustrate this:

1. Le cancer peut prendre de temps pour se développer. [Cancer can take time to develop.]
2. Cela peut durer plusieurs mois ou années. [This can take several months or years.]
3. Tu peux dire non.[You can say no.]
4. Si une femme enceinte ne veut pas garder son bébé, [...].
5. [If a pregnant woman does not wish to keep the baby, [...]]

Adverbial clause modifiers (advcl) have nearly the same relative frequency in the STs and in the ChatGPT TTs and the number is slightly higher in the human TTs. The similarity of these numbers is unexpected, as subordinal relations are not permitted by the FALC guidelines. The following examples from the TT-2_ChatGPT subcorpus illustrate the use of these clauses:

1. *Tu as le droit de dire non, si tu ne veux pas.* [You have the right to say no, if you don't want to.]
2. *Le cancer peut prendre de temps pour se développer. [Cancer can take time to develop.]*
3. *Trouver le cancer tôt permet de mieux le soigner. [Finding cancer early means better treatment.]*
4. *Il est important de commencer rapidement, pour respecter les délais. [It's important to get started quickly, to respect the deadlines.]*

The human-translated target texts include more clausal complements (ccomp) than the LLM-versions and the STs. One explanation for these higher numbers is that formulations such as "ça veut dire", "ça signifie" are used frequently to explain difficult words or concepts. Here are some examples (from TT-1_human):

1. Cela veut dire qu'ils sont secrets. [That means they are secret.]
2. Vous allez voir votre médecin cela s'appelle une consultation. [You will see your doctor, that is called a consultation.]

Clausal complements are also part of the construction "il faut X". The frequency per million tokens of the verb "falloir" is 3040 in the human TTs against 1958 (TT-2_ChatGPT), 899

(ST_StFR) and 640 (TT-3_LeChat). This explains why ccomp-relations are more frequent in the TT-1_human subcorpus.

6 Conclusion and future directions

The initial research question was whether ChatGPT and Le Chat could translate a source text into FALC and whether the output could compete with a target text that was translated by a human. Human translations are still seen as the gold standard for Easy Language translation. This is not only because automatic simplification tools either do not exist for a specific language or do not produce the desired outcome, but especially because they lack the ability to account for the different communicative needs of the very heterogenous target audience of Easy Language (Saggion, 2024). The necessary competences for an Easy Language translator include knowledge of the target audience to be able to adapt the content – both by adding and reducing the information appropriately (Maaß, 2020). We might expect that human translators are more capable of judging which information to include. However, the qualitative analysis did not confirm this, the LLMs were in some cases more consistent and omitted less information, while the human translators sometimes omitted relevant information. For example, the human translator omitted information about the time span for taking the morning-after pill, while ChatGPT and Le Chat did not. Although this is just one example, it demonstrates that assessing the adequacy of omissions is not only very difficult, but also that human judgement is error-prone. Therefore, potential content inconsistencies between ST and TT are not a sound basis to judge the capacity of ChatGPT or Le Chat to translate into FALC. As the qualitative analysis showed, the LLMs did not produce incorrect information and most of the information units was translated. Now, if we assume that a standard French ST gets translated by an LLM into FALC, we can look at the product from two perspectives: that of end user- and translator. The motivation to translate the texts differs: the user seeks information and needs a simplified version of the ST; the translator might seek inspiration or want to save time. From a user perspective, if crucial information is missing, the text might not be action-enabling as it should be (Maaß, 2020). Easy Language target audiences are unlikely to be able to search for the missing information elsewhere. Although the text might fail to enable its reader to act, based on the findings in this study, it is likely that the LLM produces a simpler text (in terms of readability and syntax), which can be interpreted as an improvement over the inaccessible ST. The situation is obviously different for translators, because they are not the end-users. If information units are missing, the translator can add them.

The results presented show that the question of whether LLMs are useful tools for FALC cannot simply be answered with yes or no. Yes, because overall the LLMs produced simpler versions of a source text. The sentences were shorter, the MATTR and the lexical density was lower (except for Le Chat) and the overall syntactic complexity decreased. Also yes, because the overall content was consistent despite some omissions. On the other hand, some of the dependency relations are more frequent in the target texts than in the source texts. This is for instance the case for adverbial clauses and open clause complements. The question is, then, to which extent each individual type of dependency relations affects the overall syntactic complexity for the target groups. Yet, this is a research desideratum, that has not yet been answered (Hansen-Schirra et al., 2020). In her study on the comprehensibility of clausal sentences in Easy German, Borghardt found that splitting them into two sentences to avoid subordination does not enhance the comprehensibility and, moreover, conjunctions have a positive impact (Borghardt, 2022). Thus, future research on FALC should focus on how specific types of dependency relations affect comprehensibility. A more fine-grained analysis of the dependency relations would be interesting as the current analysis did not account for the numbers of dependencies per sentence.

In conclusion, ChatGPT and Le Chat produced target texts that are a good starting point, but post-editing is needed. Currently, these LLMs cannot replace the work of a human translator, although the human translator did not outperform the LLMs in each category. However, if they are seen as a tool to support the translation process, especially to save time, they have a lot of potential.

The validity of the results of this pilot study is limited by the rather small corpus and the fact that the qualitative analysis could not be carried out under the four-eye-principle. Therefore, future research will focus on enlarging the corpus and including other text types and domains.

Furthermore, it would be interesting to compare different prompts and strategies. Although recommendations for prompting like assigning a role were taken into account here, more iterations and few-shot in-context examples, as suggested by (Hui Jiao et al., 2024), were not tested.

References

Abdul Rauf, S., Ligozat, A.-L., Yvon, F., Illouz, G., & Hamon, T. (2020). Simplification automatique de texte dans un contexte de faibles ressources (Automatic Text Simplification : Approaching the Problem in Low Resource Settings for French). In C. Benzitoun, C. Braud, L. Huber, D. Langlois, S. Pogodalla, & S. Schneider (Eds.), *Actes de la 6e conférence conjointe Journées d'Études sur la Parole (JEP, 33e édition), Traitement Automatique des Langues Naturelles (TALN, 27e édition), Rencontre des Étudiants Chercheurs en Informatique pour le Traitement Automatique des Langues (RÉCITAL, 22e édition). Volume 2 : Traitement Automatique des Langues Naturelles* (pp. 332–341). ATALA. https://aclanthology.org/2020.jeptalnrecital-taln.33/

Anschütz, M., Oehms, J., Wimmer, T., Jezierski, B., & Groh, G. (2023). Language Models for German Text Simplification: Overcoming Parallel Data Scarcity through Style-specific Pre-training. *Findings of the Association for Computational Linguistics: ACL 2023*, 1147–1158. https://doi.org/10.18653/v1/2023.findings-acl.74

Baker, M. (1995). Corpora in Translation Studies. An Overview and Some Suggestions for Future Research. *Target. International Journal of Translation Studies*, *7*(2), 223–243. https://benjamins.com/online/target/articles/target.7.2.03bak

Bestgen, Y. (2024). Measuring Lexical Diversity in Texts: The Twofold Length Problem. *Language Learning*, *74*(3), 638–671. https://doi.org/10.1111/lang.12630

Borghardt, L. (2022). *Die Syntax von Leichter Sprache: Reduziert die Umformulierung in Einzelsätze die Komplexität? Eine fMRT-Studie zur Verarbeitung von Kausalsätzen* [, Johannes Gutenberg-Universität Mainz]. DataCite.

Braune, E. (2024, March 14). Le succès de Mistral AI exaspère l'UE! *The Conversation*. https://theconversation.com/le-succes-de-mistral-ai-exaspere-lue-225385

Brouwers, L., Bernhard, D., Ligozat, Anne-Laure, & François, T. (2014). Syntactic sentence simplification for French. In *EACL*, Gothenburg, Sweden.

Campesato, O. (2024). *Large Language Models. An Introduction. MLI Generative AI Series*. Mercury Learning and Information. https://doi.org/10.1515/9781501520587

Canut, E., Delahaie, J., & Husianycia, M. (2020). Vous avez dit FALC? Pour une adaptation linguistique des textes destinés aux migrants nouvellement arrivés. *Langage et societe*, *171*(3), 171–201. https://www.cairn.info/revue-langage-et-societe-2020-3-page-171.htm

Cardon, R., & Grabar, N. (2019). Parallel Sentence Retrieval From Comparable Corpora for Biomedical Text Simplification. In *Recent Advances in Natural Language Processing,* Varna, Bulgaria.

Cardon, R., & Grabar, N. (2020). French Biomedical Text Simplification: When Small and Precise Helps. In D. Scott, N. Bel, & C. Zong (Eds.), *Proceedings of the 28th International Conference on Computational Linguistics* (pp. 710–716). International Committee on Computational Linguistics. https://doi.org/10.18653/v1/2020.coling-main.62

Charte d'accessibilité de la communication de l'État, 2022. https://www.gouvernement.fr/sites/default/files/contenu/piece-jointe/2023/03/sig_charte_accessibilite_v15_balise.pdf

Chehab, N., Holken, H., & Malgrange, M. (2019). *Rapport Final: Étude Recueil des besoins FALC*. http://51.91.138.70/simples/docs/SIMPLES_Etude_Recueil_desBesoins_FALC_HC.pdf

Christmann, U., & Groeben, N. (2019). Verständlichkeit: die psychologische Perspektive. In I. Rink & C. Maaß (Eds.), *Handbuch Barrierefreie Kommunikation* (pp. 123–145). Frank & Timme.

Covington, M. A., & McFall, J. D. (2010). Cutting the Gordian Knot: The Moving-Average Type–Token Ratio (MATTR). *Journal of Quantitative Linguistics*, *17*(2), 94–100. https://doi.org/10.1080/09296171003643098

Deilen, S., Hernández Garrido, S., Lapshinova-Koltunski, E., & Maaß, C. (2023). Using ChatGPT as a CAT tool in Easy Language translation. *Proceedings of the Second Workshop on Text Simplification, Accessibility and Readability*, 1–10. https://doi.org/10.26615/978-954-452-086-1_001

ELIS. (2024). *European Language Industry Survey 2024*. https://elis-survey.org/wp-content/uploads/2024/03/ELIS-2024-Report.pdf

Feng, Y., Qiang, J., Li, Y., Yuan, Y., & Zhu, Y. (2023). *Sentence Simplification via Large Language Models*. https://doi.org/10.48550/arXiv.2302.11957

François, T., Brouwers, L., Naets, H., & Fairon, C. (2014). AMesure: a readability formula for administrative texts (AMESURE: une plateforme de lisibilité pour les textes administratifs)[in French]. In *TALN,* Marseille. https://aclanthology.org/f14-2014.pdf

François, T., Müller, A., Rolin, E., & Norré, M. (2020). AMesure: A Web Platform to Assist the Clear Writing of Administrative Texts. In D. Wong & D. Kiela (Eds.), *Proceedings of the 1st Conference of the Asia-Pacific Chapter of the Association for Computational Linguistics and the 10th International Joint Conference on Natural Language Processing: System Demonstrations* (pp. 1–7). Association for Computational Linguistics. https://doi.org/10.18653/v1/2020.aacl-demo.1

Gala, N., Tack, A., Javourey-Devet, L., François, T., & Ziegler, J. C. (2020). Alector: A Parallel Corpus of Simplified French Texts with Alignments of Misreadings by Poor and Dyslexic Readers. In N. Calzolari, F. Béchet, P. Blache, K. Choukri, C. Cieri, T. Declerck, S. Goggi, H. Isahara, B. Maegaard, J. Mariani, H. Mazo, A. Moreno, J. Odijk, & S. Piperidis (Eds.), *Proceedings of the Twelfth Language Resources and Evaluation Conference* (pp. 1353–1361). European Language Resources Association (ELRA). https://aclanthology.org/2020.lrec-1.169.pdf

Gao, Y., Wang, R., & Hou, F. (2024). How to Design Translation Prompts for ChatGPT: An Empirical Study. In R. Wang, Z. Wang, J. Liu, A. Del Bimbo, J. Zhou, A. Basu, & M. Xu (Eds.), *Proceedings of the 6th ACM International Conference on Multimedia in Asia Workshops* (pp. 1–7). ACM. https://doi.org/10.1145/3700410.3702123

Grabar, N., & Cardon, R. (2018). CLEAR – Simple Corpus for Medical French. In A. Jönsson, E. Rennes, H. Saggion, S. Stajner, & V. Yaneva (Eds.), *Proceedings of the 1st Workshop on Automatic Text Adaptation (ATA)* (pp. 3–9). Association for Computational Linguistics. https://doi.org/10.18653/v1/W18-7002

Hansen-Schirra, S., Bisang, W., Nagels, A., Gutermuth, S., Fuchs, J., Borghardt, L., Deilen, S., Gros, A.-K., Schiffl, L., & Sommer, J. (2020). Intralingual Translation into Easy Language - Or how to Reduce Cognitive Processing Costs. In S. Hansen-Schirra & C. Maaß (Eds.), *Easy--Plain--Accessible: Vol. 2. Easy Language Research: Text and User Perspectives* (pp. 197–225). Frank & Timme.

Hansen-Schirra, S., & Maaß, C. (2020). Easy Language, Plain Language, Easy Language Plus: Perspectives on Comprehensibility and Stigmatisation. In S. Hansen-Schirra & C. Maaß (Eds.), *Easy--Plain--Accessible: Vol. 2. Easy Language Research: Text and User Perspectives* (pp. 17–38). Frank & Timme.

Hansen-Schirra, S., Nitzke, J., Gutermuth, S., Maaß, C., & Rink, I. (2020). Technologies for the Translation of Specialised Texts into Easy Language. In S. Hansen-Schirra & C. Maaß (Eds.), *Easy--Plain--Accessible: Vol. 2. Easy Language Research: Text and User Perspectives* (pp. 99–127). Frank & Timme.

He, S. (2024, February 29). *Prompting ChatGPT for Translation: A Comparative Analysis of Translation Brief and Persona Prompts*. http://arxiv.org/pdf/2403.00127

Hendy, A., Abdelrehim, M., Sharaf, A., Raunak, V., Gabr, M., Matsushita, H., Kim, Y. J., Afify, M., & Awadalla, H. H. (2023, February 18). *How Good Are GPT Models at Machine Translation? A Comprehensive Evaluation*. http://arxiv.org/pdf/2302.09210v1

Hui Jiao, Bei Peng, Lu Zong, Xiaojun Zhang, & Xinwei Li (2024). Gradable ChatGPT Translation Evaluation. *Procesamiento del Lenguaje Natural*, *72*(0), 73–85. http://journal.sepln.org/sepln/ojs/ojs/index.php/pln/article/view/6579

Inclusion Europe. (2009). *L'information pour tous.: Règles européennes pour une information facile à lire et à comprendre*. UNAPEI.

Jiao, W., Wang, W., Huang, J., Wang, X., Shi, S., & Tu, Z. (2023). *Is ChatGPT A Good Translator? Yes With GPT-4 As The Engine*. https://doi.org/10.48550/arXiv.2301.08745

Kettunen, K. (2014). Can Type-Token Ratio be Used to Show Morphological Complexity of Languages? *Journal of Quantitative Linguistics*, *21*(3), 223–245. https://doi.org/10.1080/09296174.2014.911506

Kew, T., Chi, A., Vásquez-Rodríguez, L., Agrawal, S., Aumiller, D., Alva-Manchego, F., & Shardlow, M. (2023). *BLESS: Benchmarking Large Language Models on Sentence Simplification*. https://doi.org/10.48550/arXiv.2310.15773

Klöser, L., Beele, M., Schagen, J.-N., & Kraft, B. (2024). *German Text Simplification: Finetuning Large Language Models with Semi-Synthetic Data*. https://doi.org/10.48550/arXiv.2402.10675

Lindholm, C., & Vanhatalo, U. (Eds.). (2021a). *Easy - plain - accessible: vol. 8. Handbook of easy languages in Europe*. Frank & Timme. https://library.oapen.org/bitstream/id/1e86bbfc-0824-4040-80f9-d24f8a6d72d0/Handbook_of_Easy_Languages_in_Europe.pdf

Lindholm, C., & Vanhatalo, U. (2021b). Introduction. In C. Lindholm & U. Vanhatalo (Eds.), *Easy - plain - accessible: vol. 8. Handbook of easy languages in Europe* (pp. 11–26). Frank & Timme.

Loi n° 2005-102 du 11 février 2005 pour l'égalité des droits et des chances, la participation et la citoyenneté des personnes handicapées, 2005. https://www.legifrance.gouv.fr/jorf/id/JORFTEXT000000809647

Maaß, C. (2020). *Easy Language - Plain Language - Easy Language Plus*. Frank & Timme.

Maaß, C., & Rink, I. (2020). Scenarios for Easy Language Translation: How to Produce Accessible Content for Users with Diverse Needs. In S. Hansen-Schirra & C. Maaß (Eds.), *Easy--Plain--Accessible: Vol. 2. Easy Language Research: Text and User Perspectives* (pp. 41–56). Frank & Timme.

Marneffe, M.-C. de, Manning, C. D., Nivre, J., & Zeman, D. (2021). Universal Dependencies. *Computational Linguistics*, 1–54. https://doi.org/10.1162/coli_a_00402

Ministère du Travail, de la Santé, des solidarités et des familles. (2025). *Accessibilité : une campagne de sensibilisation à destination des agents publics*. https://www.handicap.gouv.fr/accessibilite-une-campagne-de-sensibilisation-destination-des-agents-publics

Mistral AI. (n.d.). *Accompagner nos clients à la pointe.* Retrieved April 8, 2025, from https://mistral.ai/fr/customers

Ormaechea, L., & Tsourakis, N. (2023). Extracting Sentence Simplification Pairs from French Comparable Corpora Using a Two-Step Filtering Method. In H. Ghorbel, M. Sokhn, M. Cieliebak, M. Hürlimann, de Salis, Emmanuel, & J. Guerne (Chairs), *SwissText,* Neuchâtel, Switzerland. https://aclanthology.org/2023.swisstext-1.4/

Ormaechea, L., & Tsourakis, N. (2024). Automatic text simplification for French: model fine-tuning for simplicity assessment and simpler text generation. *International Journal of Speech Technology*, *27*(4), 957–976. https://doi.org/10.1007/s10772-024-10146-0

Parpan-Blaser, A., Girard-Groeber, S., Antener, G., Arn, C., Baumann, R., Caplazi, A., Carrer, L., Diacquenod, C., Lichtenauer, A., & Sterchi, A. (2021). Easy Language in Switzerland. In C. Lindholm & U. Vanhatalo (Eds.), *Easy - plain - accessible: vol. 8. Handbook of easy languages in Europe.* Frank & Timme.

Qi, P., Zhang, Y [Yuhao], Zhang, Y [Yuhui], Bolton, J., & Manning, C. D. (2020). Stanza: A Python Natural Language Processing Toolkit for Many Human Languages.

Qiang, J., Huang, M., Zhu, Y., Yuan, Y., Zhang, C., & Yu, K. (2025). *Redefining Simplicity: Benchmarking Large Language Models from Lexical to Document Simplification.* https://doi.org/10.48550/arXiv.2502.08281

Rink, I. (2019). Kommunikationsbarrieren. In I. Rink & C. Maaß (Eds.), *Handbuch Barrierefreie Kommunikation* (pp. 29–65). Frank & Timme. https://doi.org/10.25528/020

Rivas Ginel, M. I., & Moorkens, J. (2024). A year of ChatGPT: translators' attitudes and degree of adoption. *Tradumàtica Tecnologies De La Traducció*(22), 258–275. https://doi.org/10.5565/rev/tradumatica.369

Rodríguez Vázquez, S., Kaplan, A., Bouillon, P., Griebel, C., & Azari, R. (2022). La traduction automatique des textes faciles à lire et à comprendre (FALC) : une étude comparative. *Meta*, *67*(1), 18–49. https://doi.org/10.7202/1092189ar

Rolin, E., Langlois, Q., Watrin, P., & François, T. (2021). FrenLyS: A Tool for the Automatic Simplification of French General Language Texts. In *Proceedings of the Conference Recent Advances in Natural Language Processing - Deep Learning for Natural Language Processing Methods and Applications* (pp. 1196–1205). INCOMA Ltd. Shoumen, BULGARIA. https://doi.org/10.26615/978-954-452-072-4_135

Saggion, H. (2024). Artificial intelligence and natural language processing for easy-to-read texts. *Revista De Llengua I Dret*(82), 84–103. https://doi.org/10.58992/rld.i82.2024.4362

Seretan, V. (2012). Acquisition of Syntactic Simplification Rules for French. In N. Calzolari, K. Choukri, T. Declerck, M. Uğur Doğan, B. Maegaard, J. Mariani, . . . S. Piperidis (Chairs), *LREC,* Istanbul, Turkey. http://www.lrec-conf.org/proceedings/lrec2012/pdf/304_Paper.pdf

Siddharthan, A. (2014). A survey of research on text simplification. *ITL - International Journal of Applied Linguistics*, *165*(2), 259–298. https://doi.org/10.1075/itl.165.2.06sid

Todirascu, A., Wilkens, R., Rolin, E., François, T., Bernhard, D., & Gala, N. (2022). HECTOR: A Hybrid TExt SimplifiCation TOol for Raw Texts in French. In N. Calzolari, F. Béchet, P. Blache, K. Choukri, C. Cieri, T. Declerck, S. Goggi, H. Isahara, B. Maegaard, J. Mariani, H. Mazo, J. Odijk, & S. Piperidis (Eds.), *Proceedings of the Thirteenth Language Resources and Evaulation Conference. LREC* (pp. 4620–4630). European Language Resources Association (ELRA). https://aclanthology.org/2022.lrec-1.493/

Vandeghinste, V., Müller, A., François, T., & Clercq, O. de. (2021). Easy Language in Belgium. In C. Lindholm & U. Vanhatalo (Eds.), *Easy - plain - accessible: vol. 8. Handbook of easy languages in Europe* (pp. 53–90). Frank & Timme.

Vilar, D., Freitag, M., Cherry, C., Luo, J., Ratnakar, V., & Foster, G. (2022). *Prompting PaLM for Translation: Assessing Strategies and Performance.* https://doi.org/10.48550/arXiv.2211.09102

Yamada, M. (2023). Optimizing Machine Translation through Prompt Engineering: An Investigation into ChatGPT's Customizability. In *Proceedings of Machine Translation Summit XIX, Vol. 2: Users Track,* Macau, China.

Zhang, X., Rajabi, N., Duh, K., & Koehn, P. (2023). Machine Translation with Large Language Models: Prompting, Few-shot Learning, and Fine-tuning with QLoRA. In P. Koehn, B. Haddow, T. Kocmi, & C. Monz (Eds.), *Proceedings of the Eighth Conference on Machine Translation* (pp. 468–481). Association for Computational Linguistics. https://doi.org/10.18653/v1/2023.wmt-1.43

Zhu, W., Liu, H., Dong, Q., Xu, J., Huang, S., Kong, L., Chen, J., & Li, L. (2024). Multilingual Machine Translation with Large Language Models: Empirical Results and Analysis. In K. Duh, H. Gomez, & S. Bethard (Eds.), *Findings of the Association for Computational Linguistics: NAACL 2024* (pp. 2765–2781). Association for Computational Linguistics. https://doi.org/10.18653/v1/2024.findings-naacl.176

A Appendix: Prompts

Prompt 1 :
Tu es traductrice professionnelle. Tu fais des traductions intralinguales du français standard vers le FALC (français facile à lire et à comprendre). Le public cible a des difficultés de lecture. Le domaine de spécialité des textes originaux est la santé, plus précisément la santé sexuelle. Voici les principes de base du FALC :
Règles de rédaction :
Utiliser des phrases courtes (une seule idée par phrase).
Employer des mots simples et connus (éviter le jargon, les sigles et les abréviations).
Préférer la voix active (ex. : Marie ouvre la porte plutôt que La porte est ouverte par Marie).
Expliquer les mots compliqués si leur utilisation est indispensable.
Éviter les négations doubles (ex. : écrire C'est possible au lieu de Ce n'est pas impossible).
Faire des listes avec des puces pour organiser l'information.
Utiliser des exemples concrets pour illustrer une idée.
Mise en page et présentation :
Écrire en gros caractères (taille 14 minimum, en Arial ou Verdana).
Aérer le texte (un seul concept par ligne).
Utiliser des images ou pictogrammes pour illustrer les concepts importants.
Aligner le texte à gauche (éviter le texte justifié).
Mettre en gras les mots importants (éviter l'italique et le souligné).

Le FALC est souvent utilisé dans les documents administratifs, les brochures d'information et les sites web pour améliorer l'accessibilité. Traduit le texte suivant en FALC en appliquant les règles qui sont citées en haut et en rajoutant des explications des mots si tu le juges nécessaire. Il est important de conserver les informations clés du texte. Le texte cible doit être un texte en FALC, qui correspond aux règles. Voici le texte à traduire : [...]

Prompt 2 :
Simplifie encore plus le texte, les informations clés doivent être conservées, mais le lexique et la syntaxe peuvent être simplifiés.

Prompt 3 :
Simplifie encore le texte en prenant en compte les règles du FALC, les informations clés doivent être conservées. Simplifie le lexique et la syntaxe et rajoute des explications si c'est nécessaire pour la compréhension.

B Appendix: List of Source Texts (ST)

	Subject	Author/Editor	Link
ST_1	Breast Cancer Screening	Institut National du cancer	https://www.crcdc-hdf.fr/wp-content/uploads/2023/03/Depliant-DOCS-2022_148x210-DEPSEIN21-BD-4.pdf
ST_2	Abortion	Ministère de la Santé et de la Prévention	https://ivg.gouv.fr/sites/ivg/files/2022-11/IVG%20Guide%20complet.pdf
ST_3	Mental Health	Ministère de la Santé et de la Solidarité	https://sante.gouv.fr/IMG/pdf/sante-mentale-guide-adultes.pdf
ST_4	Sexual Health, consent	Planning familial, Région Nouvelle Aquitaine	https://cloud6.zourit.net/index.php/s/TngXksBko3DWzyb
ST_5	Gender identity and sexual orientation	Planning familial, Région Nouvelle Aquitaine	https://cloud6.zourit.net/index.php/s/HpN9kCbb3C6pmHx
ST_6	Violence and sexual assault	Planning familial, Région Nouvelle Aquitaine	https://cloud6.zourit.net/index.php/s/8jiHJDXk9QeXFgp
ST_7	Contraceptives	Planning familial, Région Nouvelle Aquitaine	https://cloud6.zourit.net/index.php/s/TsGYWdBYEWsEnF2
ST_8	Abortion	Planning familial, Région Nouvelle Aquitaine	https://cloud6.zourit.net/index.php/s/nFCzomgFxfYErEP
ST_9	Morning-after pill	Planning familial, Région Nouvelle Aquitaine	https://cloud6.zourit.net/index.php/s/s54jBx3PQs3kREt
ST_10	Menstruation	Planning familial, Région Nouvelle Aquitaine	https://cloud6.zourit.net/index.php/s/TtCzKTtcRwWjy9k
ST_11	Sexually transmitted diseases	Planning familial, Région Nouvelle Aquitaine	https://www.calameo.com/read/0075046587a946b2beb4c
ST_12	Sexually transmitted diseases	Planning familial des Pyrénées Atlantiques	https://www.tonplanatoi.fr/uploads/images/FALC_Plaquette_Planning_Familial_PAU_2024-1(1).pdf
ST_13	Contraceptives	Planning familial des Pyrénées Atlantiques	https://www.tonplanatoi.fr/uploads/images/FALC_Plaquette_Planning_Familial_PAU_2024-1(1).pdf
ST_14	Abortion	Planning familial des Pyrénées Atlantiques	https://www.tonplanatoi.fr/uploads/images/FALC_Plaquette_Planning_Familial_PAU_2024-1(1).pdf
ST_15	Violence	Planning familial des Pyrénées Atlantiques	https://www.tonplanatoi.fr/uploads/images/FALC_Plaquette_Planning_Familial_PAU_2024-1(1).pdf

Simplifying healthcare communication: Evaluating AI-driven plain language editing of informed consent forms

Vicent Briva-Iglesias
SALIS, CTTS, ADAPT Centre
Dublin City University
vicent.brivaiglesias@dcu.ie

Isabel Peñuelas Gil
CITTAC
Universidad de Valladolid
isabel.penuelas@uva.es

Abstract

Clear communication between patients and healthcare providers is crucial, particularly in informed consent forms (ICFs), which are often written in complex, technical language. This paper explores the effectiveness of generative artificial intelligence (AI) for simplifying ICFs into Plain Language (PL), aiming to enhance patient comprehension and informed decision-making. Using a corpus of 100 cancer-related ICFs, two distinct prompt engineering strategies (Simple AI Edit and Complex AI Edit) were evaluated through readability metrics: Flesch Reading Ease, Gunning Fog Index, and SMOG Index. Statistical analyses revealed statistically significant improvements in readability for AI-simplified texts compared to original documents. Interestingly, the Simple AI Edit strategy consistently outperformed the Complex AI Edit across all metrics. These findings suggest that minimalistic prompt strategies may be optimal, democratising AI-driven text simplification in healthcare by requiring less expertise and resources. The study underscores the potential for AI to significantly improve patient-provider communication, highlighting future research directions for qualitative assessments and multilingual applications.

1 Introduction

Clear communication between patients and healthcare providers is fundamental to effective healthcare delivery (Montalt-Resurrecció et al., 2024). In this context, informed consent forms (ICFs) are an essential element of this communication, ensuring that patients are aware of the reasons for the procedures they need, as well as the risks and benefits involved (Nijhawan et al., 2013). However, ICFs are usually written in highly technical language to minimise ambiguity, which could have legal consequences (Resnik, 2009). While this precision is necessary, it often results in complex texts that are difficult for patients to understand and could raise ethical concerns about the extent to which consent is truly informed. The recent popularity of generative artificial intelligence (AI) has made advanced large language models available to the public, which can facilitate language tasks such as text simplification (Brown et al., 2020). Consequently, this research aims to explore whether AI can be used in a human-centred way to augment users (Briva-Iglesias, 2024), and more specifically, intends to analyse the potential of AI in healthcare text simplification. We seek to respond to the following research questions:

RQ1. *Can AI-generated simplifications of ICFs produce documents that are statistically significantly more comprehensible for patients?*

RQ2. *What type of prompt engineering strategy yields better readability results?*

The paper is structured as follows: Section 2 presents an overview of the literature on readability and plain language practices in healthcare contexts. Section 3 describes the methodology, detailing dataset selection, the AI system utilised, the two prompt engineering approaches tested, and the evaluation metrics applied. Section 4 analyses and presents the results obtained, comparing the effectiveness of the different prompt engineering strategies. Finally, Section 5 discusses the results and outlines implications for clinical practice, patient-provider communication, and future research directions.

2 Related work

Access to information "through any media and regardless of frontiers," as stated in the Universal Declaration of Human Rights (United Nations, 1948), is a human right linked to freedom of expression and opinion. However, differences in reading comprehension, language skills and education lev-

Proceedings of the 1st Workshop on Artificial Intelligence and Easy and Plain Language in Institutional Contexts (AI & EL/PL), pages 55–65, June 23, 2025

els often become barriers to fulfilling this right (Halloran, 2023).

As society moves towards a more inclusive perspective, Easy and Plain Language (E/PL) have become essential in bridging the existing communication gaps. These approaches aim to remove linguistic barriers, with the objective of "mak[ing] content comprehensible and enabl[ing] the primary target groups to gather information as a basis for their decision-making" (Maaß, 2020). In doing so, E/PL empowers individuals to access, understand, and engage with information more effectively. Easy Language (EL) and Plain Language (PL) are considered to be "varieties of different national languages with reduced linguistic complexity" (Hansen-Schirra and Maaß, 2020); however, it is important to make a distinction between the two.

While both stand for increased comprehensibility, EL represents "the maximally comprehensible variety of a natural language" (Maaß, 2020). EL was initially established as a language variety for people with learning disabilities, that was later opened to other target groups (Ahrens, 2020), such as people with aphasia, dementia or hearing impairments, functional illiterates, and non-native speakers (Berget and Bugge, 2022). However, recent studies have shown that EL has the potential to stigmatise its users as it makes communication challenges or impairments apparent (Maaß, 2020).

As Hansen-Schirra and Maaß (2020) note, "the simplicity and uniformity of EL texts have a stigmatising effect on their users," whereas this effect is reduced in PL, which appears as an intermediate variety between EL and standard language. PL, often referred to as Plain English (PE) in Anglophone contexts, is defined in the United States Plain Writing Act of 2010 as "writing that is clear, concise, well-organized, and follows other best practices appropriate to the subject or field and intended audience," noting that what is considered plain to one group of readers may not be plain to others (United States General Administration, 2023).

As such, one of the main recommendations when writing in PL is to consider who is the target audience, a principle emphasised by organisations like the Irish National Adult Literacy Agency (NALA) (2024) or the U.S. General Services Administration (United States General Administration, 2023). NALA also stresses the importance of using personal, simple, and direct language, defining any technical terms and abbreviations used, keeping sentences concise (15-20 words long on average), and structuring information clearly in relatively short paragraphs. Visual presentation—such as clear formatting, spacing, and headings—should also be considered to ensure the text is not overwhelming (National Adult Literacy Agency, 2024).

Today, many governments have recognised the importance of PL on the road to equity. However, the legal and regulatory framework for its implementation is still in a developing stage. Some of the more notable efforts include the aforementioned United States Plain Writing Act of 2010, which requires federal agencies to use clear and concise language in their communications (United States Senate, 2010).

Progress was also made in Ireland with the Plain Language Bill of 2019, entitled "Act to ensure that all information for the public from government and State bodies is written and presented in plain language." However, it lapsed in January 2020 (Houses of the Oireachtas, 2019). More recently, New Zealand has enacted the Plain Language Act 2022, which aims to improve accessibility by requiring officials to communicate clearly with the public (New Zealand Government, 2022). At a global level, ISO 24495-1 on PL, published by the International Organisation for Standardisation (ISO) in June 2023, provides a global benchmark for clear communication.

Australia has played a key role in its development through the International Plain Language Federation (IPLF) (Plain Language Association International, 2025; ISO, 2023). In addition, Australia has actively promoted plain language across government and the private sector, and adopted the standard as an Australian Standard in 2024 (Plain Language Association International, 2025).

Some other countries have also adopted the new standard. Norway made it the national standard in December 2023, followed by South Africa, which adopted the standard in March 2024. Meanwhile, Canada has not officially adopted the standard, but its national guidelines are in line with the ISO principles (Plain Language Association International, 2025).

Furthermore, while the EU has not yet introduced comprehensive PL legislation, it does promote clear communication through specific regulations. This is the case of the General Data Protection Regulation (GDPR), which requires 'clear and plain language' (European Union, 2016) in all communications related to the processing of personal data; the European Accessibility Act (EAA), which aims to ensure that key products and services in the EU are designed to be accessible, including aspects of clear communication (European Union, 2019); or the EU Clinical Trials Regulation (CTR), which requires transparency in clinical trials, including easily accessible information in the EU database (European Union, 2014). These regulations underscore the growing recognition of PL's importance across various sectors, and healthcare is a crucial area of application.

The healthcare sector has long recognised and documented the challenges posed by low health literacy in the general population. As early as 2007, Stableford and Mettger (2007) identified PL as a "logical and flexible response" to these issues. Incorporating PL into patient-provider communication makes it easier for patients to find, understand, and use the information they need (Halloran, 2023), which can lead to better health outcomes, "including emotional health, symptom resolution, and functional status" (Yen et al., 2024).

As a result, healthcare professionals have increasingly advocated the use of PL in patient communication and patient education (e.g. Quesenberry (2017); Grene et al. (2017)). Some of these initiatives include the creation of PL materials and guides for specific medical contexts, such as Abrams and Dreyer (2008), who created a series of PL handouts for paediatric patients and their parents, recognising the importance of clear communication across different age groups; or van der Giessen et al. (2021), who created a PL guide for genetic counselling of breast cancer patients.

Recent advances in technology have opened the door to new methods of improving health literacy. Professionals have discussed the possibility of incorporating tools such as machine translation (e.g., Ugas et al. (2025, 2024); Lawson McLean and Yen (2024)) or AI (e.g., Ovelman et al. (2024); James (2024)) from both practical and ethical perspectives. This potential has been explored in studies applying PL principles to AI-based tools.

This is the case of the study conducted by Aide and the NHS (Wharton, 2023) to help patients understand their conditions and remind them to take their medication. Other example would be FactPICO (Joseph et al., 2024), a factuality benchmark for plain language summarisation of medical texts describing randomised controlled trials, which aims to assess the effectiveness of language models in this context.

However, while these technologies are promising, their implementation must be carefully considered to ensure accuracy and maintain the nuanced communication required in healthcare settings. A key area where this concern is particularly relevant is ICFs, which are complex texts that serve as ethical and legal documents outlining a patient's consent to receive specific treatments or procedures after being adequately informed about their healthcare decisions (Nijhawan et al., 2013).

In this context, adapting ICFs to PL will help patients understand the information necessary to make informed decisions about their healthcare. The following section outlines the methodology used to assess the effectiveness of generative AI to adapt ICFs for better accessibility.

3 Methodology

This study develops a methodology to systematically evaluate the effectiveness of generative AI systems in making ICFs more accessible for patients via PL. The framework consists of four distinct phases: (1) dataset and system selection, (2) readability metrics, (3) prompt design and PL ICF generation, and (4) output analysis. The following sections describe each phase in detail.

3.1 Dataset and system selection

One of the main aspects of this study concerns the selection of texts used as a sample for analysis. The ICFs should be representative of current patient-healthcare provider communication to ensure relevant conclusions that are applicable to real contexts. To this end, a corpus of ICFs was compiled partially following Seghiri Domínguez (2017) compilation protocol, which consists of four main steps: text search, download, conversion, and storage, with an additional cleaning stage incorporated.

The search focused on ICFs covering a variety of diseases, treatments, and medical specialities. This broad search process excluded only incomplete ICFs, such as templates providing drafting guidelines for specific cases. For this study, the corpus was limited to English-language texts, though the search process could be extended to other languages in future studies.

All the relevant documents found were manually downloaded in their original format (PDF) and then converted into UTF-8 TXT files using AntFileConverter (Anthony, 2014). This process seeks to prevent layout disruptions during text processing and to ensure compatibility with corpus management tools at a later date. Following conversion, a cleaning stage was applied to remove unwanted elements caused by layout interference. These elements were mostly composed of non-alphanumeric characters generated during the conversion process, which were eliminated to improve text quality for the analysis phase.

Each ICF was then assigned a unique identifier following a structured naming convention: a three-digit numerical identifier corresponding to the order of download, followed by 'ws' (indicating it was obtained via web search), an abbreviation of the general theme ('ICF'), the full download date (yyyymmdd), and a language indicator (e.g., 'EN' for English texts). For instance, the identifier 001wsICF20250213EN refers to the first document in the corpus, downloaded on 13 February 2025.

Once labelled, the files were systematically stored in folders and subfolders based on language and file format (PDF and TXT). In the case of TXT files, an additional distinction was made between raw texts and those cleaned for analysis. For efficient corpus management, a dedicated file logged key details for each document, such as its unique identifier, source URL, download date, conversion progress, thematic categorisation, and a column for additional notes.

The result is a monolingual corpus comprising 224 informed consent forms catalogued and structured for exploitation. For the present study, only a sample of 100 ICFs was used in the analysis phase, amounting to 193,979 tokens and 1,383 types. All texts of the sample were obtained from Cancer Research UK[1]. To ensure diversity within the domain, the sample includes five different types of cancer (Acute myeloid leukaemia, Breast cancer, Colorectal cancer, Gynaecological cancer, and Lung cancer) and related therapies and treatments. Each cancer type is represented by a set of 20 texts.

Although ICFs adhere to a standardised structural framework while being adapted to different diseases and treatments, the distribution of tokens and types within the corpus varies significantly. Even if recurrent legal and medical phrases lead to a high degree of repetition, the inclusion of diverse pathologies and procedures introduces considerable lexical variation.

The second main aspect of the development of this study concerns the selection of generative AI systems. In this regard, several approaches were evaluated, including whether to use one or multiple systems. In this instance, a single system was considered more appropriate, with the possibility of expanding the study to multiple AI models based on the findings of the analysis phase in future work.

When determining which AI system to use, various models were considered, including OpenAI, DeepSeek, Google, or Perplexity models. Finally, the OpenAI model gpt-4o-2024-11-20 was chosen for this study due to its current popularity among general AI users (Ginel and Moorkens, 2024). The model was accessed through API calls.

3.2 Readability metrics

The ICFs were evaluated using three different metrics that allow for a preliminary assessment of their readability: the Flesch Reading Ease (Flesch, 1948), the Gunning Fog Index (Gunning, 1952), and the SMOG Index (Mc Laughlin, 1969). These metrics were measured for each of the clean TXTs compiled.

The Flesch Reading Ease (FRE), based on sentence length and syllable count, is the most general of the three, as it measures the overall reading difficulty and accessibility of a text. FRE results are presented on a scale ranging from 0 to 100, where higher scores indicate easier readability. Texts that score under 50 are considered to be difficult, where 50 indicates an undergraduate reading level and 30 a postgraduate reading level.

Meanwhile, the Gunning Fog Index (GFI) serves as a broader measure of readability. It incorporates into its analysis both sentence length and the frequency of complex words, defined as words with three or more syllables. As a result, it provides insight into some aspects of structural and lexical difficulty. GFI results estimate the number of years of education required to understand a text, with scores typically ranging from 1 to 17, where 17 or higher suggests a postgraduate reading level.

In contrast, while the GFI takes into account complex words in general, the SMOG Index is specifically designed to focus on polysyllabic words, making it particularly useful for identifying complex or specialised terminology. When it comes to medical texts and, therefore, ICFs, the prevalence of technical terms can significantly affect text accessibility for patients (Dahm, 2012). The results provided by SMOG indicate the minimum school grade, based on the United States schooling system, needed to fully understand a text.

[1]Link: https://www.cancerresearchuk.org/health-professional/treatment-and-other-post-diagnosis-issues/consent-forms-for-sact-systemic-anti-cancer-therapy

Similarly to the GFI, the scale typically stops at 17, where texts that score 17 or higher require a post-graduate knowledge level. However, unlike in the previous index, the scale starts at 4.

Each of the metrics addresses specific surface-level features of readability and, when combined, they offer a preliminary analysis of textual difficulty, including sentence complexity and word length. However, it is important to note that these indices do not account for deeper aspects of language, such as discourse structure, conceptual clarity, or terminological consistency in the theoretical sense. As such, they serve as an initial tool for exploring textual accessibility, particularly in a pilot context. These readability metrics are essential to address the research questions posed by this study and were run simultaneously using a Python script that processed all texts at once and returned the scores on their respective scales.

3.3 Prompt design and PL ICF generation

Having selected the model gpt-4o-2024-11-20 as the AI system for this study, the next step was to design the prompts. This study used two distinct prompt engineering strategies to generate PL ICFs (see Table 1 in Appendix A for observing the detailed prompts). The objective was to assess which approach yielded more effective results in terms of readability and comprehensibility.

The first approach employed a simple, minimalistic prompt strategy, primarily instructing the generative AI system to simplify texts into PL without extensive additional guidance (hereafter, "Simple AI Edit"). The Simple AI Edit allowed us to evaluate the AI system's innate ability to independently produce accessible text simplifications.

The second approach involved a more detailed, structured prompt, explicitly providing comprehensive instructions aligned with officially recognised best practices in PL (hereafter, "Complex AI Edit"). The prompt of the Complex AI Edit included clear guidance on readability, text structure, and formatting, explicitly encouraging the use of short paragraphs, lists, and other elements aimed at enhancing accessibility and comprehension. Besides, the prompt included an attached document, namely the "Writing and design tips" document of the Irish National Adult Literacy Agency (2024), which provides best practices on how to write and design documents and materials so that they are easier to read, understand and use.

Both prompt strategies were systematically applied to the original TXT files through 200 API calls. The outputs were initially generated in Markdown format and subsequently converted to plain UTF-8 TXT files to remove formatting that could affect readability metric calculations. These simplified texts were then processed using the readability metrics outlined in Section 3.2.

Following best practices in transparency and reproducibility, the complete dataset (including original and simplified texts) and the Python script to run the readability metrics and visualise the graphs are publicly available for replication, open research and further analysis at the following Zenodo link.

3.4 Statistical analyses

To assess whether AI-based PL editing statistically significantly altered the readability of the ICFs, paired sample t-tests were conducted. Given that the same set of documents was analysed under three different configurations (Original, Simple AI Edit, and Complex AI Edit), this statistical test was deemed appropriate to account for within-subject differences. For each of the metrics in Section 3.2, paired-sample t-tests were conducted to compare the following conditions: (i) Original vs. Simple AI Edit; (ii) Original vs. Complex AI Edit; (iii) Simple AI Edit vs. Complex AI Edit. A significance threshold of 0.05 was applied.

4 Results

The analyses conducted on the readability of ICFs reveal significant differences across the three document conditions assessed: Original, Simple AI Edit, and Complex AI Edit. Figure 1 demonstrates that, overall, the documents simplified through the Simple AI Edit approach yielded the best readability metrics. Documents generated using the Complex AI Edit strategy followed, while the original, unedited documents consistently showed the worst readability scores.

4.1 SMOG Readability Score

A series of paired-sample t-tests were conducted to determine whether AI-based PL editing significantly affected SMOG scores. A statistically significant reduction in SMOG scores ($t(99) = 52.17$, $p < .001$) was observed when comparing the Original version ($M = 13.88$; $SD = 0.34$) and the Simple AI Edit version ($M = 11.26$; $SD = 0.46$), indicating that the Simple AI Edit significantly simplified the texts.

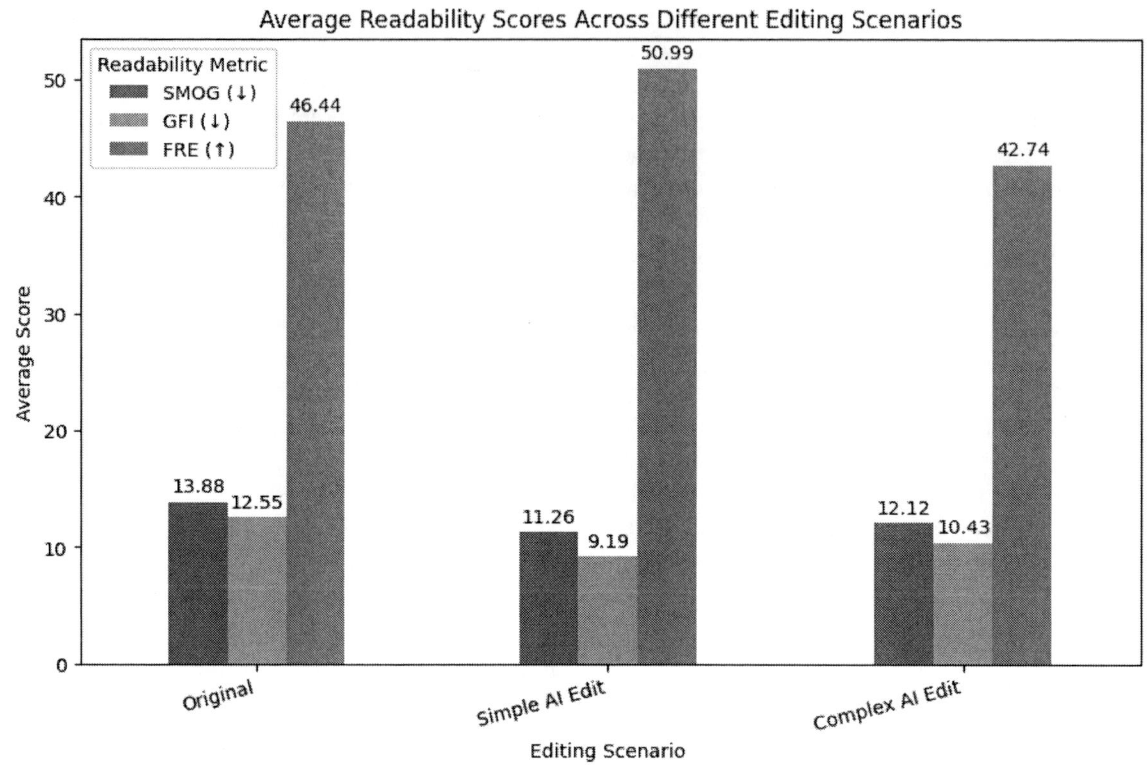

Figure 1: Readability Results.

SMOG scores were also statistically significantly lower (t(99) = 29.77, p < .001) in the Complex AI Edit (M = 12.12; SD = 0.48) compared to the Original version. Furthermore, the difference between the Simple AI Edit and Complex AI Edit was also statistically significant (t(99) = -14.35, p < .001), indicating that the Simple AI Edit resulted in greater simplification.

4.2 Gunning Fog Index (GFI)

Similar analyses were performed for the GFI metric. When comparing Original documents (M = 12.55; SD = 0.52) to the Simple AI Edit documents (M = 9.19; SD = 0.48), a statistically significant decrease in GFI scores was found (t(99) = 48.76, p < .001), confirming substantial text simplification by the Simple AI Edit.

Likewise, the Complex AI Edit documents (M = 10.43; SD = 0.67) showed a significant reduction in GFI scores compared to the Original documents (t(99) = 22.57, p < .001). Again, the difference between the two AI editing strategies was statistically significant (t(99) = -15.66, p < .001), reinforcing the greater effectiveness of the simpler prompt in reducing text complexity.

4.3 Flesch Reading Ease (FRE)

Regarding FRE scores, the comparison between Original documents (M = 46.44; SD = 4.22) and Simple AI Edit documents (M = 50.99; SD = 4.14) revealed a significant increase in readability scores (t(99) = -8.40, p < .001), indicating improved readability in the AI-edited documents. Interestingly, when comparing the Original vs Complex AI Edit documents (M = 42.74; SD = 4.04), results share a different story. In this comparison, the statistically significant difference (t(99) = 6.65, p < .001) indicates that the Original documents have higher readability than the documents generated via the Complex AI Edit.

Finally, when directly comparing Simple AI Edit and Complex AI Edit, the Simple AI Edit documents also demonstrated statistically significantly higher readability improvements (t(99) = 14.68, p < .001), underscoring the superior effectiveness of the simpler prompt strategy.

5 Discussion of the results

The findings of this study highlight the considerable potential of AI to significantly enhance the readability and comprehensibility of ICFs, essential documents within patient-provider communication (Nijhawan et al., 2013). Overall, the Simple AI Edit prompt consistently demonstrated superior effectiveness in simplifying text compared to both the Complex AI Edit and the original documents, suggesting that minimalistic yet clear instructions to generative AI systems might yield optimal results in this specific use case (see Table 2 in Appendix A for consulting a brief excerpt from the results).

Interestingly, this finding democratises the use of AI-driven PL editing, as the effort and expertise required to achieve excellent readability results are significantly reduced. Thus, healthcare providers and institutions with limited resources or technical expertise can easily integrate AI-driven simplification strategies to improve patient-healthcare provider communication.

The statistically significant reductions observed across SMOG and GFI scores clearly indicate that AI can effectively reduce text complexity, particularly through simplifying medical terminology and sentence structures. This improvement is critical in healthcare contexts where patient comprehension directly influences the quality of consent and decision-making. The Simple AI Edit strategy, with its straightforward prompt, consistently produced greater readability improvements than the more detailed and structured Complex AI Edit, which incorporated extensive PL guidelines. This result underscores the importance of simplicity and directness when guiding generative AI systems in readability enhancement tasks.

Another interesting result was that AI Plain Language editing consistently outperformed original documents across all readability metrics, except in the case of the FRE score when comparing Original documents with Complex AI Edit documents. This deviation suggests that overly detailed prompt instructions may inadvertently limit the AI system's natural simplification abilities, potentially resulting in outputs that remain closer to the original texts in terms of readability. This is supported by previous research on the importance of appropriate prompt engineering in every specific use case (Sahoo et al., 2024). Consequently, future prompt designs might benefit from balancing specificity with flexibility to optimise AI-generated readability improvements.

6 Conclusion

This study demonstrated the significant potential of AI for enhancing the readability and comprehensibility of ICFs. The findings revealed that simpler prompt instructions (Simple AI Edit) consistently achieved better readability outcomes than more complex prompts (Complex AI Edit), highlighting the feasibility and efficiency of minimalistic prompt strategies in healthcare communication contexts.

Despite these promising results, certain limitations should be acknowledged. Primarily, this research was conducted exclusively in English, thereby restricting the generalisability of the conclusions to other languages, particularly minor languages that may have different linguistic and structural complexities and less training data for AI systems, resulting in lower quality AI output (Briva-Iglesias, 2022; Briva-Iglesias et al., 2024).

Additionally, the analysis conducted was strictly quantitative, leaving qualitative aspects unexplored—specifically, whether the AI-driven simplifications inadvertently suppress crucial medical or legal information necessary for informed patient decision-making. Future research should therefore incorporate qualitative evaluations to comprehensively assess the content integrity and accuracy of AI-generated simplified documents. Such analyses will ensure that readability improvements do not compromise critical informational elements essential for informed consent.

Expanding this research to other languages and healthcare domains beyond informed consent forms could also provide further insights into the broader applicability and effectiveness of generative AI in terms of PL simplification strategies, ultimately contributing to improved patient-healthcare provider communication across diverse linguistic and medical contexts.

Furthermore, future studies should explore the impact of model size on the effectiveness of AI-driven simplification strategies. The present research utilised a large language model; however, investigating smaller models is crucial, given the importance of token usage, computational resource consumption, and sustainability considerations (Moorkens et al., 2024). Analysing the trade-off between output quality and resource efficiency could provide valuable insights into optimising generative AI applications in healthcare communications.

The implications of these results extend into clinical practice, suggesting that healthcare providers and administrators could efficiently implement simple AI-based text editing methods to produce clearer, more comprehensible documents. This could significantly enhance patient autonomy and participation in healthcare decisions, fostering more ethical and effective patient care. Additionally, this research contributes valuable insights to the broader fields of health literacy and patient-provider communication by illustrating practical strategies to bridge the persistent gap between medical precision and patient comprehension.

Acknowledgements

This research was conducted within the framework of the 'Programa Investigo' of the Spanish State Public Employment Service and the European Union, with funding from the European Union – NextGenerationEU.

References

Mary Ann Abrams and Benard P. Dreyer, editors. 2008. *Plain Language Pediatrics: Health Literacy Strategies and Communication Resources for Common Pediatric Topics*, 1st edition. American Academy of Pediatrics, Elk Grove, IL.

Sarah Ahrens. 2020. Easy language and administrative texts: Second language learners as a target group. In Silvia Hansen-Schirra and Christiane Maaß, editors, *Easy Language Research: Text and User Perspectives*, pages 67–97. Frank & Timme.

Laurence Anthony. 2014. AntConc (Version 3.4.3) [Computer Software]. Tokyo, Japan: Waseda University.

Gerd Berget and Hanna Bovim Bugge. 2022. The Development and Production of Literature Within an Easy Language and a Universal Design Perspective. *Publishing Research Quarterly*, 38(2):308–325.

Vicent Briva-Iglesias. 2022. English-Catalan Neural Machine Translation: State-of-the-art technology, quality, and productivity. *Tradumàtica*, (20):0149–176.

Vicent Briva-Iglesias. 2024. *Fostering Human-Centered, Augmented Machine Translation: Analysing Interactive Post-Editing*. Doctoral thesis, Dublin City University.

Vicent Briva-Iglesias, Gokhan Dogru, and João Lucas Cavalheiro Camargo. 2024. Large language models "ad referendum": How good are they at machine translation in the legal domain? *MonTI. Monografías de Traducción e Interpretación*, (16):75–107.

Tom B. Brown, Benjamin Mann, Nick Ryder, Melanie Subbiah, Jared Kaplan, Prafulla Dhariwal, Arvind Neelakantan, Pranav Shyam, Girish Sastry, Amanda Askell, Sandhini Agarwal, Ariel Herbert-Voss, Gretchen Krueger, Tom Henighan, Rewon Child, Aditya Ramesh, Daniel M. Ziegler, Jeffrey Wu, Clemens Winter, Christopher Hesse, Mark Chen, Eric Sigler, Mateusz Litwin, Scott Gray, Benjamin Chess, Jack Clark, Christopher Berner, Sam McCandlish, Alec Radford, Ilya Sutskever, and Dario Amodei. 2020. Language Models are Few-Shot Learners. *Preprint*, arXiv:2005.14165.

Maria Dahm. 2012. Coming to Terms with Medical Terms – Exploring Insights from Native and Non-native English Speakers in Patient-physician Communication. *HERMES - Journal of Language and Communication in Business*, (49):79–98.

European Union. 2014. Regulation (EU) No 536/2014 of the European Parliament and of the Council of 16 April 2014 on clinical trials on medicinal products for human use. Eur-Lex.

European Union. 2016. Regulation (EU) 2016/679 of the European Parliament and of the Council of 27 April 2016 on the protection of natural persons with regard to the processing of personal data and on the free movement of such data. Eur-Lex.

European Union. 2019. Directive (EU) 2019/882 of the European Parliament and of the Council of 17 April 2019 on the accessibility requirements for products and services. Eur-Lex.

Rudolph Flesch. 1948. A new readability yardstick. *Journal of Applied Psychology*, 32(3):221–233.

María Isabel Rivas Ginel and Joss Moorkens. 2024. A year of ChatGPT: Translators' attitudes and degree of adoption. *Tradumàtica tecnologies de la traducció*, (22):258–275.

Margaret Grene, Yvonne Cleary, and Ann Marcus-Quinn. 2017. Use of Plain-Language Guidelines to Promote Health Literacy. *IEEE Transactions on Professional Communication*, 60(4):384–400.

Robert Gunning. 1952. *The Technique of Clear Writing*. McGraw-Hill.

Emily Halloran. 2023. Plain language supports equity, accessibility and inclusion. Plain English Foundation.

Silvia Hansen-Schirra and Christiane Maaß. 2020. *Easy Language – Plain Language – Easy Language Plus: Perspectives on Comprehensibility and Stigmatisation*. Frank & Timme.

Houses of the Oireachtas. 2019. Plain Language Bill 2019.

ISO. 2023. ISO 24495-1:2023 on Plain Language. Part 1: Governing principles and guidelines.

Lisa Chamberlain James. 2024. Plain language summaries of clinical trial results: What is their role, and should patients and AI be involved? *Medical Writing*, 33:34–37.

Sebastian Antony Joseph, Lily Chen, Jan Trienes, Hannah Louisa Göke, Monika Coers, Wei Xu, Byron C. Wallace, and Junyi Jessy Li. 2024. FactPICO: Factuality Evaluation for Plain Language Summarization of Medical Evidence. *Preprint*, arXiv:2402.11456.

Aaron Lawson McLean and Tui Lin Yen. 2024. Machine Translation for Multilingual Cancer Patient Education: Bridging Languages, Navigating Challenges. *Journal of Cancer Education: The Official Journal of the American Association for Cancer Education*, 39(5):477–478.

Christiane Maaß. 2020. *Easy Language–Plain Language–Easy Language plus: Balancing Comprehensibility and Acceptability*. Frank & Timme.

G. Harry Mc Laughlin. 1969. SMOG Grading-a New Readability Formula. *Journal of Reading*, 12(8):639–646.

Vicent Montalt-Resurrecció, Isabel García-Izquierdo, and Ana Muñoz-Miquel. 2024. *Patient-Centred Translation and Communication*. Taylor & Francis.

Joss Moorkens, Sheila Castilho, Federico Gaspari, Antonio Toral, and Maja Popović. 2024. Proposal for a triple bottom line for translation automation and sustainability: An editorial position paper. *Journal of Specialised Translation*, (41):2–25.

National Adult Literacy Agency. 2024. Plain english writing, structure and design tips.

New Zealand Government. 2022. Plain Language Act 2022. Public Act No 54 – New Zealand Legislation.

Lokesh P. Nijhawan, Manthan D. Janodia, B. S. Muddukrishna, K. M. Bhat, K. L. Bairy, N. Udupa, and Prashant B. Musmade. 2013. Informed consent: Issues and challenges. *Journal of Advanced Pharmaceutical Technology & Research*, 4(3):134.

Colleen Ovelman, Shannon Kugley, Gerald Gartlehner, and Meera Viswanathan. 2024. The use of a large language model to create plain language summaries of evidence reviews in healthcare: A feasibility study. *Cochrane Evidence Synthesis and Methods*, 2(2):e12041.

Plain Language Association International. 2025. Plain language around the world.

Alexandria C. Quesenberry. 2017. Plain Language for Patient Education. *Journal of Consumer Health on the Internet*, 21(2):209–215.

David B. Resnik. 2009. Do informed consent documents matter? *Contemporary Clinical Trials*, 30(2):114–115.

Pranab Sahoo, Ayush Kumar Singh, Sriparna Saha, Vinija Jain, Samrat Mondal, and Aman Chadha. 2024. A Systematic Survey of Prompt Engineering in Large Language Models: Techniques and Applications. *Preprint*, arXiv:2402.07927.

Miriam Seghiri Domínguez. 2017. Metodología de elaboración de un glosario bilingüe y bidireccional (inglés-español/español-inglés) basado en corpus para la traducción de manuales de instrucciones de televisores. *Babel: Revue Internationale de la Traduction = International Journal of Translation*, 63(1):43–64.

Sue Stableford and Wendy Mettger. 2007. Plain Language: A Strategic Response to the Health Literacy Challenge. *Journal of Public Health Policy*, 28(1):71–93.

Mohamed Ugas, Maria Anna Calamia, Jessica Tan, Ben Umakanthan, Christine Hill, Karen Tse, Angela Cashell, Zaynab Muraj, Meredith Giuliani, and Janet Papadakos. 2025. Evaluating the feasibility and utility of machine translation for patient education materials written in plain language to increase accessibility for populations with limited english proficiency. *Patient Education and Counseling*, 131:108560.

Mohamed Ugas, Meredith Giuliani, and Janet Papadakos. 2024. When is good, good enough? On considerations of machine translation in patient education. *Journal of Cancer Education*, 39(5):474–476.

United Nations. 1948. Universal Declaration of Human Rights.

United States General Administration. 2023. What is plain language? Plain Language Action and Information Network.

United States Senate. 2010. An act to enhance citizen access to Government information and services by establishing that Government documents issued to the public must be written clearly, and for other purposes. U.S. Government Printing Office.

J. A. M. van der Giessen, M. G. E. M. Ausems, E. van Riel, A. de Jong, M. P. Fransen, and S. van Dulmen. 2021. Development of a plain-language guide for discussing breast cancer genetic counseling and testing with patients with limited health literacy. *Supportive Care in Cancer*, 29(6):2895–2905.

Ian Wharton. 2023. Achieving 75% adherence in asthma and type 2 diabetes: Our NHS England pilot results. Aide Health.

Renata W. Yen, Robert Hagedorn, Marie-Anne Durand, JoAnna K. Leyenaar, A. James O'Malley, Catherine H. Saunders, Talia Isaacs, and Glyn Elwyn. 2024. Clinician-Spoken Plain Language in Health Care Encounters: A Qualitative Analysis to Assess Measurable Elements. *Academic Medicine*, 99(6):663.

A Appendix

This Appendix contains Table 1 (the prompts used for both the Simple AI Edit and the Complex AI Edit) and Table 2 (a small excerpt from one of the ICFs analysed with the results with the original and both AI edits).

Condition	Prompt
Simple AI Edit	Transform the following document into Plain Language so that it is more understandable. Do not suppress or remove any of the information.
Complex AI Edit	Transform the following document into Plain Language by considering the enclosed document and the following recommendations. Do not suppress or remove any of the information. **Writing Style** *Know Your Audience* Consider who will read your text and what they already know. Use familiar words and concepts. Keep the tone and detail level appropriate for your audience. *Use Clear and Direct Language* Prefer "we" (for your organisation) and "you" (for the reader). Make it clear who is responsible for actions (e.g., "We will contact you" instead of "You will be contacted"). *Choose Simple Words* Avoid jargon, corporate language, and complex words. If a simpler word conveys the same meaning, use it (e.g., "use" instead of "utilise"). *Explain Technical Terms and Abbreviations* If a technical term is necessary, define it the first time. Spell out abbreviations when first mentioned and limit their use. *Keep Sentences Concise* Aim for 15–20 words per sentence. Express one idea per sentence. Avoid unnecessary phrases. **Structure** *Prioritise Reader's Needs* Present information in a logical order. Start with the most important points. *Use Visual Formatting to Guide Readers* Include bullet points and subheadings to break up text. Leave white space to make content more readable. *Keep Paragraphs Short* Each paragraph should focus on one idea. Avoid long blocks of text.

Table 1: Prompts for the AI plain language transformation

Condition	Resulting text
Original	Common chemotherapy side effects. Affecting more than 10 in every 100 (>10%) people - An increased risk of getting an infection from a drop in white blood cells – it is harder to fight infections and you can become very ill. - If you have a severe infection this can be life- threatening. Contact your doctor or hospital straight away if: - your temperature goes over 37.5°C or over 38°C, depending on the advice given by your chemotherapy team - you suddenly feel unwell (even with a normal temperature) - Thinning of the hair or sometimes complete hair loss, watery/sore eyes, sore mouth/ulcers, feeling sick (nausea) and being sick (vomiting), tummy (abdominal) pain. diarrhoea, tiredness and feeling weak (fatigue). - Low blood pressure during treatment, fluid build- up in legs and ankles with weight gain, change in skin colour, mild allergic reactions (rash, flushing).
Simple AI Edit	Common Side Effects (happens in more than 10 out of 100 people) - Infections: A weakened immune system makes infections harder to fight. Severe infections can be life-threatening. Call a doctor if: - Your temperature is above 37.5°C or 38°C (as advised by your medical team). - You feel suddenly unwell, even with a normal temperature. - Thinning or loss of hair. - Watery or sore eyes. - Sore mouth and ulcers. - Nausea and vomiting. - Abdominal (tummy) pain. - Diarrhoea. - Tiredness and weakness (fatigue). - Low blood pressure during treatment. - Fluid build-up in the legs and ankles, leading to weight gain. - Skin color changes, mild allergic reactions (rash, flushing).
Complex AI Edit	Common Side Effects (More than 10% of patients may experience these) - Increased risk of infections due to low white blood cells. Severe infections can be life-threatening. - Seek medical help if your temperature is over 37.5°C or 38°C (based on chemotherapy team advice). - Contact your doctor if you suddenly feel unwell, even with a normal temperature. - Thinning of hair or complete hair loss. - Nausea, vomiting, diarrhoea, abdominal pain. - Sore mouth and ulcers. - Fatigue, weakness. - Muscle and joint aches and pain (which may be severe). - Numbness or tingling in hands and feet (temporary or permanent). - Fluid build-up in ankles and legs with weight gain. - Low blood pressure during treatment.

Table 2: Small excerpt from one ICF after the plain language transformation

Translating Easy Language administrative texts: a quantitative analysis of DeepL's performance from German into Italian using a bilingual corpus

Christiane Maaß
University of Hildesheim / Germany
maass@uni-hildesheim.de

Chiara Fioravanti
National Research Council of Italy
Institute of Legal Informatics and Judicial Systems / Italy
chiara.fioravanti@cnr.it

Abstract

This study evaluates the performance of DeepL as an AI-based translation engine, in translating German Easy Language Texts into Italian. The evaluation is quantitative and based on a corpus of 26 German fact sheets and their Italian human translations. The results show that DeepL's translations exhibit significant errors in terminology, accuracy, and language conventions. The machine-translated texts often lack consistency in terminology, and the use of technical or unfamiliar words is not adapted to the difficulty level of the target language. Furthermore, the translations tend to normalize the texts towards standard administrative language, making them less accessible. The study highlights the need for human post-editing to ensure both accuracy and suitability of the translated texts. The findings of this study will help identify where to prioritize post-editing efforts and facilitate comparisons with the results obtained from other artificial intelligence tools used for interlingual translation of Easy Language texts in the administrative domain.

1 Introduction

Easy Language, a comprehensibility-optimized form of a natural language that makes content accessible to people with communication impairments (Maaß, 2015; Bredel & Maaß, 2016; Maaß, 2020; Maaß & Schwengber, 2022), can play an important role in institutional communication, enabling greater civic participation and inclusion. However, the extent to which it is adopted for legal and administrative texts is not the same from an international perspective (Lindholm & Vanhatalo, 2021a), leading to very different amounts of texts that are available for the different European languages. In German-speaking countries, for example, like Germany, Switzerland, and Austria, the use of Easy Language in public communication is a common and well-established approach (see Maaß et al., 2021; Parpan-Blaser et al., 2021; Fröhlich & Candussi, 2021). In this perspective, interlingual translation could be a valuable asset in expanding the use of Easy Language, all the more so with AI tools at hand.

In a previous study (Maaß & Fioravanti, in press) we examined the feasibility of utilizing DeepL, an AI-based translation engine, recognized for its high accuracy (Fitria, 2023; Kaplan, 2021), as a machine translation tool for interlingual translation into Easy Language within the domain of administrative communication for the language pair German and Italian. The performance analysis of DeepL was based on a corpus derived from texts in Easy Language produced, both in German and Italian, by the administration of the Province of Bolzano/Bozen (a multilingual geographical area in Italy).

In this study, we quantify the errors present in the machine-translated Italian target texts in comparison with the gold standard human translations.

2 Related Work

2.1 Easy Language

Easy Language (also referred to as Easy-to-read, on terminological issues see Lindholm & Vanhatalo, 2021b, and the contributions for the various languages in the *Handbook of Easy Languages in Europe* (Lindholm & Vanhatalo, 2021a)) is a comprehensibility-optimized version of a natural language (for German, see the work of Maaß, 2020; Bredel & Maaß, 2016; for Italian, see the work of Sciumbata, 2022, and Perego, 2021). Vanhatalo & Lindholm (2021a) describe the situation of Easy Language for 20 European countries. In doing so, they not only look at regulations and the legal situation, but also at the text types and domains for which Easy Language texts are available for the various languages. A particularly large number of legal-administrative communication texts are available for German (Rink, 2020; Maaß et al., 2021; Maaß & Rink, 2021). It is therefore reasonable to make these texts usable for other languages via interlingual translation. Particularly in the case of European legal topics or in multilingual regions and communities (Ahrens & Fioravanti, 2022) an increase in the number of available texts for the various languages involved can be expected.

It is also important to acknowledge that legal and administrative texts require a significant effort for translation into Easy Language due to their specialized terminology, complex syntax, and reliance on knowledge of legal procedures (Maaß & Rink, 2021). It is logical, then, to adapt an established best practice across different languages. This approach was implemented in the Province of Bolzano/Bozen, where legal and administrative texts were first translated intralingually into Easy German and subsequently into Easy Italian.

2.2 Machine Translation into or between Easy Languages

Recently, there has been growing interest in exploring machine translation in the context of Easy Language and Plain Language. However, the focus has always been on intralingual translation (see, for example, the work of Deilen et al., 2023, Deilen et al., 2024a, Deilen et al., 2024b). This is obvious, as most translations into Easy Language and Plain Language are intralingual (Maaß, 2020; Maaß, 2024). However, Pedrini (2024) shows that interlingual translation into Plain Language is also a common practice. There is significant research desideratum here. In a previous study (Maaß & Fioravanti, in press), the authors of this paper have already explored the possibilities of interlingual machine translation between the language pair German-Italian (both directions).

2.3 Evaluating the quality of translations via MQM

In the present paper, the Multidimensional Quality Metrics (MQM) framework was employed. MQM offers a comprehensive catalog of more than 100 issue types that encompass all key translation quality assessment metrics. These issues serve as a "master catalog" from which the most relevant metrics can be selected to evaluate specific translation quality tasks. As an open and freely available framework, MQM can be adopted and expanded to suit various needs (Lommel et al., 2014).

From the MQM CORE Typology error the following four categories were chosen in line with the approach of Ahrens et al. (in press), who have analyzed errors in machine translation of simplified texts: Terminology, Accuracy, Language conventions and Audience appropriateness. However, Ahrens et al. (in press) focus on intralingual translation.

3 Research Design

The analysis of DeepL's performance was based on a corpus extracted from texts in Easy Language from the Province of Bolzano/Bozen in Italy, a bilingual region where both German and Italian are official languages

These texts were produced, in German and Italian, through a collaboration between the provincial administration and Okay, the Easy Language Office of the non-profit organization Lebenshilfe ("live aid"). The Easy language texts are available on the official website of the Province of Bolzano, in a dedicated section (https://lingua-facile.provincia.bz.it/).

The German Easy Language texts were created following the rules established by the Research Centre for Easy Language at the University of Hildesheim, as outlined by Maaß (2015) and Bredel & Maaß (2016). They were proof-read by readers with intellectual disabilities (on Easy Language for this target group in Germany see

Maaß & Maaß, 2024). The Italian Easy Language texts originate from the translation of the German versions while also incorporating specific guidelines for Italian Easy Language, as defined by Sciumbata (2022). Like the German texts, the Italian translations were reviewed by individuals with intellectual disabilities to ensure their accessibility.

The source corpus comprises 26 German fact sheets (defined "Corpus Bolzano German") and their Italian human translation (defined "Corpus Bolzano Italian").

For the purpose of our study, we translated the "Corpus Bolzano German" into Italian with the help of DeepL, which led to the creation of the "Corpus DeepL Italian". We used the free version of DeepL. The style was set to "automatic". No post-editing was carried out. The "Corpus Bolzano German" (source corpus) contains a total of 12.416 words and 69.616 characters, while the "Corpus DeepL Italian" (target corpus) comprises a total of 15.453 words and 74.817 characters. The source German texts have an average length of 486,8 tokens, and the target Italian texts have an average length of 594,6 tokens.

The human translations of the "Corpus Bolzano German" (Corpus Bolzano Italian) served as gold standards for the evaluation of the DeepL performance. The evaluation followed the MQM criteria as adapted to Easy Language by Ahrens et al. (in press).

4 Results

Table 1 shows the quantification of the errors in the Corpus DeepL Italian compared to the gold standard texts (Corpus Bolzano Italian) following the MQM criteria. We followed the categorization put forward in Ahrens et al. (in press) with respect to the subcategories of the MQM core and added the category "incorrect explanation" (category: "accuracy") for cases of incorrect or inappropriate explanations of technical or unfamiliar words. The category "Hallucination" was also added.

We used the category "Audience Appropriateness" for all issues related to deviations from the rules of Italian Easy Language. This is because such deviations make the text unsuitable for the target audience, either by increasing complexity and potentially causing misunderstandings or bearing the risk of stigmatization.

Errors and issues in the DeepL translation in Italian were annotated, evaluated and then discussed by both authors who have a native-level proficiency in Italian.

MQM Error type	Quantity in the Corpus DeepL Italian
Terminology	
Inconsistent terminology	15
Wrong term	52
Accuracy	
Mistranslations and semantic shifts	8
Hallucinations	2
Untranslated	24
Wrong explanation	7
Language conventions	
Grammar	7
Audience appropriateness *Deviations from the EL rules*	196
TOTAL	311

Table 1: The quantification of the errors in the Corpus DeepL Italian compared to the gold standard texts (Corpus Bolzano Italian)

5 Discussion

5.1 Terminology

Terminology-related issues regarding the DeepL translation were critical. The machine-translated text versions exhibited problems with the correct translation of technical or domain-specific terminology, where substituting synonyms would result in a loss of contextual clarity. This issue was particularly evident in the translation of names related to legal institutions, administrative bodies, services and professional titles. A specific difficulty arose in the translation of the names of administrative units in the municipality of Bolzano, which were generalized according to the German standard, causing the original terms in Italian to be omitted in the retranslation. For example, the "Sportello unico per l'assistenza e la cura" ("One-stop-shop for care and support") was called "Punto di contatto per l'assistenza e il supporto" ("Contact point for care and support") in the DeepL translation, while the "Sportello informativo per il cittadino" ("Citizen information point") became the generic "Servizio al cittadino" ("Citizen service").

The question of correct terminology also comprised abbreviations that were not translated in the target text but remained unaltered in their source text version, although they have a correspondence in the target text that is not identical to the source text. In a bilingual region like Bolzano, each language has its own set of abbreviations for the same institutions and processes, usually derived from their full forms. For example, the German abbreviation "EEVE" appeared in place of the Italian "DURP" in texts translated with DeepL. These untranslated abbreviations pose a risk of not being recognized or linkable to their full forms, especially if these full forms also appear in the text.

5.2 Accuracy

The evaluation of the Easy Language texts translated by DeepL revealed several significant issues related to accuracy. Semantic shifts due to incongruent synonymy were observed in the DeepL corpus. These errors arose when terms in the source language had a different scope or meaning, resulting in the use of inappropriate equivalents in the target language that did not align with the intended context. For example, this happened with the word "indennità" ("allowance") becoming "paghetta" ("child's pocket money") and "amministratore di sostegno" ("legal guardian") becoming "custode" ("guard").

This also concerned the use of modal verbs in the translated texts. In several instances, these verbs were altered from their original form in the source text, resulting in substantial semantic shifts in both the German and Italian versions. An example of the Italian translation is the sentence from the Corpus Bolzano Italian "Anche le cooperative sociali devono guadagnare soldi" (Even social cooperatives must earn money) that appears as "Anche le cooperative sociali vogliono guadagnare soldi" ("Even social cooperatives want to earn money") in the Corpus DeepL Italian.

Another category of errors involved non-translated sequences. In both translation directions, certain phrases remained unchanged from the source text, though this occurred in a very limited number of instances. For example, the names of Bolzano's administrative units remained in German in the Italian text and in Italian in the German text, but not consistently. This inconsistency was also observed in the reverse translation direction, where different toponyms were either translated or left untranslated compared to the other direction, showing a lack of systematic approach.

5.3 Hallucinations

Furthermore, the Corpus DeepL Italian displays some fragments of English with no relation to the source text. As the source text is in German they were labelled hallucinations. These 'hallucinations' in English create an additional obstacle to understanding complex content, such as that typical of administrative texts.

5.4 Untranslated fragments

In as many as 24 cases, untranslated fragments from the source text remained in the target text. They mainly concern toponyms for which both German and Italian terms are available. There is no consistency here in the target texts, which significantly reduces comprehensibility, especially for an audience with intellectual disabilities or other vulnerabilities in terms of understanding content.

5.5 Language conventions

Grammatical errors were identified in some of the machine-translated texts. While these errors were not numerous, they were recurrent within specific syntactic structures, affecting the overall grammatical accuracy of the texts.

5.6 Deviations from the rules of German and Italian Easy Language

DeepL's translations of Easy Language texts do not adhere to the established German (Bredel & Maaß, (2016; Maaß, 2020) or Italian guidelines (Sciumbata, 2022; Perego, 2021), as the system is trained on standard and specialized language corpora rather than Easy Language rules. A qualitative analysis revealed several key deviations from these guidelines.

First, the translations tended to normalize the texts towards standard administrative language. This results in longer sentences and more complex vocabulary, often replacing simpler words with more high register synonyms, making the text less accessible. For example, the sentence from the Corpus Bolzano Italian, "Nel contratto di lavoro c'è scritto…" ("In the employment contract it says…") is rendered in a more institutional tone in the Corpus DeepL Italian as "il contratto di lavoro stabilisce che…" ("The employment contract states that…"). Similarly, "La persona può lavorare"

("The person can work") becomes "la persona è idonea al lavoro" ("the person is suitable for work") and "altre informazioni" ("other information") appears as "ulteriori informazioni" ("further information") in the DeepL translation.

Second, the use of verbal tenses, modes, and voice does not align with Easy Language restrictions. While Easy Language guidelines limit German to the present and perfect tenses and discourage the subjunctive, and Italian similarly minimizes grammatical complexity, DeepL translations frequently include a broader range of tenses, including the conditional, gerund, future, and passive constructions. Here are two examples of translations that highlight these issues: "questa persona non può andare a lavorare" ("this person cannot go to work") became "questa persona potrebbe non essere in grado di lavorare" ("this person might not be able to work") and "gli esperti assistono le persone" ("experts assist people") appeared as "le persone sono assistite da esperti" ("people are assisted by experts"). Another issue arose with impersonal constructions and double negatives. Easy Language favors action-oriented sentences that clarify actors and contact persons, avoiding impersonal and passive forms. Furthermore, negative statements and double negatives, which can obscure meaning, are discouraged. However, DeepL-generated texts frequently contained these structures, making the content harder to understand. For example: "lei trova le informazioni qui" ("you find the information here") becomes "per informazioni si veda qui" ("for information see here" which is impersonal and grammatically requires the Italian subjunctive rendering this solution more complex in more respects) and "il libro è gratis" ("the book is free") is "il libro non costa nulla" ("the book costs nothing") in the DeepL translation.

Consistency in terminology is also compromised. Easy Language guidelines require using the same term for the same concept throughout a document to enhance cohesion and clarity. DeepL translations, however, operate at the sentence level, failing to maintain consistency even within sections. For example in the same text, both "medico di famiglia" ("family doctor") and "medico di base" ("general practitioner") are used to refer to the same profession, whereas "parlamentari" ("parliamentarians") are also called "membri del parlamento" ("members of parliament").

Finally, the handling of difficult terms does not follow Easy Language principles. Technical or unfamiliar words should be explained when necessary, but DeepL does not adapt explanations to the difficulty level of terms in the target language. As a result, some complex terms remain unexplained when they should be, while others are unnecessarily explained, sometimes incorrectly, leading to a heavier and less effective text.

6 Conclusion and future work

The previous evaluation indicated that DeepL has achieved good, however not outstanding, results in interlingual translation of administrative texts into Easy Language. These texts present a risk of misinterpretation or misunderstanding among the target groups, primarily due to inaccuracies or a lack of compliance with Easy Language rules, which can hinder comprehension.

Moreover, administrative-legal communication is highly sensitive, requiring a level of accuracy comparable to that of health communication. As discussed in Deilen et al. (2023, 2024a, 2024b) for health-related texts, any content-related errors render a text unsafe. Consequently, automatic translation into Easy Language cannot be directly provided to the intended audience (e.g., via an institutional website) without human post-editing to ensure both accuracy and suitability.

This additional analysis using the MQM method will help identify where to prioritize post-editing efforts and facilitate comparisons (Lommel, Uszkoreit & Burchardt, 2014) with the results obtained from other artificial intelligence tools used for interlingual translation of Easy Language texts in the administrative domain.

References

Sarah Ahrens, Silvana Deilen, Sergio Hernández Garrido, Ekaterina Lapshinova-Koltunski, Christiane Maaß. 2025 in press. Evaluation of Translations into Plain German Produced by Humans and MT Systems Including ChatGPT. *SKASE Journal of Translation and Interpretation.*

Sarah Ahrens, Chiara Fioravanti. 2022. Cultural implications in Easy Language texts for migrants. Theoretical considerations and insights from practice in Germany and in Italy. *Trans-kom - Journal of Translation and Technical Communication Research*, 15 (2) 2022: 270–292.

Ursula Bredel, Christiane Maaß. 2016. *Leichte Sprache. Theoretische Grundlagen*, Orientierung für die Praxis, Duden, Berlin.

Silvana Deilen, Sergio Hernández Garrido, Ekaterina Lapshinova-Koltunski, Christiane Maaß. 2023. Using ChatGPT as a CAT tool in Easy Language translation. In *Proceedings of the Second Workshop on Text Simplification, Accessibility and Readability*, Varna, Bulgaria. INCOMA Ltd., Shoumen, Bulgaria; 2023: 1–10. https://aclanthology.org/2023.tsar-1.1

Silvana Deilen, Ekaterina Lapshinova-Koltunski, Sergio Hernández Garrido, Julian Hörner, Christiane Maaß, Vanessa Theel, Sophie Ziemer. 2024a. Evaluation of intralingual machine translation for health communication. In: *Proceedings of the 25th Annual Conference of the European Association for Machine Translation (Volume 1)*:469-479.

Silvana Deilen, Ekaterina Lapshinova-Koltunski, Sergio Hernández Garrido, Christiane Maaß, Julian Hörner, Vanessa Theel, Sophie Ziemer. 2024b: Towards AI-supported Health Communication in Plain Language: Evaluating Intralingual Machine Translation of Medical Texts. In *Proceedings of the First Workshop on Patient-Oriented Language Processing (CL4Health)@* LREC-COLING 2024, 44–53.

Tira Nur Fitria. 2023. Performance of Google Translate, Microsoft Translator, and DeepL Translator: Error Analysis of Translation Result. Al-*Lisan: Jurnal Bahasa (e-Journal)*, Vol. 8.2, 2023.

Walburga Fröhlich, Klaus Candussi. 2021. Easy Language in Austria. In Lindholm C, Vanhatalo U (eds.): *Handbook of Easy Languages in Europe*Frank & Timme, Berlin: 191-218.

Abigail Kaplan 2021. *Suitability of Neural Machine Translation for Producing Linguistically Accessible Texts. Exploring the Effects of Pre-Editing on Easy-to-Read Administrative Documents*. Manuscript of the PhD thesis, University of Geneva.

Camilla Lindholm, Ulla Vanhatalo (eds. 2021a). *Handbook of Easy Languages in Europe*. 2021. Frank & Timme, Berlin. DOI: 10.26530/20.500.12657/52628; https://library.oapen.org/handle/20.500.12657/52628

Camilla Lindholm, Ulla Vanhatalo (2021b): Introduction. In Lindholm C, Vanhatalo U (eds. 2021a) *Handbook of Easy Languages in Europe*. Frank & Timme, Berlin: 11-26. DOI: 10.26530/20.500.12657/52628; https://library.oapen.org/handle/20.500.12657/52628

Arle Lommel, Hans Uszkoreit, Aljoscha Burchardt. 2014. Multidimensional quality metrics (MQM): A framework for declaring and describing translation quality metrics. *Tradumatica*, 12:0455–463.

Christiane Maaß. 2015. *Leichte Sprache*. Das Regelbuch, Berlin.

Christiane Maaß. 2020. *Easy language – Plain Language – Easy Language* Plus. Balancing comprehensibility and acceptability, Frank&Timme, Berlin,

Christiane Maaß. 2024. Intralingual Translation in Easy Language and in Plain Language. In Pillière L, Berk Albachten Ö; Hrsg (eds), *The Routledge Handbook of Intralingual Translation*, Routledge; London. doi:https://doi.org/10.4324/9781003188872

Christiane Maaß, Chiara Fioravanti. 2025 in print, *Evaluating the performance of DeepL as translation tool between German and Italian Easy Language administrative texts*, RIID 1/2025.

Christiane Maaß, Laura Marie Maaß. 2024, *Leichte Sprache bei intellektuellen Beeinträchtigungen*. In *Sprache - Stimme – Gehör, s.p.* DOI: 10.1055/a-2302-7802.

Christiane Maaß, Isabel Rink. 2021. Translating legal texts into Easy language. In Chiara. Fioravanti (ed) *Communicating the law and public information to vulnerable audiences*. JOAL Vol.9 n.1. https://ojs.law.cornell.edu/index.php/joal/article/view/109

Christiane Maaß, Isabel Rink, Silvia Hansen-Schirra. 2021. *Easy Language in Germany*. in: C Lindholm, U. Vanhatalo (eds.), Handbook of Easy Languages in Europe, Frank & Timme; 2021. https://www.frank-timme.de/de/programm/produkt/handbook_of_easy_languages_in_europe?file=/site/assets/files/4477/2021_of_easy_languages_in_europe.pdf

Christiane Maaß, Schwengber Laura Marie. 2022. Easy Language and Plain Language in Germany. In *Rivista internazionale di tecnica della traduzione International Journal of Translation*, 24: 43–61. doi: 10.13137/2421-6763/

Anne Parpan-Blaser, Simone Girard-Groeber, Gabriela Antener, Christina, Baumann Rita, Alexandra Caplazi, Luisa Carrer, Cindy Diacquenod, Annete Lichtenauer, Andrea Sterchi. 2021. Easy Language in Switzerland. In Lindholm C, Vanhatalo U (eds.), *Handbook of Easy Languages in Europe*. 2021, Frank & Timme, Berlin: 573-622.

Giulia Pedrini. 2024. *Medical communication between Plain Language and Einfache Sprache. A corpus analysis of layperson summaries of clinical trials in*

English, German, and Italian. Frank & Timme, Berlin.

Elisa Perego. 2021. Easy Language in Italy, In Lindholm C, Vanhatalo U (eds.), *Handbook of Easy Languages in Europe*. 2021, Frank & Timme, Berlin: 275 -304.

Isabel Rink. 2020. Rechtskommunikation und Barrierefreiheit. Zur Übersetzung juristischer Informations- und Interaktionstext. In *Leichte Sprache,* Frank & Timme, Berlin.

Carlotta Sciumbata. 2022. *Manuale dell'Italiano facile da leggere e da capire*, Franco Cesati editore, Firenze.

Do professionally adapted texts follow existing Easy-to-Understand (E2U) language guidelines? A quantitative analysis of two professionally adapted corpora

Andreea Deleanu and **Constantin Orăsan** and **Shenbin Qian** and **Anastasiia Bezobrazova** and **Sabine Braun**
Centre for Translation Studies
University of Surrey, UK
{m.deleanu, c.orasan, s.qian, a.bezobrazova, s.braun}@surrey.ac.uk

Abstract

Easy-to-Understand (E2U) language varieties have been recognised by the UN Convention on the Rights of Persons with Disabilities as a means to prevent communicative exclusion of those facing cognitive barriers and guarantee the fundamental right to Accessible Communication. However, guidance on what it is that makes language 'easier to understand' is still fragmented and vague, leading practitioners to rely on their individual expertise. For this reason, this article presents a quantitative corpus analysis to further understand which features of E2U language can more effectively improve verbal comprehension according to professional practice. This is achieved by analysing two parallel corpora of standard and professionally adapted E2U articles to identify adaptation practices implemented according to, in spite of or in addition to official E2U guidelines analysed by the research team (Deleanu et al., 2024). The results stemming from the corpus analysis, provide insight into the most effective adaptation strategies that can reduce complexity in verbal discourse. This article will present the methods and results of the corpus analysis.

1 Introduction

Accessibility has recently been defined in the European Standard EN 17161 (2019) as the "extent to which products, systems, services, environments and facilities can be used by people from a population with the widest range of user needs, characteristics and capabilities to achieve identified goals in identified contexts of use". Contexts of use include interaction between people and Accessible Communication, as advocated by the UNCRPD (2006), has therefore called for alternatives to be supplied when users cannot (completely) access information in its original form (Greco, 2016). To date, efforts in Accessible Communication have focused on tackling barriers in written verbal communication (Maaß, 2020; Perego, 2020) and have offered 'Easy-to-Understand language varieties' as a means to overcome verbal communication barriers for a plethora of users (UNCRPD, 2006).

Easy-to-understand (E2U) is an umbrella term that encompasses a wide range of "functional language varieties of different national languages with reduced linguistic complexity, which aim to improve comprehensibility" (Hansen-Schirra and Maaß, 2020). These language varieties thus differ from standard language as they are user-oriented and their main function is to help understand and use information provided (Hansen-Schirra and Maaß, 2020), regardless of individual (dis)abilities or cultural and expert knowledge. This is achieved by adapting content to match users' abilities guarantee its function is fulfilled. E2U varieties enhance written comprehension for a wide range of users, including functional illiterates, vulnerable age groups (Maaß, 2020) and people with diverse cognitive abilities[1]. *Plain Language* and *Easy Language* are the most widely used and known E2U language varieties (Perego, 2020). They deviate from standard language and decrease in complexity, as shown in Figure 1.

Plain Language and *Easy Language* are two distinct language varieties that rely, to different extents, on verbal and non-verbal strategies to make language more accessible and meaning easier to retrieve and perceive (Perego, 2020), thus matching content to end users' abilities. Although there are currently several official guidelines for both

[1]'People with diverse cognitive abilities' and 'cognitively diverse individuals' are used as umbrella terms to identify individuals with temporarily reduced cognitive abilities (due to fatigue, inattention, a learning difficulty, age and/or injury-related cognitive decline) and individuals with permanent impairments. These include, but are not limited to, the conditions identified by the American Psychiatric Association as 'mental disorders' (American Psychiatric Association, 2013)

Proceedings of the 1st Workshop on Artificial Intelligence and Easy and Plain Language in Institutional Contexts (AI & EL/PL), pages 73–93, June 23, 2025

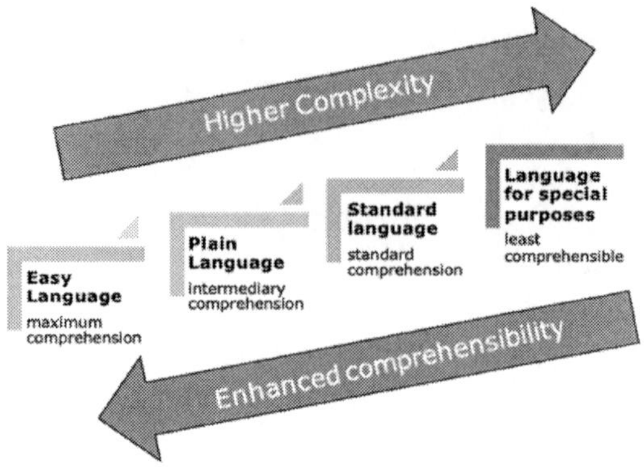

Figure 1: Natural language varieties.

Plain Language and *Easy Language* to be used in context-specific written communication, several issues arise, undermining the success of these two language varieties.

Firstly, the UNCRPD (2006) does not (yet) provide practical guidance on E2U principles to be followed nor specifies which conditions end-users have, leaving signatories to develop guidelines and best practices at company, national[2] or transnational[3] level. Secondly, reception studies with end users in the field of Accessible Communication are scarce and often rely on individual endeavours. This contributes to the absence of an official E2U taxonomy and a growing pool of vague, context-specific or unreliable guidelines created by academia and the public and private sectors. This in turn results in the proliferation of official and non-official guidelines based on intuition or individual preference, leaving professional and amateur content-creators to navigate through a multitude of recommendations, often in contrast with one other, as shown in our guidelines analysis (see Section 2). Thirdly, official guidance regarding the application of *Plain Language* and *Easy Language* principles in spoken interactions, audiovisual and multimodal formats is yet to be established (Maaß and Hernández Garrido, 2020; Maaß, 2020; Perego, 2020) with a few exceptions[4], further excluding people with diverse cognitive abilities from a truly accessible communicative environment.

This research is conducted within the framework of a project in Media Accessibility, with a focus on overcoming cognitive barriers in audiovisual formats. The final goal was to identify best practice and recommendations applicable to audiovisual content, and more specifically, to the adaptation of film narratives for cognitively diverse audiences. This has resulted in the creation of an audiovisual mode called 'Accessible Cues'.

To achieve this, we carried out a review and classified existing official E2U guidelines to identify shared recommendations, discrepancies and grey areas (Deleanu et al., 2024). In this paper, we focus on analysing E2U practice to identify to what extent guidelines are applied in professionally adapted texts. This has been pursued by analysing two professionally adapted parallel standard vs. E2U language corpora, the FIRST corpus (Orasan, Evans and Mitkov, 2018) and the Guardian Weekly corpus (Onestopenglish, 2007).

Our contributions can be summarised as follows:

(1) we conduct a comprehensive quantitative analysis of two professionally adapted English text corpora to identify strategies covered by existing guidelines. The analysis was also conducted to explore how professionals have tackled elements which have been found to be grey areas and discrepant in official E2U guidelines and whether any other strategies not mentioned by the guidelines have been consistently used.

(2) we provide an alternative methodology to analyse standard and adapted corpora, beyond the use of readability indices.

Related work will be reviewed in Section 2, with a focus on readability measures and an overview on the framework used for the guidelines analysis we conducted. This will be followed by Section 3 on the corpus analysis which will focus on presenting the corpora and methodology used. Section 4 will cover the corpus analysis results and discussion. Section 5 will provide conclusions and an overview on future work. Section 6 will conclude with a brief discussion on limitations. Section 7 provides the references while Section 8 provides the links to the resources used for the corpus analysis.

2 Related Work

2.1 Assessing complexity: readability indices

The expected level of difficulty of a text or the appropriate grade level score can be captured by

[2] See UNE 153101:2018 EX, Accessibility Standard on Easy Language (here called easy to read)

[3] See Lindholm & Vanhatalo (2021) for a discussion on the application of E2U language varieties across the EU

[4] See the EU project SELSI (Spoken Easy Language for Social Inclusion) on spoken Easy Language and the EU project EASIT (Easy Access for Social Inclusion Training) on training materials for the adaptation of existing audiovisual access services.

readability[5] indices. Metrics such as Gunning-Fox Index, Flesch-Kincaid Grade level, Flesch Reading Ease scale, Simple Measure of Gobbledygook (SMOG) and Coh-Metrix have been traditionally used to assess the complexity of standard texts and Easy-to-Understand (E2U) texts (Daghio et al., 2006; Pothier et al., 2008; Crossley et al., 2008; Yaneva, 2015; Štajner, 2021; Arfé et al., 2018). In general, readability indices rely on statistical averages and analyse sentence length to determine syntactic complexity, as well as word length, number of syllables, and word frequency to determine semantic difficulty. Their use to assess verbal complexity has, however, often been criticized. For example, the presence of high-frequency words may boost readability but could result in a higher number of polysemic words, while shorter sentences could result in grammatical errors or alteration of meaning, thus increasing complexity (Crossley et al., 2007; Allen, 2009; Fajardo et al., 2014; Saggion, 2018). Moreover, while some official E2U guidelines are in favour of the use of readability indices (Inclusion Europe, 2010), (PLAIN, 2011), others (McGee, 2010) warn against their use, as reading grade levels can differ significantly depending on the formula chosen, proving unreliable.

The corpora investigated in this research have been manually adapted according to professional expertise rather than according to a structural approach based on readability testing and age of acquisition wordlists (Allen, 2009). For this reason, it was deemed more effective to explore a different approach to establish the readability of and identify the strategies adopted in the adapted *FIRST* and *Guardian Weekly* corpora.

2.2 Guidelines Analysis

A set of 10 *Plain Language* and *Easy Language* guidelines have been analysed, classified and compared to identify shared recommendations, discrepancies and grey areas in official E2U guidelines developed for Anglophone countries by organisations such as the *International Federation of Library Associations and Institutions, Inclusion Europe*, the *Plain Language Action and Information Network* and Australian and British disability service providers such as *Scope* and *Mencap*. We have presented a comprehensive analysis of the guidelines in (Deleanu et al., 2024) and have relied on the guidelines classification framework and analysis results to establish the methodology to be used in the corpus analysis for this paper. The categories identified in the guidelines analysis encompassing lexical, syntactic, and adaptation strategies have been used to explore the behaviour of the adapted texts in the *FIRST* corpus (Orasan, Evans and Mitkov, 2018) and the *Guardian Weekly* corpus (Onestopenglish, 2007).

3 Corpus analysis

To gauge the extent to which the above-mentioned guidelines are followed in practice, this research has opted for a corpus analysis to identify expected and unexpected language-dependent phenomena that characterise professionally adapted texts in the Easy-to-Understand (E2U) language varieties.

The FIRST corpus, the code used for the analysis and the corresponding generated data developed as part of this project are available upon request. Please contact the 1st or 2nd author for more information.

3.1 Corpora

Because there are no substantial standard vs. *Plain* or *Easy Language* parallel corpora available – nor audiovisual corpora for that matter – the analysis has focused on data sets that contain a type of adapted language closely related to E2U. The data set includes two plain text corpora, namely the parallel corpus developed for the *A Flexible Interactive Reading Support Tool* (FIRST) project (Orasan, Evans and Mitkov, 2018) and the *Guardian Weekly* (GW) parallel corpus (Onestopenglish, 2007). Neither of the adapted texts in these corpora were *explicitly* created following the official E2U guidelines analysed in previous work (Deleanu et al., 2024), with FIRST and GW content-creators relying on their experience and in-house standards. Nevertheless, the list of adaptation recommendations used in the FIRST project can be found in Table A in Appendix.

The FIRST project[6] addresses the needs of people with Autism Spectrum Disorder, who have been identified as end users of *Easy Language* (IFLA, 2010). The corpus developed in the FIRST project comprises a total of 62 texts, divided into 31 orig-

[5]Readability relates to language-dependent variables that determine text complexity. It represents the degree to which printed information is unambiguous based on the reader's language fluency, the message communicated, and the quantity and the quality of text delivered (Perego, 2020).

[6]See the 2011–2014 EU project FIRST (Flexible Interactive Reading Support Tool)

inal texts and their 31 manually adapted counterparts. The texts were manually adapted by five professionals who work with people with autism. The texts were selected based on the user requirements and include extracts from novels, book and film plot summaries and reviews, scientific articles, news items and leaflets in plain text.

The GW corpus is made up of 300 adapted texts, which are equally divided into three different levels of ascending language proficiency: elementary, intermediate and advanced. These are the adapted versions of 100 original articles from *The Guardian* newspaper, selected and adapted by four experts to provide relevant online material for English learners (Allen, 2009). As the original articles are no longer available and the advanced texts present minor changes compared to their original counterparts (Allen, 2009), the advanced texts have been used as the standard against which to compare the elementary texts. Intermediate texts have not been considered in this analysis in order to mirror the structure of the FIRST corpus, i.e., have only one standard and one adapted version of each article.

3.2 Resources used in the analysis

Five secondary resources related to the creation and evaluation of accessible language were used to support the data analysis. These resources were used to identify any recurring patterns or preferences in the adapted versions at lexical and syntactic level. These resources can be accessed following the URLs provided in section 8.

(1) The *UK Subtlex word frequency database* built on a corpus of words extracted from BBC broadcasts (van Heuven et al., 2014) was used to assign a word frequency score to each type and token in the FIRST and GW subcorpora as an indicator of their difficulty.

(2) *Concreteness ratings* by Brysbaert et al. (2014) were assigned to types and tokens in the subcorpora to understand to what extent abstract words are removed or replaced by experience-based words, as advised by guidelines (Deleanu et al., 2024).

(3) The *English Vocabulary Profile* (EVP) grading database (University of Cambridge et al., 2011) used by Text inspector (Bax, 2012) was used to grade the lexical proficiency of types and tokens in the subcorpora. EVP uses the Common European Framework of Reference for Languages (CEFR) (Council of Europe, 2001) as its reference scale. We assigned a score (1-6) to the proficiency levels (A1 to C2), and 0 to the EVP's *Unlisted* words, to facilitate the analysis.

(4) Over 200 words to be avoided and their preferred *Plain Language* counterparts in domain-specific communication (PLAIN, 2011b) were also checked in the corpora to explore which adaptation strategies have been used for phrases (e.g., *by means of, in accordance with*), phrasal verbs (e.g., *set up, give up*), collocations (e.g., *interpose no objection, pursuant to*), and technical terms (e.g., *notwithstanding, remuneration*).

(5) As far as linking words are concerned, the list provided by PLAIN, (2011a) was used to evaluate the extent to which they are maintained, added or replaced in adapted texts.

3.3 Methodology

The first step was to clean the corpora of special characters, typos, grammatical errors, duplications and encoding problems which would have interfered with our analysis. The two corpora were analysed using corpus linguistic, computational and statistical methods, in line with previous studies (Crossley et al., 2012). A manual analysis was also performed.

Our analysis covers **lexical** and **syntactic** features and **adaptation** strategies (simplification and easification strategies and narrative choices) used by professionals at type and token level. Narrative choices will not be discussed in this paper, as their analysis was conducted in order to identify best practices to inform the creation of 'Accessible Cues' for audiovisual formats. For this reason, they are beyond the scope of this paper. Table B in Appendix provides an overview of the analysed elements per category.

3.3.1 Automatic processing

In order to carry out the analysis of lexical and syntactic features, we used Stanza (Qi et al., 2020) to tokenise, lemmatise and add part-of-speech (POS) information to all texts in the two corpora. We replaced American spelling with British spelling for the comparison with resources in Section 3.2. Sentences were extracted from the processed texts via Stanza. The length of each sentence and the number of sentences in each text were computed thereafter.

Tokenised lemmas were compared with the words in the *UK Subtlex frequency database, the Concreteness* ratings list, the PLAIN lists of content words (2011b) and linking words (2011a) to count their occurrences for the analysis of lexical frequency and concreteness rating, lists of words to be avoided and linking words respectively. The count of personal pronouns and negations was based on a list of personal pronouns and negative words.

POS labels were used to identify contractions, tenses, passive voice, and clauses. More specifically, we used string matching for contracted formats such as *'s* and checked their POS labels to detect contractions. Labels such as *VBZ* were used to detect tenses and passive voice with the help of auxiliary verbs such as *will*. Words such as *who, when, which* and their corresponding POS labels were used to find types of clauses and count their occurrences in the corpora.

We calculated the Mean (M) and the Standard Deviation (SD) of each text in the corpora for the convenience of comparing standard *vs* adapted versions. Results have been rounded to the first decimal point.

3.3.2 Manual checking

A manual check was conducted when statistical results per article were below or above the average of the subcorpora, and when results were unexpected. We also conducted a manual check to identify and confirm simplification and easification strategies used. This was done by manually consulting each adapted and parallel article and noting the presence of simplification and easification strategies used for each article.

4 Results and Discussion

Although we have explored all phenomena mentioned in Table B in Appendix as part of our project, due to space restrictions and the scope of this paper, the analysis will focus on the following lexical features: lexical frequency and proficiency, concreteness, personal pronouns, tenses and use of passive voice. The following syntactic features will also be presented: sentence counts and clauses. With regard to adaptation strategies, easification and simplification devices will be discussed. Information about data distribution and extensive examples and definitions for each of the analysed lexical, syntactic and easification and simplification features can be found in Tables C, D and E in the Appendix.

4.1 Lexical features

With regard to lexical frequency, the Mean (M) scores of the standard and adapted FIRST subcorpora suggest that the words used belong mainly to the high-frequency range established by van Heuven et al. (2014), with minimal variation between individual texts as shown by the Standard Deviation (SD) in Table 1. The GW subcorpora behave similarly, with a lack of significant difference between the standard and adapted subcorpora.

	FIRST Standard	FIRST Adapted	GW Standard	GW Adapted
M	5.7	5.8	5.8	5.9
SD	1.4	1.4	1.4	1.3

Table 1: Mean and Standard Deviation of lexical frequency of types in the *FIRST* and *GW* corpora

As the results did not provide evidence of a clear division between standard and adapted texts, we have extracted the words that were not present in the *UK Subtlex database* (van Heuven et al., 2014) for each article across all four subcorpora, to clarify whether the lack of difference lays in the database's nature. Surprisingly, we found no notable differences, as words that are *not part* of the *UK Subtlex*, and can therefore be considered too low-frequency, are *still* present in both subcorpora. This suggests that domain-specific and low frequency words can be *kept* in adapted versions as content-creators expect their audiences to cope with both technical and low-frequency terms especially because high-frequency alternatives could prove ambiguous and unsuited, regardless of the "use familiar, high-frequency words" maxim present in all guidelines analysed (Deleanu et al., 2024). While some domain-specific concepts were introduced and terms, foreign words or low-frequency words were explained[7], others were either kept with no further information[8], removed[9], replaced[10] or all of the above within the same text[11], suggesting that word frequency is not a reliable marker for comprehensibility and that multiple strategies can be used simultaneously.

In order to understand whether adapted texts are actually easier to understand based on the CEFR proficiency level (see Section 3.2, EVP) we have analysed the proficiency level of types in all 4 subcorpora using the *English Vocabulary Profile* (EVP)

[7]See Text 1, GW in Table C in Appendix.
[8]See Text 6, FIRST and 37, GW in Table C.
[9]See Text 47, GW in Table C.
[10]See Text 21, GW in Table C.
[11]See Text 32, GW in Table C.

database. The results are shown in Table 2.

	FIRST Standard	FIRST Adapted	GW Standard	GW Adapted
Unlisted	23.8%	21.2%	37.8%	31.8%
A1	23.7%	25.0%	14.8%	20.5%
A2	19.6%	20.9%	16.4%	21.2%
B1	23.4%	23.7%	25.9%	28.7%
B2	21.1%	20.2%	24.9%	20.7%
C1	7.0%	6.4%	9.6%	5.3%
C2	5.2%	3.9%	8.4%	3.7%

Table 2: Proficiency level of types in the *FIRST* and *GW* corpora according to the EVP

In terms of the distribution of *Listed* types, words tend to belong to B1 and B2 levels for the GW and A1 and B1 for the FIRST in the standard versions. C1 and C2 are also present. On the contrary, a decrease in complexity can be observed in the adapted versions. The percentage of types steadily increases in the *elementary* (A1-A2) and *intermediate* (B1-B2) levels to the detriment of B2, C1 and C2 types for both the GW and the FIRST corpus, (e.g., C2 types *paradoxes* and *albeit* disappear), as advised by Easy-to-Understand (E2U) guidelines (Deleanu et al., 2024). However, *upper intermediate* levels (B2, C1 and C2) do not *completely* disappear in the adapted versions although their numbers do decrease as they are replaced with higher-frequency and therefore lower proficiency level synonyms[12], or removed because they are considered non-relevant information according to content-creators' expertise[13].

In the case of the FIRST corpus, 23.8% of all standard types were unlisted in the EVP database, compared with 21.2% of all adapted types. While the numbers suggest that lexical variety is lower in the adapted version due to the lower number of types and higher number of tokens compared to the standard counterpart[14], the high incidence of *Unlisted* words represents a limitation of the EVP, as differences between the subcorpora could drastically change if a level was allocated to each word. The results are similar in the GW corpus, with 37.8% of types in the standard and 31.8% of types in the adapted subcorpus being *Unlisted*, and thus potentially problematic.

As *Unlisted* words are mainly lexical rather than grammatical in nature (e.g., words such as *nucleotide, Obama, Oscars, Pakistan, plunder* or *punchy* in the FIRST and *fatality, Felix, Lufthansa, Havana, incoming* or *leftist*, in the GW) they can be assumed to belong to *intermediate* and *advanced* levels. These also tend to be removed or explicitated[15], suggesting that when words are perceived as less frequent, and therefore less known, content-creators *have* intervened to contextualise terms, in line with guidelines recommendations.

The extent to which the expertise-based strategies applied to reduce *intermediate, advanced* and *Unlisted* occurrences improve comprehension for end-users, is however not fully confirmed. It can be argued that removal, explanations and replacement depend on content-creators subjective perception of relevance, which can result in bias, information loss, misinterpretation and increased grammatical intricacy and thus text complexity (Halliday, 2008; To, 2017) as lexical units are removed[16]. As a case in point, low-frequency or high-proficiency level words have been kept in many cases[17], suggesting that high-frequency and low-proficiency level words do not necessarily entail more comprehensible output. Often enough higher-frequency and lower-proficiency level words can be polysemic in nature resulting in some texts preferring the use of the specific term to the phrasal verb[18].

In terms of concreteness, there are again no notable differences between the standard and adapted subcorpora. Concreteness ratings (Brysbaert et al., 2014) for both corpora suggest that abstract and concrete words are consistently used across the board and that any topic can undergo adaptation as suggested by 2 out of 10 guidelines analysed. See Table E in Appendix for the distribution.

In order to dispel the vagueness of the guidelines on pronoun use, referencing patterns have been explored for both object and subject personal pronouns, as shown in Table 3. Token occurrences of personal pronouns have been normalized against the total number of tokens per subcorpora. Pronouns can be a hurdle for autistic readers and therefore guidelines provided for the adaptation of

[12]For example, huge (A2) for mammoth (C2) in Text 21, GW and argued (B1) for quarrelled (B2) in Text 5, FIRST. See Table C.

[13]See Text 13, FIRST and 21, GW in Table C.

[14]See Table D in Appendix for type and token distribution.

[15]For example, *destitute children* becomes *poor orphans and street children* in Text 76, GW.

[16]See Text 28, FIRST in Table C for an overview of misinterpretations and mistakes due to adaptation.

[17]See Text 8 FIRST in Table C.

[18]*To take on a case* becomes to *defend a case* in text 28, GW in Table C.

the FIRST corpus suggested their resolution (Jordanova et al., 2014). However, adapted FIRST texts seem to rely more on personal pronouns than their standard counterparts[19], highlighting the inconsistencies between guidelines, expertise-based practice and the needs of end-users (Tavares et al., 2015; Hawthorne and Loveall, 2021). Similar results have been found in the GW adapted subcorpora, suggesting that, contrary to some guidelines, the replacement of pronouns with proper nouns is not consistently carried out as an adaptation technique, with creative alternatives also being preferred[20].

	FIRST Standard	FIRST Adapted	GW Standard	GW Adapted
Pers. Pron. %	3%	4%	4%	5%

Table 3: Personal pronoun percentage against total tokens in the FIRST and GW corpora

While the number of verbs has increased in the adapted FIRST subcorpus, it has significantly decreased in the adapted GW, as shown in Table 4. Percentages have been obtained by calculating the number of analysed tokens against the total number of tokens identifying verbs for each subcorpora.

	FIRST Standard	FIRST Adapted	GW Standard	GW Adapted
Total verbs	1410	1605	9822	7981
Simple present	35.9%	41.0%	40.7%	48.2%
Simple Past	28.5%	33.0%	29.2%	33.1%
Simple Future	1.8%	2.1%	2.1%	3.5%
Others	33.8%	22.9%	28.0%	15.3%
Passive	11.5%	10.8%	8.6%	4.0%

Table 4: Distribution of tenses and passives in the *FIRST* and *GW* corpora

The different number of verbs in the adapted subcorpora could be due to different adaptation strategies being used: removal of information, and therefore sentences, in the GW subcorpus as also suggested by sentence counts (see Table 5 in the next Section); and explicitation of nominalised or hidden verbs PLAIN, 2011a and increase in the number of simple sentences in the FIRST subcorpus (see Table 6 in the next Section).

[19]See Text 19, FIRST in Table C.

[20]See text 94, GW in Table C.

Simple tenses are used in abundance in the adapted subcorpora, to the detriment of compound tenses such as auxiliaries, perfects, progressive forms or past participle ('others'), as shown in Table 4. However, 'others' do not disappear, suggesting that *consecutio temporum* is maintained regardless of their numbers being significantly reduced in the adapted versions as advised by guidelines (Deleanu et al., 2024). Also contrary to the guidelines, the simple past is vastly represented in the adapted subcorpora. The same is applicable to the simple future, thus contradicting the ban on future tenses and use of uncertain future[21]. These percentages suggesting that practitioners believe target users to be able to cope with and infer temporal information beyond the simple present, allowing for the production of more natural language in adapted texts[22].

While all guidelines suggest avoiding passives, passive voices have still been kept[23] or introduced[24] in the adapted subcorpora, albeit to a lesser extent (see percentages in Table 4). Passive voices have been significantly reduced in the adapted texts, and especially the GW, with 1 passive out of 2 replaced by an active form[25] or being removed altogether. The presence of passives in the adapted subcorpora could however be justified by a series of reasons, such as the text-type (i.e., articles); the need to improve literacy by gradually introducing passive voices and the underlying pragmatic implications of the original author's intention. Additional reasons are the use of passive to mark order of importance in the sentence and the impossibility of transforming the agent in the performer of the action[26] (Shintani, 1979). These results, once more, highlight how suggestions by official guidelines are ignored in favor of more natural language being produced.

4.2 Syntactic features

In terms of the number of sentences, this increases in the adapted FIRST subcorpus, while it decreases in the adapted GW subcorpus. The figures are presented in Table 5. This could be due to different adaptation strategies being adopted: the GW

[21]Constructed with *might happen* or *should do* ((ILSMH European Association, 1998), PLAIN, 2011a.

[22]See the use of preset and past simple, conditional and present perfect in text 30, FIRST in Table C.

[23]See *has been accused of* in Text 28, GW in Table C.

[24]See Text 5, FIRST in Table C.

[25]See Text 5, FIRST in Table C.

[26]See *to be born* in Text 34, GW in Table C.

content-creators mainly resorted to elimination as preferred E2U strategy while the FIRST project participants have relied on bullet point, extensive text re-organization and explanations to make content more accessible.

	FIRST Standard	FIRST Adapted	GW Standard	GW Adapted
Sentence count	584	1004	4010	3904

Table 5: Sentence counts in the *FIRST* and *GW* corpora

The total number of verbless clauses, single sentences, coordinate clauses and subordinate clauses has been compared against the total number of clauses in the text. Percentages can be found in Table 6. These numbers were estimated using the part of speech information.

Clause type	FIRST Standard	FIRST Adapted	GW Standard	GW Adapted
Verbless	3.4%	2.3%	1.5%	1.3%
Simple	27.6%	45.4%	29.3%	31.7%
Coordinate	61.0%	43.9%	69.0%	66.6%
Subordinate	39.7%	27.5%	40.0%	36.3%

Table 6: Distribution of clauses in the *FIRST* and *GW* corpora

Several verbless clauses have been identified in the adapted subcorpora. These are titles, creative devices to maintain engagement[27] or ellipsis of the verb. These elements are surprising, as, intuitively, they could lead to more misunderstandings.

Simple sentences, i.e., independent clauses with one main verb, represent the majority in the adapted versions, in line with guidelines (Deleanu et al., 2024).

Coordinate conjunctions include both syndetic (*or, and, but* and *so*) and asyndetic (commas and semicolon) coordination used in independent clauses. These are largely preferred to subordinate (dependant) clauses, which have been transformed in either coordinates or simple sentences[28] in the adapted texts, as advised by official guidelines.

Interestingly enough, subordinates have not disappeared[29], suggesting that their use is essential for the cohesion and coherence of the overall text as suggested by PLAIN (2011a) and its proposed list of linking words to be used.

[27]For example: *Tense? Angry? Can't get online?* in Text 90, GW and *Rain is our national weather. Snow can cause us problems, yes, and very hot weather, like last summer, causes difficulties, too. But rain?* in Text 99, GW.

[28]See clauses **in bold** in Text 19, FIRST in Table C.

[29]See underlined clauses in Text 19, FIRST in Table C.

4.3 E2U adaptation strategies: easification and simplification

Easification makes texts more accessible by developing in the reader specific learning strategies (Bhatia, 1983). This includes guiding readers, raising awareness of potential ambiguities and difficulties (van den Bos et al., 2007) and restructuring, reorganising or rearranging information in the text at verbal and visual level (Caro, 2020). Simplification is the process of transforming a text into a more understandable equivalent (Saggion et al., 2011) by reducing linguistic complexity (WCAG 2.1, 2019). Easification and simplification strategies are used to different degrees in each adapted subcorpus, with the number of types and tokens and linking words across levels partially indicating whether any elimination, reiteration, exemplification or explanation strategies have been used. Nevertheless, not all strategies have been applied, especially those belonging to easification, as confirmed by our manual checks. Table 7 presents an overview of the E2U adaptation strategies identified in the subcorpora. Ticks indicate strategies that have been used while crosses indicate those that have not. Dashes indicate that the strategy has only been partially applied.

	FIRST Adapted	GW Adapted
Summary	X	X
Introduction	X	✓
Glossary	X	✓
Elimination	✓	✓
Reiteration	–	–
Exemplification	X	✓
Explanation	✓	✓
Context Clue	✓	✓
Definition	X	✓
Paraphrase	✓	✓
Inference	✓	✓

Table 7: Overview of easification and simplification strategies used in the *FIRST* and *GW* corpora

In terms of adaptation strategies, summaries have not been used in the subcorpora, while introductions[30] have been rarely used in the adapted GW. Glossaries are hardly used in the standard texts[31] but existing ones have been, alongside an existing footnote[32] partially adapted and kept at the bottom of the text. No glossaries have been created specifically for adapted versions.

[30]See Text 82, GW in Table C.

[31]See Text 12, GW in Table C.

[32]See Text 85, GW in Table C.

As discussed previously, simplification strategies shared by adapted subcorpora are primarily **elimination**[33], **explanation** (*meaning, meaning that*, definitions, context clues and paraphrase)[34] and **spelling out of implications**[35]. However, practice has not always been consistent between the GW and FIRST adapted subcorpora, with **exemplification**[36] being used in the former rather than the latter. **Reiteration** strategies in the form of repetitions, have not been found in the GW or FIRST corpus. However, reiteration has encompassed a consistent use of lexicon and reiteration of syntactical structures[37].

These results do not mean that all strategies should be simultaneously used in the same text but only when required. Nevertheless, there is a risk of corrupting meaning as personal interpretation can always interfere, as in the following text in Table 8.

In the example in Table 8, 'shells' are a means to *predict* the dissolution of the implant in the original version, rather than a means to *control* it, as suggested in the adapted FIRST subcorpus.

Standard	Adapted
Getting the electronics to fade away in a controlled manner relies on two scientific developments – getting the electronics to dissolve at all and **using a shell to control when that happens**.	Electronics melt away in a controlled manner. It relies on two scientific developments. One is to get the electronics to dissolve. **The other is to use a shell to control what happens.**

Table 8: Distortion of meaning in Text 18, FIRST corpus

4.4 Discussion

There are several strategies used by content-creators which have been banned by guidelines. For example, the analysed guidelines have rejected the use of negations, passives and contractions. On the other hand, the analysed adapted subcorpora have instead preserved or added them. This strategy was used by content-creators to maintain or explicitate the meaning intended by the original text and to avoid creating non-grammatical and disconnected sentences, i.e., more complex sentences. However, these opposite strategies provide food for thought. A major problem in Media Accessibility, i.e., the field in which this research was conducted, are time constraints: subtitles for the Deaf and Hard of Hearing and Audio Description are part of the post-production process and therefore depend on the pace and the pauses in the original soundtrack. Resorting to the Saxon Genitive, verb contractions, negations, abbreviations (when previously explicitated, familiar and meaningful in the given context) and pronouns or glosses (when non-ambiguous and reiterated), for instance, could potentially help overcome the media limitation or allow for longer processing time in audiovisual formats, such as films.

Nevertheless, shared patterns have also been identified, such as the elimination of words banned by PLAIN (2011b) or the preference for simple sentences, coordinating conjunctions and elimination and explanation strategies in the adapted subcorpora. Elimination has been the most consistently applied simplification strategy in the analysed adapted subcorpora. The results have shown that higher proficiency terms belonging to *intermediate* and *advanced* levels, alongside *Unlisted* words which can be considered too low-frequency to be graded by the English Vocabulary Profile (EVP) database (Capel, 2010, 2012), have been mostly eliminated during adaptation. It can, however, be argued that adaptation should not be solely guided by a reductive approach, as it is not a matter of subjectively choosing between relevant or irrelevant eliminable information but a matter of identifying which relevant elements can be easily inferred from the available information or the visual aids provided.

As no database of prevalent vocabulary possessed by cognitively diverse individuals has been collated by psycholinguistics (Jordanova et al., 2014), the corpus analysis has relied on the EVP and the *UK Subtlex* (van Heuven et al., 2014) databases to determine which words fall under the category of 'difficult' or 'low-frequency' words to be avoided, as prescribed by the analysed guidelines (Deleanu et al., 2024). In the adapted subcorpora, content-creators have relied on different and often contradictory strategies to address technical or B1 to C2 terms, due to individual expertise-based practice and a lack of a proofreading and validation phase to confirm and unify adaptation strategies within a given text. If both phases had

[33] See Text 33, GW in Table C.
[34] See Text 2, 5, 9 and 28 FIRST in Table C.
[35] See Text 45, GW in Table C.
[36] See Text 3, FIRST in Table C.
[37] See Text 3, FIRST in Table C.

been pursued by content-creators of the FIRST and GW corpora, the E2U strategies used and therefore the results of this analysis might have been different.

5 Conclusions

The effectiveness of Easy-to-Understand (E2U) language varieties is still under-researched, and limitations have been highlighted (Fajardo et al., 2014; Hurtado et al., 2014). Yet, findings from reception studies with individuals with diverse cognitive abilities (Fajardo et al., 2014; Yaneva, 2016; Säuberli et al., 2024) have shown that Easy Language *does* partially address language complexity and thus support comprehension. Language, and especially accessible language, could therefore be instrumental to achieving Accessible Communication for all. However, adapting standard texts into E2U is no easy feat. Often enough, content-creators find themselves juggling different alternatives and having to settle for the one they deem most comprehensible to the majority of their end users. For this reason, it can be argued that adaptation depends on individual instances. This entails that the use of different and often conflicting but valid strategies ought to be acceptable as no universal set of guidelines can be drafted. However, giving content-creators a toolbox of options from which to choose could enable them to adapt standard texts more swiftly and accurately. The existence of a toolbox could also increase awareness and reflexion on what it is about language that makes meaning-making a complex process.

Only a few of the official guidelines that we have analysed (Deleanu et al., 2024)) have stressed the preference for the use of spoken language in adaptations, including to the detriment of natural grammar. Our corpus analysis has highlighted the preference of content-creators for natural language that end-users are familiar with and the often-contradictory presence of elements that guidelines have deemed unapproachable. While improving literacy *does* play an important role in the corpora we have analysed, it could be argued that only end-users can have the final say on *how much* an adapted text has been made accessible. Validation with end-users could help overcome biased interpretations and provide an indication of how much background information is necessary. However, this can prove time consuming and expensive, which is why a toolbox could be the first step towards the production of a higher number of E2U texts. This could include the corpus analysis resources and the guidelines and corpus analysis framework, providing users with an overview of shared *and* contrasting practice.

In the future, we intend to develop a toolbox and make the E2U guidelines recommendations developed in this project available in the future. The toolbox could then be used in the process of training AI models and provide an environment in which standard texts could be efficiently and consistently adapted into E2U. The methodology applied could also be used to assess automatically generated simplified outputs obtained using AI tools, to better understand the 'black box' strategies these tools apply and help detect differences between original and the offered multiple adapted versions. As we conducted this research in the context of a project in Media Accessibility, we also intend to address the gap in Accessible Communication by applying best identified E2U strategies to an audiovisual format.

6 Limitations

We acknowledge that our analysis framework, developed through a qualitative guidelines analysis is, to some extent, subjective and tailored to a project in Media Accessibility. The corpus analysis was conducted using a limited sample of texts (131 standard texts and 131 adapted texts) and only two corpora as our focus was on *professionally* adapted parallel standard vs. E2U texts and few alternatives were available. Although analysed corpora do not specifically fall under the category of either *Plain* or *Easy Language*, the adapted output does represent an E2U language variety meant to reduce verbal complexity for language learners and autistic readers, i.e., primary audiences of *Plain* and *Easy Language* respectively.

References

David Allen. 2009. A study of the role of relative clauses in the simplification of news texts for learners of english. *System*, 37:585–599.

American Psychiatric Association. 2013. *Diagnostic and Statistical Manual of Mental Disorders*, 5th edition. American Psychiatric Publishing, Arlington, VA.

Barbara Arfé, Lucia Mason, and Inmaculada Fajardo. 2018. Simplifying informational text structure for struggling readers. *Reading and Writing*, 31:2191–2210.

S Bax. 2012. Text inspector. *Online text analysis tool.* Retrieved from https://languageresearch.cambridge.org/images/pdf/theenglishprofilebooklet.pdf.

Vijay K Bhatia. 1983. Simplification vs. easification — the case of legal texts. *Applied linguistics*, 4(1):42–54.

Marc Brysbaert, Amy Beth Warriner, and Victor Kuperman. 2014. Concreteness ratings for 40 thousand generally known English word lemmas. *Behavior research methods*, 46:904–911.

Annette Capel. 2010. A1–B2 vocabulary: insights and issues arising from the English Profile Wordlists project. *English Profile Journal*, 1. Retrieved from http://www.englishprofile.org/wordlists.

Annette Capel. 2012. Completing the English vocabulary profile: C1 and C2 vocabulary. *English Profile Journal*, 3.

Rocío Bernabé Caro. 2020. New taxonomy of easy-to-understand access services1. *Monografias de Traduccion e Interpretacion (MonTI)*, 12:345–380.

Council of Europe. 2001. Common European Framework of Reference for Languages: Learning, Teaching, Assessment (CEFR). Retrieved from https://www.coe.int/en/web/common-european-framework-reference-languages.

Scott A. Crossley, David Allen, and Danielle S. McNamara. 2012. Text simplification and comprehensible input: A case for an intuitive approach. *Language Teaching Research*, 16(1):89–108.

Scott A Crossley, David F Dufty, Philip M McCarthy, and Danielle S McNamara. 2007. Toward a new readability: A mixed model approach. In *Proceedings of the annual meeting of the cognitive science society*, volume 29, pages 197–202.

Scott A. Crossley, Jerry Greenfield, and Danielle S. McNamara. 2008. Assessing text readability using cognitively based indices. *Tesol Quarterly*, 42(3):475–493.

M. Monica Daghio, Giuseppe Fattori, and Anna V. Ciardullo. 2006. Assessment of readability and learning of easy-to-read educational health materials designed and written with the help of citizens by means of two non-alternative methods. *Advances in Health Sciences Education: Theory and Practice*, pages 123–132.

Maria Andreea Deleanu, Constantin Orăsan, and Sabine Braun. 2024. Accessible Communication: a systematic review and comparative analysis of official English Easy-to-Understand (E2U) language guidelines. In *Proceedings of the 3rd Workshop on Tools and Resources for People with REAding DIfficulties (READI)*, pages 70–92. ELRA and ICCL.

European Standard EN 17161. 2019. Design for all. https://universaldesign.ie/about-universal-design/products-and-services/standard-i-s-en-171612019-design-for-all.

Inmaculada Fajardo, Vicenta Ávila, Antonio Ferrer, Gema Tavares, Marcos Gómez, and Ana Hernández. 2014. Easy-to-read texts for students with intellectual disability: linguistic factors affecting comprehension. *Journal of applied research in intellectual disabilities*, 27:212–225.

Gian Maria Greco. 2016. On accessibility as a human right, with an application to media accessibility. *Researching audio description: New approaches*, pages 11–33.

Michael A. K. Halliday. 2008. *Complementarities in language*. Beijing: The Commercial Press.

Silvia Hansen-Schirra and Christiane Maaß. 2020. Easy language, plain language, easy language plus: Perspectives on comprehensibility and stigmatisation. In Christiane Maaß, editor, *Easy Language Research: Text and User Perspectives*, pages 17 – 38. Frank & Timme, Berlin.

Kara Hawthorne and Susan J Loveall. 2021. Interpretation of ambiguous pronouns in adults with intellectual disabilities. *Journal of Intellectual Disability Research*, 65(2):125–132.

Barbara Hurtado, Lara Jones, and Francesca Burniston. 2014. Is easy read information really easier to read? *Journal of Intellectual Disability Research*, 58(9):822–829.

IFLA. 2010. Guidelines for easy-to-read materials. Available at: https://www.ifla.org/wp-content/uploads/2019/05/assets/hq/publications/professional-report/120.pdf.

ILSMH European Association. 1998. Make it simple: European guidelines for the production of easy-to-read information for people with learning disability. Available at: https://docplayer.net/142050357-Ilsmh-europeanassociation-make-it-simple-european-guidelinesfor-the-production-of-easy-to-read-information-for-people-with-learning-disability.html.

Inclusion Europe. 2010. Information for all: European standards for making information easy to read and understand. https://www.inclusion-europe.eu/wp-content/uploads/2017/06/EN_Information_for_all.pdf.

Vesna Jordanova, Richard Evans, and A Cerga Pashoja. 2014. D7.2: Benchmark report (results of piloting task).

Christiane Maaß. 2020. *Easy Language – Plain Language – Easy Language Plus: Balancing Comprehensibility and Acceptability*, volume 3. Frank & Timme, Berlin.

Christiane Maaß and Sergio Hernández Garrido. 2020. Easy and plain language in audiovisual translation. In Christiane Maaß, editor, *Easy Language Research: Text and User Perspectives*, pages 131–161. Frank & Timme, Berlin.

Jeanne McGee. 2010. *Toolkit for making written material clear and effective*. Centers for Medicare and Medicaid Services, Department of Health and Human.

Elisa Perego. 2020. *Accessible Communication: A Cross-country Journey*, volume 4. Frank & Timme, Berlin.

Louise Pothier, Rachael Day, Catherine Harris, and David D Pothier. 2008. Readability statistics of patient information leaflets in a speech and language therapy department. *International journal of language & communication disorders*, 43(6):712–722.

Peng Qi, Yuhao Zhang, Yuhui Zhang, Jason Bolton, and Christopher D. Manning. 2020. Stanza: A Python natural language processing toolkit for many human languages. In *Proceedings of the 58th Annual Meeting of the Association for Computational Linguistics: System Demonstrations*.

Horacio Saggion. 2018. Text simplification. In Ruslan Mitkov, editor, *The Oxford Handbook of Computational Linguistics*, 2 edition. Oxford University Press.

Horacio Saggion, Elena Gómez-Martínez, Esteban Etayo, Alberto Anula, and Lorena Bourg. 2011. Text simplification in simplext: Making texts more accessible. *Procesamiento del lenguaje natural*, (47):341–342.

Andreas Säuberli, Franz Holzknecht, Patrick Haller, Silvana Deilen, Laura Schiffl, Silvia Hansen-Schirra, and Sarah Ebling. 2024. Digital comprehensibility assessment of simplified texts among persons with intellectual disabilities. In *Proceedings of the 2024 CHI Conference on Human Factors in Computing Systems*, pages 1–11.

Michiko Shintani. 1979. *The frequency and usage of the English passive*. University of California, Los Angeles.

Sanja Štajner. 2021. Automatic text simplification for social good: Progress and challenges. *Findings of the Association for Computational Linguistics: ACL-IJCNLP 2021*, pages 2637–2652.

Gema Tavares, Inmaculada Fajardo, Vicenta Avila, Ladislao Salmerón, and Antonio Ferrer. 2015. Who do you refer to? how young students with mild intellectual disability confront anaphoric ambiguities in texts and sentences. *Research in developmental disabilities*, 38:108–124.

Vinh To. 2017. Grammatical intricacy in efl textbooks. *International Journal of English Language Education*, 5:127–140.

UNCRPD. 2006. United Nations, convention on the rights of persons with disabilities. https://www.un.org/development/desa/disabilities/convention-on-the-rights-of-persons-with-disabilities.html. Retrieved from the United Nations website. Accessed May 24, 2025.

University of Cambridge, British Council, University of Bedfordshire, and English UK. 2011. English Profile: Introducing the CEFR for English. Retrieved from https://languageresearch.cambridge.org/images/pdf/theenglishprofilebooklet.pdf.

KP van den Bos, H Nakken, PG Nicolay, and EJ Van Houten. 2007. Adults with mild intellectual disabilities: Can their reading comprehension ability be improved? *Journal of Intellectual Disability Research*, 51(11):835–849.

Walter JB van Heuven, Pawel Mandera, Emmanuel Keuleers, and Marc Brysbaert. 2014. SUBTLEX-UK: A new and improved word frequency database for British English. *Quarterly journal of experimental psychology*, 67(6).

WCAG 2.1. 2019. The web content accessibility guidelines. Retrieved from https://www.w3.org/WAI/WCAG21/quickref/.

Victoria Yaneva. 2015. Easy-read documents as a gold standard for evaluation of text simplification output. In *Proceedings of the Student Research Workshop*, pages 30–36.

Victoria Yaneva. 2016. *Assessing text and web accessibility for people with autism spectrum disorder*. Ph.D. thesis, University of Wolverhampton.

7 Language Resource References

7.1 Corpora used in the analysis

Onestopenglish. (2007). *News lessons. Macmillan English Campus.* Retrieved from http://www.onestopenglish.com

Orasan, C., Evans, R.J., & Mitkov, R. (2018). Intelligent Text Processing to Help Readers with Autism. *Intelligent Natural Language Processing: Trends and Applications*, Springer.

7.2 Resources used in the analysis

Bax, S. (2012). *Text Inspector.* Online text analysis tool. Retrieved from https://textinspector.com

Peng Qi, Yuhao Zhang, Yuhui Zhang, Jason Bolton, and Christopher D. Manning. 2020. Stanza: A python natural language processing toolkit for many human languages. In *Proceedings of the 58th Annual Meet-ing of the Association for Computational Linguistics:System Demonstrations*, pages 101–108. Association for Computational Linguistics.

PLAIN. 2011a. Federal Plain Language Guidelines. Available at https://www.plainlanguage.gov/guidelines/

PLAIN. 2011b. *Plain Language: Use Simple Words and Phrases.* Available at https://www.plainlanguage.gov/guidelines/words/use-simple-words-phrases/

Walter J. B. van Heuven, Paweł Mandera, Emmanuel Keuleers, and Marc Brysbaert. 2014. Subtlex-UK: A new and improved word frequency database for British English. *Quarterly Journal ofExperimental Psychology*, 67(6).

Marc Brysbaert, Amy Beth Warriner, and Victor Kuperman. 2014. Concreteness ratings for 40 thousand generally known English word lemmas. *Behavior Research Methods*, 46:904–911. https://doi.org/10.3758/s13428-013-0403-5

Appendix

Table A: FIRST Recommendations	
1.	Detect infrequent words and substitute them with simpler synonyms, definitions or explanations.
2.	Identify figurative expressions such as idioms and metaphors and replace with simpler words or definitions. Provide inferred meaning for non-lexicalized metaphors.
3.	Identify jargon or specialised terms and replace with specific definitions.
4.	Identify phraseological units and polysemic words and replace with specific definitions. Highlight the domain. Avoid using the easier synonym.
5.	Identify and divide long paragraphs.
6.	Detect long sentences and divide them into shorter easier to understand chunks.
7.	Rewrite complicated sentences to make them easier to understand.
8.	Identify and resolve anaphora.
9.	Replace infrequent abbreviations and acronyms with full version.
10.	Use bullet points if necessary to break down the text in easier parts.
11.	Break sentences into segments no longer than 15 words. Prefer simple sentences.
12.	Avoid semicolon, suspension points and special characters.
13.	Substitute infrequent slang with simpler synonym or provide simple definitions to explain slang.
14.	Disambiguate temporal adjectives.

Table B: Analysed elements per each category	
Lexical Features	• Frequency • Concreteness ratings • Proficiency level • Types and tokens distribution • Object & subject personal pronouns • Contractions (Saxon Genitive and Verbs) • Lists of words to be avoided (PLAIN, 2011b) • Compound words • Tenses • Passive voice • Negations
Syntactic Features	• Sentence length • Sentence counts • Clauses counts (verbless clauses with absent or nominalised verbs, single sentences, subordinates, coordinates) • Linking words
Adaptation Strategies	• Elimination • Reiteration • Exemplification • Explanations (context clues, definitions and glossaries) • Summaries • Introductions • Explicitation of inferences

Table C: Examples extracted from the corpora		
	Standard	**Adapted**
TEXT 1, GW (Introducing the topic and explaining low-frequency technical terms)	John Prescott, has been praised by medical experts for his 'brave' admission that he struggled with the **eating disorder bulimia** for **two decades**".	**Anorexia** and **bulimia** are both illnesses where people have problems with **eating problems** known as **eating disorders**. **People who suffer from anorexia** do not eat enough food and they soon become very thin. **People who suffer from bulimia** eat a large amount of food but they usually vomit after eating it. Both these eating disorders can be very dangerous for your health [. . .] John Prescott, has published his autobiography. In the book he says that he suffered from **bulimia** for **twenty years**.
TEXT 6, FIRST (Technical terms kept or adapted)	In **trauma patients** who have undergone heavy **blood loss**, these **molecules** are **in short supply**, and its makers claim MP40X can deliver an **oxygen boost** to organs and tissue in the body reducing the risk of organ failure.	**Patients** who suffered **trauma and lost lots of blood**, have a **shortage** of these **chemicals**. People who made MP40X claim that it can deliver an **oxygen boost** to organs and tissue in the body. In this way the risk of **organ failure** will be reduced.
Text 37, GW (Foreign words and domain-specific terms are *kept* or *wrongly used* to replace other domain-specific ones)	In recent years the US army has been forged into a motivated, effective tool for large-scale military operations overseas. But it has never been suited to combating **insurgency**. **Guerrillas** and **suicide bombers** can impose a deadly corrosion on *conventional forces*.	In recent years the US army has become a very effective army for big military operations in other countries, but it has never been effective against **insurgents**. It is very difficult for *regular armies* to fight against **guerrillas** and **suicide bombers**.
TEXT 47, GW (Removal of foreign words)	Life for the housewife is an endless ***faena***, a round of tasks to ensure the comfort of every (other) member of the family.	Many women, especially older woman, like to serve the rest of the family. They work very hard to make the rest of the family comfortable.
Text 21 GW (Low-frequency words **replaced** by high-frequency yet polysemic ones) (Removal of non-relevant domain-specific information) (Addition of temporal contextualization)	Six years after 9/11, bin Laden is **maddeningly out of reach**. Despite the world's largest manhunt and a \$25m **bounty**, he **remains at large**, the Scarlet Pimpernel of jihad. [. . .] The Pakistani army thought it had **cornered** in a village in the lawless North Waziristan tribal agency in 2003. A year later the Spanish newspaper El Mundo claimed to have **located** him inside a Muslim **enclave** of western China. After the **mammoth** earthquake that devastated northern Pakistan, Senator Harry Reid from Nevada **announced** that bin Laden had died under the rubble.	Six years after 9/11, bin Laden is **still free**. The world's largest manhunt and a possible **reward** of \$25 million have **not managed to find** him. [. . .] The Pakistani army thought it had **found** him in a village in North Waziristan in 2003. A year later, the Spanish newspaper El Mundo said he **was** in a Muslim **area** of western China. One US senator **said** that bin Laden had died in the **huge** earthquake in Pakistan last year.

Table C: Examples extracted from the corpora (continued)		
	Standard	**Adapted**
Text 32, GW (Simultaneous lexical strategies)	Tourists could also visit some of Britain's **ancient architectural treasures** which, she says, **risk becoming derelict** because of a **lack of funding**. Strawberry Hill, Sir Horace Walpole's **folly in Twickenham**, west London, **which sparked the Gothic revival in the early 19th century**, is **struggling** to raise £8m. One of the oldest **parish churches** in England, St Mary's, in Stow in Lindsey, Lincolnshire, needs £3m for renovations. Another London **landmark**, Battersea power station, becomes more **run-down** every day as government, developers and **local community boards** argue over its future [...] West points out that the guidebook's message is not all **gloom**.	Tourists should also visit some of Britain's **ancient architectural treasures** which, she says, are in **danger of falling down** because there is **no money** to save them. Strawberry Hill, Sir Horace Walpole's **building** in west London **needs** £8m. One of the oldest **churches** in England, St Mary's, in Stow in Lindsey, Lincolnshire, needs £3m. Another London **landmark**, Battersea power station, becomes more **run-down** every day as government, property developers and the **local people** argue about its future [...] West points out that the guidebook's message is not all **gloom**.
TEXT 13, FIRST (Removal of non-relevant information *including* higher-proficiency words)	To celebrate their first wedding anniversary in April, Jeremy Forrest and his photographer wife Emily spent two **idyllic** weeks in Thailand and Malaysia.	Jeremy Forrest and his wife Emily celebrated their first wedding anniversary on a holiday in Thailand and Malaysia.
Text 28, FIRST (**Bending** of meaning and **mistakes** due to adaptation) (Domain-specific term replaces phrasal verb) (Passive voice kept) (Explanation: paraphrase)	Atticus decides to take on a case involving a black man named Tom Robison who has been accused of raping a very poor white girl [...] Because Atticus is defending a black man, **Scout and Jem find themselves whispered at and taunted, and have trouble keeping their tempers**. At a family Christmas gathering, Scout beats up her cloying relative Francis when he accuses Atticus of ruining the family name by being a "nigger-lover". Jem cuts off the tops of an **old neighbour's** flower bushes **after she** derides Atticus, and as punishment, has to read out loud to **her** every day.	Atticus decides to defend a case involving a black man named Tom Robinson. This man has been accused of raping a very poor white girl [...] **Scout and Jem gossip about Atticus** defending a black man. **They are very disapproving of him. They become annoyed.** At a family Christmas gathering, Scout beats up her cloying relative Francis. Scout does this because he accuses Atticus of ruining the family name by being sympathetic to black people. Jem cuts off the tops of **her neighbour's** flower bushes. **She** derides Atticus. As punishment, **she** has to read out loud to her every day. **Scout is a female character, Atticus, Jem and Francis are male characters. The neighbour is female.*
Text 8, FIRST (Higher-proficiency words are kept rather than replaced by lower-proficiency ones).	The story starts shortly after the **sudden** death of Barry Fairbrother, a kind-hearted member of the **parish council**.	The story starts shortly after the **sudden** death of Barry Fairbrother, a kind-hearted member of the **parish council**. **Sudden* (EVP: B2) could have been removed or replaced by *fast* (A1) or *quick* (EVP: A2) **Parish* (Unlisted, possible C1/C2) could have been replaced by *community* (EVP: A2) and *council* (EVP: B1) by *group* (EVP: A1)

Table C: Examples extracted from the corpora (continued)		
	Standard	**Adapted**
Text 19, FIRST (Use of anaphoric references) (Dependent and independent clauses **replaced** by main clauses. With the exception of two dependent clauses in the adapted version – a kept infinitive and an added conditional clause).)	Teenager Marty McFly [. . .] **gets sent back** to 1955 **where** he **runs into** his mother and father and **prevents** their union. **Meeting** up with younger Doc, Marty **hatches** a plan to get his parents together **before** he **gets erased** from existence.	He **sends** teenager Marty McFly back to 1955. He **meets** his mother and father. He **stops** them from getting together. He **meets** Doc as a young man. Marty and Doc **plan** to get his parents together. If they are not together, he **cannot** be born. He would **cease** to exist.
Text 94, GW (Modifying the existing gloss to avoid asides in the adapted version)	In what seems to have been another misjudged remark, **Obama's wife, Michelle**, campaigning for **him** in South Carolina, also brought up race.	On the other side, **Michelle Obama**, campaigning for **her husband** in South Carolina, also mentioned race.
Text 30, FIRST (Kept *consecutio temporum*)	The standardised house design **has led** some to believe that there **was** no hierarchy of rank within the settlement at Skara Brae, and that all villagers **were** equal. Whether or not this **is** true **is debatable**. However, it **is likely** that life here **was probably** quite comfortable for the Neolithic people. The villagers **kept** sheep and cattle and **grew** wheat and barley. They **probably traded** these commodities for pottery. They **would have hunted** red deer and boar for their meat and skins. They **would also have consumed** fish, seal and whale meat, and the eggs of sea birds. The skin and bones of these animals **would have provided** tools such as needles and knives. Flint for cutting tools **would have been traded** or **gathered** from the shore.	The uniform house design **has led** some to believe that there **was** no rank order within the village at Skara Brae. The standardised house design **has led** some to believe that all villagers **were** equal. This **is uncertain**. However, it **is likely** that life here **was probably** quite comfortable for the Neolithic people. The villagers **kept** sheep and cattle. The villagers **grew** wheat and barley. The villagers **probably traded** wheat and barley for pottery. They **would have hunted** red deer and boar for their meat and skins. The villagers **would also have consumed** fish, seal and whale meat, and the eggs of sea birds. The skin and bones of these animals **would have provided** tools such as needles and knives. Flint for cutting tools **would have been traded** or **gathered** from the shore.
Text 5, FIRST (High-proficiency **replaced** by low-proficiency equivalent) (Passive voice added to paraphrase) (Passive voice replaced with active voice)	The children ran wild all over the house; the English governess **quarrelled** with the housekeeper [. . .] Three days after the **quarrel**, Prince Stepan Arkadyevitch Oblonsky – Stiva, as he was called in the fashionable world – woke up at his usual hour, that is, at eight o'clock in the morning [. . .]	The children ran around the house and nobody looked after them all day. An English woman who was paid to look after the children **argued** with the woman who looked after the house [. . .] Three days after the **argument** between the husband and the wife had finished, Prince Stepan Arkadyevitch Oblonsky – Stiva woke up at eight o'clock in the morning. Only people who called him Stepan Arkadyevitch Oblonsky – Stiva were from the upper class [. . .]
TEXT 34, GW (Passive voice kept)	They know that they are father and daughter, that Ryann **was conceived** thanks to sperm **donated** by Mr Harrison in the 1980s.	They know that Ryann **was born** thanks to sperm **given** by Mr Harrison in the 1980s.

Table C: Examples extracted from the corpora (continued)		
	Standard	**Adapted**
TEXT 82, GW (Introduction added)		Many animals around the world are very rare, gorillas and tigers, for example. There is a danger that in a few years time these animals will disappear from the world forever and we will only see them in photographs. Animals like these are known as endangered species and there are laws which protect endangered species. However, some people are buying and selling rare and endangered animals on the internet.
Text 12, GW (Glossary kept)	Near-Earth objects Comets and asteroids pulled into orbits near the Earth by the gravitational attraction of planets. Most NEOs are made of ice and dust, or are bits of rock from the asteroid belt between Jupiter and Mars. Outside chance Apophis had been tracked since its discovery in June 2004. [. . .] Slight gravitational attraction Everything in the universe that has mass attracts anything else with mass via the force of gravity. If a gravity tractor is placed near an asteroid, the asteroid will move fractionally towards it. [. . .]	Near-Earth objects Comets and asteroids that start to circle very near the Earth. Most NEOs are made of ice and dust, or are bits of rock from the asteroid area between Jupiter and Mars. Outside chance Astronomers discovered Apophis in June 2004. [. . .] Slight gravitational attraction Everything in the universe that has mass attracts anything else with mass because of gravity. If a "gravity tractor" is placed near an asteroid, the asteroid will move very slightly nearer to it. [. . .]
Text 85, GW (Footnote kept)	* Note: In the UK, so-called 'public' schools are not public at all. They are private schools for the children of rich parents.	* Note: In the UK, so-called 'public' schools are not public at all. They are private schools for the children of rich parents.
Text 33, GW (Elimination)	There is a fear that the film will stop people buying all African diamonds, **something both the industry and the campaigners want to avoid. "It would be terrible if the film meant that people saw Sierra Leone as a pariah,"** said Sanders. "Quite a few African countries have weak control systems."	Some people are worried that the film will stop people buying all African diamonds. "Quite a few African countries have weak control systems," says Sanders.
Text 2, FIRST (Explanation: definition)	The **twenty-five metre** pool is available for recreational swimming from seven to nine in the morning and twelve thirty to one thirty on weekdays, and ten am to four pm on Saturdays.	**Recreational swimming means not swimming in lanes.** The 25 metre pool is available for **recreational swimming** from 07:00–09:00 and 12:30–13:30 on weekdays. The 25 metre pool is available for recreational swimming from 10:00 – 16:00 on Saturdays.

Table C: Examples extracted from the corpora (continued)

	Standard	Adapted
Text 9, FIRST (Explanation: paraphrase)	About half of this **shrinkage is due to change in distribution and abundance**, the remainder to **changes in physiology**.	Half of the **shrinkage is because of location of the fish and their number**. The other half is because of the **changes in the structure and function of their bodies**.
Text 45, GW (Spelling out implications)	Not since Hamelin has the discovery of a rat provoked so much **alarm**. It was only a single creature, but it had no business being on the island of Santa Fe in the **isolated Galapagos archipelago, where conservationists now strive to keep foreign wildlife at bay as effectively as hundreds of miles of open ocean did for millions of years**.	About 1,000 km west of the coast of Ecuador in the middle of the Pacific Ocean is a group of islands called the Galapagos Islands. Because the Galapagos Islands are so far away from the rest of South America, **the wildlife there is unique and plants and animals found in other parts of the world do not exist on the islands**. There are no rats, for example. But now a rat has been found on the island of Santa Fe and the conservationists who are working to stop foreign wildlife reaching the islands are **very worried**.
Text 3, FIRST (Exemplification)	Students will receive guidance from their **tutors** on how best to conduct research and write it up effectively.	**A tutor is like a teacher who gives private lessons**. Students will be guided by their tutors on how to do research.
Text 3, FIRST (Reiteration of structure)	Our **pre-sessional courses** are ideal for students who have a conditional place at a British university, but who need to achieve a certain level of English in order to be accepted. The **course** aims to provide students with the English language and study skills that they need in order to be successful at university or another academic establishment.	**Pre-sessional courses** are courses to prepare people for university. Our **pre-sessional courses are ideal for students who** have a conditional place at a British university. The **pre-sessional courses are ideal for students who** need to achieve a certain level of English in order to be accepted.

Table D: Type and token distribution

	FIRST Standard	FIRST Adapted	GW Standard	GW Adapted
Type count	3 089	2 818	10 902	7 026
Token count	10 850	11 171	74 527	61 569

Table E: Concreteness rating distribution

	FIRST Standard	FIRST Adapted	GW Standard	GW Adapted
Mean	3.1	3.1	3.2	3.2
Standard Deviation	1.1	1.1	1.1	1.1

Quantifying word complexity for *Leichte Sprache*: A computational metric and its psycholinguistic validation

Umesh Patil[1], Jesús Calvillo[1], Sol Lago[2], Anne-Kathrin Schumann[1]

[1]t2k GmbH, Dresden, Germany, [2]Goethe University Frankfurt, Germany

umesh.patil@text2knowledge.de j.calvillo@text2knowledge.de

sollago@em.uni-frankfurt.de ak.schumann@text2knowledge.de

Abstract

Leichte Sprache ("Easy Language" or "Easy German") is a strongly simplified version of German geared toward a target group with limited language proficiency. In Germany, public bodies are required to provide information in *Leichte Sprache*. The initial rules for *Leichte Sprache* were developed instinctively by non-linguists, without grounding in linguistic research or cognitive science, and lacked precise criteria for assessing the complexity of linguistic structures (Bock and Pappert, 2023).[1] Although more recent rulebooks have introduced scientifically grounded guidelines for *Leichte Sprache* (Bredel and Maaß, 2016), there remains a need for a computational metric to evaluate language complexity. In response, this paper proposes a model for determining word complexity by training an XGBoost classifier using word-level linguistic features, corpus-level distributional data, frequency information from an in-house *Leichte Sprache* corpus, and human-annotated complexity ratings. We psycholinguistically validate our model by showing that it captures human word recognition times above and beyond traditional word-level predictors. Moreover, we discuss a number of practical applications of our classifier, such as the evaluation of AI-simplified text and detection of CEFR levels of words. To our knowledge, this is one of the first attempts to systematically quantify word complexity in the context of *Leichte Sprache* and to link it directly to real-time word processing.

1 Introduction

1.1 German *Leichte Sprache*

Text Simplification (TS), Complex Word identification (CWI) and Lexical Complexity Prediction (LCP) are popular NLP tasks that have attracted widespread attention due to increased awareness regarding the importance of making information easily accessible to diverse audiences. In the European Union, this awareness has led to legislation, for instance, in the form of the European Accessibility Act (Eur, 2019) and the German *Behindertengleichstellungsgesetz*:[2] In certain scenarios, texts are required to be translated intralingually from standard German into *Leichte Sprache* (Hansen-Schirra et al., 2020). *Leichte Sprache* is a strongly simplified version of German that uses a reduced inventory of German linguistic forms and structures (Maaß, 2020; Maaß et al., 2021; Bock and Pappert, 2023). For illustration, examples (1) and (2) show two versions of the same text: a standard German input text and its translation in *Leichte Sprache*, created by our (*t2k GmbH's*) simplification model. As can be seen, sentences in *Leichte Sprache* are shorter and avoid abstract nouns (such as “Paradigmenwechsel”, meaning ‘paradigm change’) or complex nominalisations, and also avoid complex syntactic structures. Remaining compound nouns are visually split ("Lebens-Bereich" instead of "Lebensbereich", both meaning ‘sphere of life’) to further facilitate processing.

1. Der mit der Konvention verbundene **Paradigmenwechsel** weg von Fürsorge und Integration hin zur Inklusion betrifft alle Menschen und nahezu jeden Lebensbereich.

2. Alle Menschen mit und ohne Behinderung sollen sich besser um die Menschen mit Behinderung kümmern. Und das in fast jedem **Lebens-Bereich**.

Given the difficulty of generating *Leichte Sprache* translations, an automated complexity met-

[1]The DIN Institute's DIN SPEC 33429:2025-03 provides an overview and discussion of these rules, see Deutsches Institut für Normung (DIN) (2025).

[2]Literally meaning "law to prevent discrimination against people with disabilities", see https://www.gesetze-im-internet.de/bgg/__11.html

Proceedings of the 1st Workshop on Artificial Intelligence and Easy and Plain Language in Institutional Contexts (AI & EL/PL), pages 94–107, June 23, 2025

ric is a vital requirement not only for model development and tuning, but also for output evaluation. It is also required for data curation and quality-checking AI- or human-generated simplifications. Naturally, this metric needs to be psycholinguistically valid to actually measure processing difficulty in human comprehenders. None of these specific requirements has been covered by existing research in text simplification and complex word identification.

1.2 Word Complexity

Word complexity is considered as the perceived difficulty of a word by language users, and is typically assessed from the perspective of a target group with limited language proficiency, consisting of individuals with cognitive impairments, second language learners or children (North et al., 2023). The text simplification process, geared towards such target groups, requires the identification of complex words that can then be substituted in the final simplified text (North et al., 2024).

1.2.1 Word Complexity in NLP

After determining CWI as a stand-alone task in Shardlow (2013), it has been researched through various shared tasks that focused on classifying words or expressions as complex or non-complex, for example CWI–2016 at SemEval (Paetzold and Specia, 2016), CWI–2018 at BEA (Yimam et al., 2018) and ALexS–2020 at SEPLN (Ortiz-Zambrano and Montejo-Ráez, 2020). Later on, CWI has been extended with the Lexical Complexity Prediction (LCP) task (e.g. LCP–2021 at SemEval (Shardlow et al., 2021)) which denotes the complexity of a word or phrase on a continuous scale rather than assigning a binary "complex" or "non-complex" label. Both CWI and LCP tasks have primarily focused on English (in terms of the dataset size and the frequency of being part of such tasks), but at times also included French, German, and Spanish as parallel tasks. German was part of the CWI-2018 shared task, which involved a binary classification task (predicting whether a target word was complex or simple) and a probabilistic classification task (predicting the probability of a target word being complex). The best performing system for German, which was submitted by Kajiwara and Komachi (2018), used a random forest classifier and regressor, and features such as two types of word frequency estimates, and the length of the word or phrase.

So far, the primary resources for German word complexity analysis–both datasets and models–have predominantly come from the CWI-2018 shared task. As a result, research specifically targeting German remains limited, which emphasizes the importance of our current effort.

1.2.2 Word Complexity in Psycholinguistics

A major limitation in current CWI and LCP research is the lack of psycholinguistic validation. The primary objective of simplification is to facilitate readability and comprehension for low language proficiency groups (Shardlow, 2014; Al-Thanyyan and Azmi, 2021). Most CWI and LCP models are trained and evaluated with annotations collected from participants who indicated which words or phrases they found difficult for themselves or for a specific low language proficiency group. These annotations are untimed, however, it is key to evaluate complexity models with real-time comprehension data, ideally collected from participants with low language proficiency.[3]

In the domain of real-time word recognition, psycholinguists seek to identify the variables that determine processing effort. A variety of methods can be used to measure word recognition time, with the most common being lexical decision, word naming, and reading eye-tracking (Ferrand et al., 2011; Kliegl et al., 2010; Kuperman et al., 2013; New et al., 2006). Of specific relevance for this study is the lexical decision task, in which participants see strings of letters and press different keys depending on whether they think that a string corresponds to a word in their language or not. Their response times and accuracy are recorded.

The main properties that affect response times in word recognition tasks are word length (New et al., 2006; Barton et al., 2014), word frequency (Brysbaert et al., 2016, 2018; Kuperman and Van Dyke, 2013; Ferrand et al., 2011; Kliegl et al., 2010), and the size of a word's orthographic neighborhood (Mathey, 2001; Yarkoni et al., 2008; Schröter and Schroeder, 2017; Chen and Mirman, 2012). While these factors are often studied individually, a contribution of the CWI word complexity metric proposed here is that it combines them into a single metric to quantitatively describe word complexity.

[3]Although, in some cases, real-time lexical comprehension data are available from psycholinguistic studies with low language proficiency groups (e.g. the lexical decision task in Pappert and Bock, 2020), they are typically smaller in size than the data required for training CWI or LCP models.

Recent psycholinguistic work also shows that properties of speakers (i.e., their language experience) can affect word recognition (Brysbaert et al., 2016; Keuleers et al., 2015; Kuperman and Van Dyke, 2013; Davies et al., 2017). For example, it has been shown that corpus-based (objective) word frequencies are worse at predicting lexical decision times than subjective ratings, especially with less skilled readers (Kuperman and Van Dyke, 2013). Similarly, frequency effects differ between university students with larger vs. smaller vocabularies, as well as between native vs. non-native (second language) speakers, which suggests that differences in language experience affect word recognition (Keuleers et al., 2015; Cop et al., 2015). Because of this, it is important to create complexity measures that are informed by the different types of text that readers might have access to, including simplified texts. To do this, the CWI model reported in this article incorporated word frequency estimates based on an in-house proprietary dataset of *Leichte Sprache*, which may better capture the type of linguistic input available to second language learners, as well as individuals with lower literacy and/or language impairments.

1.2.3 Application: CEFR Level Detection

Psycholinguistic research shows that simplifying text at different levels of proficiency may help comprehension in second language learners (Crossley et al., 2014; Rets and Rogaten, 2021). This idea aligns naturally with the Common European Framework of Reference for Languages (CEFR), a widely accepted standard that categorizes second language proficiency into six levels (A1–C2). These levels help instructors design materials and courses, and institutions/employers to understand candidates' linguistic proficiency.

Intuitively, the CEFR levels lie between CWI and LCP, classifying language proficiency into distinct levels yet maintaining a progressive continuity of complexity (A1 < A2 < B1 < etc.). Regarding *Leichte Sprache*, we can expect that the vocabulary range at the initial levels (A1, A2) complies with its lexical requirements, while the middle levels (B1, B2) would require more careful assessment, and vocabulary from the advanced levels (C1, C2) is likely to be avoided. While complexity can differ between second language learners and native speakers, one may expect a considerable overlap between these two groups (North and Zampieri, 2023). Moreover, *Leichte Sprache* is also intended to help second language learners with limited proficiency (BMAS, 2014).

Despite the wide acceptance of CEFR levels, the classification of a linguistic unit into a level is usually done manually based on somewhat vague guidelines that can lead to inconsistencies. Some efforts have been made to automatically classify text as per CEFR levels in many languages (e.g., François and Fairon, 2012; Santucci et al., 2020; Velleman and van der Geest, 2014; Branco et al., 2014). However, to our knowledge, only a few studies have been carried out for German (Hancke and Meurers, 2013; Vajjala and Rama, 2018), which were mainly targeted towards classifying bigger segments of text (e.g. essays). This shows the need of having a word-level classifier for German CEFR levels.

1.3 Approach and Summary of Contributions

Language complexity can be conceptualized as both a continuum and a multidimensional construct, spanning various levels of linguistic analysis (e.g. pragmatic, syntactic, lexical). Correspondingly, the task of language simplification needs to be approached at different points along this continuum and across different linguistic levels, depending on the needs of the target audience (Maaß, 2020).

The main objective of this work is to develop a word complexity metric tailored to the requirements of the target groups for *Leichte Sprache*—the "Easy Language target groups" as defined in Maaß (2020), which includes individuals with dyslexia, cognitive disability, dementia, prelingual hearing impairment, aphasia, functional illiteracy, and learners of German as a second language. However, the development and evaluation of such a tool is inherently constrained by the availability of relevant resources. In our case, these resources include: (i) the CWI dataset, annotated considering the target group involving children, language learners, and individuals with reading impairments; (ii) the CEFR wordlists, developed primarily for second language learners; and (iii) the DeveL dataset, compiled using data from young and adult speakers.

Although the metric is constructed using data from diverse target groups, we propose that its quantifiable nature helps progress in mapping word complexity along this complexity continuum. Given that different target groups have distinct complexity requirements, this metric holds potential for broader applicability—not only for *Leichte*

Sprache, but also for other simplified language contexts. This perspective aligns with the "chest of drawers" approach proposed by Maaß (2020), which advocates for differentiated simplification strategies tailored to specific audiences.

The contributions of our article are as follows. First, we train a novel word complexity classifier for German and evaluate it in comparison with earlier work reported in Yimam et al. (2018). Second, since we are interested in CWI in the context of *Leichte Sprache*, we extend traditionally used CWI features using information derived from *Leichte Sprache* data to better account for the specific needs of our target group. Third, we demonstrate the psycholinguistic validity of the model. Fourth, by integrating various features into the model, we effectively produce a unified psycholinguistic measure of word complexity. Finally, we show that the model can be extended to detect CEFR levels of words.

2 CWI Model

Quantifying word complexity is not a straightforward task. Lexical complexity is subjective and it also depends on the context. For the task of CWI we make the simplifying assumptions that a word has a fixed complexity level and that it can be classified as either complex or non-complex.

2.1 Dataset

We used the CWI-2018 dataset, which was released for the second CWI shared task organized as part of the BEA 2018 workshop (Yimam et al., 2018). The dataset consists of offline responses where participants rated single- and multi-word expressions (MWE) on complexity. Participants were shown 5–10 sentences and asked to annotate words or phrases that could pose difficulty in understanding them for a given target reader such as children, language learners or people with reading impairments. The entire dataset consists of English, German, Spanish and French, but we used only the German part. The German dataset was annotated by a mixture of native and non-native speakers (n=23 out of which 12 were native speakers). This led to 7,905 words and MWEs (6,151 training, 795 development and 959 testing instances).

2.2 (Re-)Define Complex Word Label

In the CWI-2018 task a word or MWE was considered complex if at least one of the annotators annotated it as complex. We deem this definition overly simplistic because: (i) an instance could get classified as complex simply because one of the annotators by mistake labeled it complex—it has been observed that CWI can have low inter-annotator agreement (Zampieri et al., 2017); (ii) many proper names such as 'Wikipedia', 'UNICEF' and 'Hannover' (a city in Germany) were rated as complex.

We followed the following procedure to define which words are complex and which are not.

(a) *Complexity Threshold*: We combined all occurrences of a word and calculated the complexity proportion of the word as the ratio of the number of times it was rated as complex to the number of times it received a rating. We defined a threshold for complexity proportion to consider the word as complex or not; for this we again made use of the information in our *Leichte Sprache* dataset.[4] All words with a complexity proportion value above or equal to the threshold were labeled as complex, and below as non-complex.

(b) *Annotation correction*: We experimented with the classification process with an earlier version of the CWI classifier that used heuristics and only a subset of the final features. In the output of the heuristics-based classifier we found that some misclassified instances could have been labeled incorrectly in the dataset. We manually corrected those labels for further use of the dataset. In total 927 labels were manually corrected.

(c) *Proper names are non-complex*: Although, in theory, some proper names can be more complex than others because of their familiarity, pronunciation or cross-linguistic complexity —e.g. 'Berlin' vs. 'Thiruvananthapuram', the capital of the Indian state of Kerala—, we limited the scope of the model to classifying word classes that were not

[4]For determining the threshold we used the *Leichte Sprache* training dataset which consists of input text in standard German and output text in *Leichte Sprache*. For the CWI-2018 dataset we created two classes of words: words that occur in the target texts (the negative class) and words that occur only in the input texts (the positive class). Using the entire range of the difficulty proportion values as the threshold and the binary class labels as the ground truth we computed the True Positive Rate (TPR) and False Positive Rate (FPR) for the positive class. This was done by using the *roc_curve()* function from the `scikit-learn` library (Pedregosa et al., 2018). We chose the optimal threshold to be the one that maximized the difference between the TPR and FPR.

proper names, and we assumed that all proper names are non-complex even if some participants rated them as complex.

(d) *A1-level words are non-complex*: We referred to two wordlists for second language learners of German at the CEFR A1-level. The first wordlist is published by the Goethe-Institut, a globally recognized cultural institute of the Federal Republic of Germany that offers German language courses, and administers German language exams. The second wordlist is published by telc GmbH, an organization known for its language proficiency exams.[5] We defined all words from the dataset that occur in the wordlists to be non-complex even if some participants rated them as complex.

(e) *Drop MWEs*: Since our goal was to capture word-level complexity using lexical and sub-lexical features, we dropped all MWEs.

2.3 Feature Selection & Engineering

For each word we used the following features.

(a) *POS*: Part-of-Speech tag returned by the `spaCy` library employing the medium-sized German language model `de_core_news_md` (Honnibal et al., 2020). We used the Universal POS, a tagset consistent across languages.

(b) *freq_word*: Word frequency estimate returned by the `wordfreq` library (Speer, 2022).

(c) *freq_lemma_word*: The lemma frequency of the word. For calculating the lemma frequency, we first calculated the lemma of each word using two libraries, `spaCy` and `Stanza` (Qi et al., 2020). Based on the POS of the word we picked the best lemma from the two lemmas: `spaCy` lemma for nominal and punctuations (NOUN, PRON, PROPN, NUM and PUNCT) and `Stanza` lemma for the rest (in an experiments for testing the lemmatization accuracy of `spaCy` and `Stanza`, we found that this strategy lead to more accurate final lemmas). To calculate the frequency of the best lemma, we first lemmatized all words from the `wordfreq` library and added the word frequency values for the same lemma entry. We considered these cumulative frequency values to be the frequency estimates of the best lemma.

(d) *length*: Word length in terms of the number of characters.

(e) *freq_LS_target*: The frequency of the word in the entire target part of the *Leichte Sprache* training dataset. The rationale behind adding these frequencies was that the more often a word occurs in the target translation for *Leichte Sprache*, the more likely it is to be a non-complex word.

(f) *freq_proportion_LS*: The proportion of source to target text frequency of the word in the *Leichte Sprache* training dataset. The rationale behind adding this proportion was that if a word occurs very frequently in the source text but very rarely in the target text, it is probably because it is complex.

(g) *is_in_LS_source*: A binary value denoting if the word occurs in the source text of the *Leichte Sprache* training dataset.

(h) *is_in_a1_wordlist*: A binary value denoting if the word occurs in A1 wordlists release by the Goethe-Institute and telc GmbH.

2.4 Training & Evaluation

We combined all three splits—training, development and testing—from the CWI-2018 dataset. After applying the data cleaning procedure described above (see 2.2), we were left with 4,892 unique instances (2,316 complex and 2,576 non-complex). We split this dataset into training (80%) and test (20%) sets. Our dataset included a single categorical variable (`POS`) and multiple continuous features. To ensure consistent handling of the categorical feature, we identified all possible `POS` values across the entire dataset and used that set for one-hot encoding in subsequent experiments. Following the results from Hartmann and dos Santos (2018), who found that a feature-engineered XGBoost model outperformed multiple neural network architectures in the CWI domain, we used the `XGBClassifier` in binary classification mode (Chen and Guestrin, 2016). We carried out five-fold cross-validation to discover an optimal set of hyperparameters. The search drew 5,000 random samples from a predefined distributions of these hyperparameters (see Table A1.1 in Appendix B).

[5]The lists are available at `https://www.goethe.de/pro/relaunch/prf/de/A1_SD1_Wortliste_02.pdf` from the Goethe-Institut and `https://www.telc.net/fileadmin/user_upload/Downloads_Verlag/Einfach_gut/Wortschatzlisten/Einfach_gut_A1_Wortschatzliste_alphabetisch.pdf` from telc GmbH.

Upon completion of cross-validation, the best hyperparameters were automatically selected according to the highest macro-averaged F1 score. The best model that emerged from the cross-validation process had an F1 score of 0.85 on the held-out test set. For an informal comparison, our classifier performed much better than the best system at CWI-2018 shared task for German, which had an F1 score of 0.75 (Yimam et al., 2018). Since we used a different split of the dataset for testing and adjusted the definition of labels, the performance of our classifier cannot be compared directly with the ones from the CWI-2018 task; nevertheless, it offers an approximate indication of the classifier's performance.

To leverage all available data, we refitted the best model from the cross-validation process on the entire dataset. This model was then used as the final model for further analysis, validation and applications of the classifier.

3 CWI Model: Validation & Applications

3.1 Lexical Complexity Prediction Using The CWI Model

An `XGBClassifier`, after being trained on the dataset, can also generate probability estimates of a data point being of a given class; in our case the probability of a word being "complex" or "non-complex" based on its features. We assume that the predicted probability of a word being "complex" is a proxy of the complexity of the word (0 denotes minimal complexity and 1 corresponds to maximal complexity). We use these word complexity values for further evaluation and applications of the model.

3.2 Psycholinguistic Validation

To provide a psycholinguistic validation of the complexity estimates generated by the CWI model, we re-analyzed a dataset of 1152 German nouns from the Developmental Lexicon Project (DeveL, Schröter and Schroeder, 2017). The DeveL dataset was created by a large scale developmental study conducted with 800 children from school grades 1–6, as well as 43 younger (20–30 years) and 41 older adults (65–75 years). We focused on the adults, because some predictors in our analysis (word frequency and orthographic neighborhood size) were specific to adult populations—a supplementary analysis with the child group can be found in Appendix C. Because all adults were native German speakers with no history of reading or language impairment, they can't be classified as a primary target group for *Leichte Sprache*. However, given the absence of an equivalent dataset with *Leichte Sprache* users, our analysis provides a first step to validating word simplification methods—which should be further validated with psycholinguistic datasets from other populations once they become available.

All groups completed a lexical decision task and a naming task. We analyzed the noun recognition times from the lexical decision task. The DeveL dataset provides the recognition time estimated for each noun in each speaker group. We predicted that nouns with higher CWI complexity should increase processing difficulty and therefore elicit longer recognition times.

As expected, more complex nouns showed longer recognition times (Figure 1). Next, we sought to identify the effect of CWI complexity above and beyond the linguistic variables previously shown to predict recognition times in the DeveL dataset by Schröter and Schroeder (2017). For this purpose, we ran a mixed-effects linear regression model with CWI complexity as a predictor together with the following variables: noun length, trigram frequency, noun type frequency, and orthographic neighborhood size.[6] Note that with the exception of trigram frequency and orthographic neighborhood size, the other variables were used for training the CWI model. Thus, the estimated effect of word complexity in the statistical model incorporating these variables as covariates should reflect the unique contribution of CWI complexity in explaining recognition times, i.e., the contribution of complexity in explaining variance in the data that is not shared with the other variables.

With the exception of CWI complexity, all other variables were taken from the DeveL dataset (Schröter and Schroeder, 2017). Specifically, noun length was operationalized as the number of letters in each noun. Trigram frequency was based on the childLex corpus (version 0.16, December 2015, see Schroeder et al., 2015) and it was the sum of the frequencies of a sequence of three let-

[6]Following Schröter and Schroeder (2017), we initially included two different frequency estimators: noun type (or form) frequency and noun lemma frequency. However, type and lemma frequency were highly correlated (i.e., above 0.93) and caused high collinearity in the statistical model, as evidenced by variance inflation factors above 10 (James et al., 2013). To address this problem, only noun type frequency was kept in the final model—reported in Table 1.

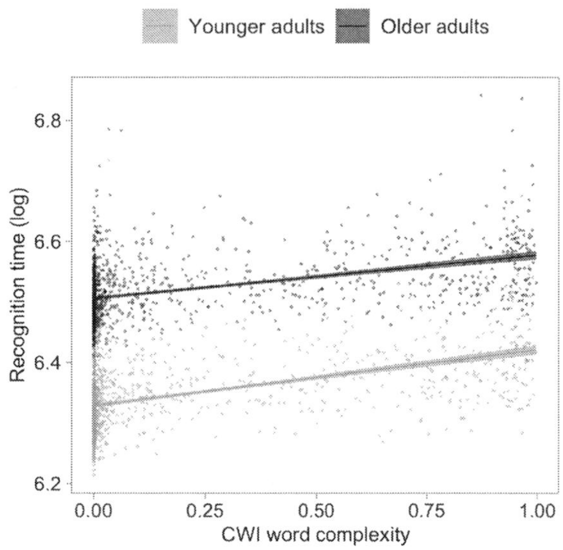

Figure 1: Relationship between CWI complexity and recognition time for the 1152 German nouns in the DeveL dataset (Schröter and Schroeder, 2017). Lines show the effect of word complexity estimated without any covariates in a linear regression model with log-transformed word recognition time as the dependent variable. Ribbons show 95% confidence intervals. Dots correspond to the mean recognition time of each noun in the younger and older adults.

ters within a noun, treating the word beginning and end as separate letters. Noun type (or form) frequency was the number of occurrences of a distinct noun form per million tokens in the DWDS corpus (Digitales Wörterbuch Deutscher Sprache, version 0.4, January 2014; see Geyken, 2007). The orthographic neighborhood size was estimated using the mean Levenshtein Distance from a noun to its 20 closest orthographic neighbors in the DWDS corpus—with this distance being a function of the minimum number of changes, i.e. substitutions, additions and deletions, that are required to turn one word into another (Yarkoni et al., 2008; Schröter and Schroeder, 2017).

All variables mentioned above, together with CWI complexity, were entered in the statistical model as fixed effects nested under the categorical predictor "group" (younger/older adults). This allowed estimating the effect of each variable in the young and old groups separately. Continuous variables were centered. Following Schröter and Schroeder (2017), noun recognition times were log-transformed to account for the right skew of response time distributions. The model included a random intercept by noun, because each noun was seen by both the younger and older group. The data was analyzed using the package lme4 (v.1.1-36; Bates et al., 2015) in R (version 4.5.0, R Core Team, 2025).

The results of the statistical model showed the expected effects of noun length, frequency, and orthographic neighborhood on recognition times (Table 1). Crucially, the effect of CWI complexity was significant after adjusting for these variables: recognition time increased with increasing complexity in both the younger and older adult groups. These results demonstrate that the CWI complexity measure predicted noun recognition difficulties, and that it continued to do so after being adjusted for the effects of frequency, length, and neighborhood size reported in previous research (Schröter and Schroeder, 2017).

3.3 Word Complexity for CEFR Level Detection

In order to address the lack of a German CEFR classifier capable of assigning words to specific levels, we tested the CWI model on this task. The goal was to use the word complexity values to determine the threshold between different CEFR levels. We assume that a word's CEFR level is determined by its complexity value—words from lower CEFR levels should have lower complexity values and complexity values should progressively increase from level A1 (lowest level) to level C2 (highest level). Note that the CEFR framework defines nested levels, meaning that all A1 words are a subset of A2, which in turn is a subset of B1, and so forth. Considering this nested structure, we defined the classification task as follows: for a given word the classifier has to predict the *lowest possible CEFR level* that can be assigned to it. This effectively amounts to first finding out the optimum thresholds for the complexity value that separates the adjacent levels, and then comparing the complexity of a word with the thresholds to determine its level.

To perform this task, we used data from various word lists freely available online that correspond to CEFR levels A1 through C1. Because CEFR levels are nested and also because there are only vague guidelines for defining the levels, these lists initially contained overlapping words. Next, we transformed the lists into mutually exclusive sets by iteratively removing words already assigned to a lower level: first, all words appearing in A1 were removed from the A2 list, then all A2 words were

	Estimate	Std. Error	t-value	p-value
Intercept (younger adults)	6.349	0.001	4723.517	0.000*
Older adults	0.173	0.001	124.187	0.000*
Length: younger adults	0.005	0.001	3.306	0.001*
Length: older adults	0.003	0.001	2.377	0.018*
Trigram frequency: younger adults	0.000	0.000	4.362	0.000*
Trigram frequency: older adults	0.000	0.000	3.945	0.000*
Type frequency: younger adults	–0.013	0.001	–11.768	0.000*
Type frequency: older adults	–0.010	0.001	–9.448	0.000*
Orthographic neighborhood size: younger adults	0.011	0.007	1.656	0.098
Orthographic neighborhood size: older adults	0.023	0.007	3.458	0.001*
CWI complexity: younger adults	0.036	0.005	6.891	0.000*
CWI complexity: older adults	0.020	0.005	3.763	0.000*

Table 1: Output of the statistical model with CWI word complexity as a predictor, together with noun length, trigram frequency, noun type frequency, and orthographic neighborhood size. R model structure: `lmer(log(Noun recognition time) ~ Group / (Length + Trigram frequency + Type frequency + Orthographic neighborhood size + CWI complexity) + (1 | Noun))`. Effects significant at the alpha .05 level are marked with asterisks. Further details of the model: `AIC` $= -7781$, `BIC` $= -7701$, `Log Likelihood` $= 3905$, `Number of observations` $= 2304$, `Number of groups:Noun` $= 1152$, `Variance:Noun (Intercept)` $= 0.000$, `Variance:Residual` $= 0.000$.

removed from B1, and so on. We did not prepare any list for the C2 level since C2 is essentially the entire lexicon of German; furthermore, we assume that words that are above the B2 level are anyway too difficult for the target group, hence it is sufficient to identify C1–C2 words as being above B2 level. This procedure yielded five distinct lists, each capturing the lowest possible CEFR level for the words in it. From these lists, we extracted a held-out test set of 200 words per level and used the remaining items for training.

An examination of these five wordlists revealed that the A2- and B1-level words share closely related lexical and distributional properties, making it difficult to identify a precise boundary between them. Consequently, we merged A2 and B1 into a single level, thereby reducing the classification task to identifying three thresholds: (1) A1 vs. A2-B1, (2) A2-B1 vs. B2, and (3) B2 vs. C1. We followed the following procedure for determining each threshold: (i) create a balanced set of words from the train split that belonged to all levels, but more for the two adjacent levels on either side of the threshold, (ii) assign them binary class labels based on the side of the threshold they are expected to belong to, (iii) compute the F1 scores of both classes for a range of complexity values as the threshold and the binary class labels as the ground truth, and finally, (iv) select the complexity value that optimizes the performance for the two classes (the point where two F1 scores intersect). We evaluated the performance of these thresholds on the held-out test set.

CEFR levels	F1 score (train)	F1 score (test)
A1	0.78	0.69
A2–B1		0.9
A2–B1	0.68	0.79
B2		0.71
B2	0.56	0.81
C1		0.45

Table 2: Performance of the classification procedure on determining the word complexity thresholds between different CEFR levels. The F1 score (train) is the same for both classes in each group since it is the optimum complexity threshold selected for the two classes.

All F1 scores are listed in Table 2. Based on the F1 scores, the thresholds distinguishing A1 from A2–B1 and A2–B1 from B2 perform well; however, further refinement is needed to improve discrimination between words at the B2 and C1 levels. Overall, these findings indicate that CEFR level classification using word complexity scores effectively identifies words at the A1, A2–B1, and B2 levels, and further show promising potential for distinguishing C1-level words from those at the B2 level.

4 General Discussion

We present a German word complexity classifier and evaluate its performance using existing resources. Given our focus on *Leichte Sprache* ("Easy German"), a strongly simplified version of German for the Easy Language target groups, we complement the standard feature sets for complexity prediction with additional features derived from *Leichte Sprache* datasets. Our results confirm the psycholinguistic validity of the resulting model, and illustrate how the model improves downstream tasks such as text simplification and CEFR-level identification.

Although official guidelines for *Leichte Sprache* do not quantitatively define complexity, making texts accessible critically requires quantitative methods to identify complex words. Our model meets this need by offering a measure of word complexity, validated through word recognition measures in humans, demonstrating its direct impact on readability and comprehensibility. Crucially, once complex words are identified, they can be simplified, which supports both automated text simplification tools and human *Leichte Sprache* translators in tailoring content for less proficient readers. Extending the classifier to map words onto CEFR levels provides additional practical benefits for second language learners of varying proficiency. By aligning text to an appropriate CEFR level, authors and educators can ensure more accessible reading material that is optimally matched to the intended audience.

Limitations

Although the word complexity metric can generate complexity values for all word classes, our psycholinguistic evaluation was restricted to nouns, as the DeveL dataset only contains nouns. It would be informative to extend the evaluation to other word classes, but we are not aware of a dataset with properties comparable to those of DeveL. Furthermore, although our findings suggest that reduced lexical complexity can facilitate reading, this effect is yet to be validated with *Leichte Sprache* users.[7] Again, the absence of suitable datasets currently prevents a direct assessment of whether our results extend to the primary target group of *Leichte Sprache*. Finally, our proposed CEFR classification approach requires additional refinements, particularly for identifying words beyond the B2 level. We see clear potential for improvement, especially by integrating different computational methodologies—such as neural network architectures and word embeddings—and by using larger and/or cleaner datasets.

[7]See Schiffl (2022) who investigated the effects of individual word-level features, such as word length and frequency, comparing a target group of participants with cognitive impairments to a control group. Their study did not find any significant effects for these individual factors.

Data and Code Availability

All non-proprietary data and code used in this paper are publicly available at: `https://github.com/text2knowledge/word-complexity-leichtesprache`.

Acknowledgments

The work leading to this paper was partially funded by the Federal German Ministry for Labour and Social Affairs through the Civic Innovation Platform[8] and through the MuvAko project,[9] financed by the Sächsische Aufbaubank. We are grateful to our colleague Felix Dittrich for providing technical help and insightful discussion during the development of this work, and also to Johann Seltmann and Tobias Wittig for their contributions to the data collection and curation process. We thank the anonymous reviewers for their insightful comments and constructive feedback, which helped improve the quality of this work.

References

2019. Directive (eu) 2019/882 of the european parliament and of the council on the accessibility requirements for products and services (european accessibility act). https://eur-lex.europa.eu/eli/dir/2019/882/oj. Official Journal of the European Union, L 151, 7.6.2019, pp. 70–115. Accessed: 2025-03-13.

Suha S. Al-Thanyyan and Aqil M. Azmi. 2021. Automated text simplification: A survey. *ACM Comput. Surv.*, 54(2).

Jason J. S. Barton, Hashim M. Hanif, Laura Eklinder Björnström, and Charlotte Hills. 2014. The word-length effect in reading: A review. *Cognitive Neuropsychology*, 31(5-6):378–412.

Douglas Bates, Martin Mächler, Ben Bolker, and Steve Walker. 2015. Fitting Linear Mixed-Effects Models Using lme4. *Journal of Statistical Software*, 67:1–48.

[8]https://www.knowledgegraph.de/.

[9]https://xr-interaction.com/projects-muvako/.

BMAS. 2014. Leichte Sprache – Ein Ratgeber. https://www.bmas.de/DE/Service/Publikationen/Broschueren/a752-leichte-sprache-ratgeber.html. Accessed: 2025-03-14.

Bettina M. Bock and Sandra Pappert. 2023. *Leichte Sprache, Einfache Sprache, verständliche Sprache*. Narr, Tübingen.

António Branco, Joao Rodrigues, Francisco Costa, Joao Silva, and Rui Vaz. 2014. Rolling out text categorization for language learning assessment supported by language technology. In *Computational Processing of the Portuguese Language: 11th International Conference, PROPOR 2014, São Carlos/SP, Brazil, October 6-8, 2014. Proceedings 11*, pages 256–261. Springer.

U. Bredel and C. Maaß. 2016. *Leichte Sprache: Theoretische Grundlagen ?Orientierung für die Praxis*. Duden - Ratgeber. Duden.

Marc Brysbaert, Paweł Mandera, and Emmanuel Keuleers. 2018. The Word Frequency Effect in Word Processing: An Updated Review. *Current Directions in Psychological Science*, 27(1):45–50. Publisher: SAGE Publications Inc.

Marc Brysbaert, Michaël Stevens, Paweł Mandera, and Emmanuel Keuleers. 2016. The impact of word prevalence on lexical decision times: Evidence from the Dutch Lexicon Project 2. *Journal of Experimental Psychology: Human Perception and Performance*, 42(3):441–458. Place: US Publisher: American Psychological Association.

Qi Chen and Daniel Mirman. 2012. Competition and cooperation among similar representations: Toward a unified account of facilitative and inhibitory effects of lexical neighbors. *Psychological Review*, 119(2):417–430. Place: US Publisher: American Psychological Association.

Tianqi Chen and Carlos Guestrin. 2016. XGBoost: A scalable tree boosting system. In *Proceedings of the 22nd ACM SIGKDD International Conference on Knowledge Discovery and Data Mining*, KDD '16, pages 785–794, New York, NY, USA. ACM.

Uschi Cop, Emmanuel Keuleers, Denis Drieghe, and Wouter Duyck. 2015. Frequency effects in monolingual and bilingual natural reading. *Psychonomic Bulletin & Review*, 22(5):1216–1234.

Scott A. Crossley, H.S. Yang, and Danielle McNamara. 2014. What's so simple about simplified texts? a computational and psycholinguistic investigation of text comprehension and text processing. *Reading in a Foreign Language*, 26:92–113.

Rob A. I. Davies, Ruth Arnell, Julia M. H. Birchenough, Debbie Grimmond, and Sam Houlson. 2017. Reading through the life span: Individual differences in psycholinguistic effects. *Journal of Experimental Psychology. Learning, Memory, and Cognition*, 43(8):1298–1338.

Deutsches Institut für Normung (DIN). 2025. DIN SPEC 33429:2025-03 – Empfehlungen für Deutsche Leichte Sprache. Technische Regel [NEU], PAS-Verfahren. 60 pages. Original language: German. Accessible PDF available. English title: *Guidance for German Easy Language*.

Ludovic Ferrand, Marc Brysbaert, Emmanuel Keuleers, Boris New, Patrick Bonin, Alain Méot, Maria Augustinova, and Christophe Pallier. 2011. Comparing Word Processing Times in Naming, Lexical Decision, and Progressive Demasking: Evidence from Chronolex. *Frontiers in Psychology*, 2. Publisher: Frontiers.

Thomas François and Cédrick Fairon. 2012. An "AI readability" formula for french as a foreign language. In *Proceedings of the 2012 joint conference on empirical methods in Natural Language Processing and computational natural language learning*, pages 466–477.

Alexander Geyken. 2007. The DWDS Corpus: A reference corpus for the German language of the 20th century. In C. Fellbaum, editor, *Idioms and collocations: Corpus-based linguistics and lexicographic studies*, pages 23–41. Continuum, New York, NY.

Julia Hancke and Detmar Meurers. 2013. Exploring cefr classification for german based on rich linguistic modeling. *Learner Corpus Research*, pages 54–56.

S. Hansen-Schirra, W. Bisang, A. Nagels, S. Gutermuth, J. Fuchs, L. Borghardt, S. Deilen, A.-K. Gros, L. Schiffl, and J. Sommer. 2020. Intralingual translation into easy language – or how to reduce cognitive processing costs. In S. Hansen-Schirra and C. Maaß, editors, *Easy Language Research: Text and User Perspectives*, pages 197–225. Frank & Timme, Berlin.

Nathan Hartmann and Leandro Borges dos Santos. 2018. NILC at CWI 2018: Exploring feature engineering and feature learning. In *Proceedings of the Thirteenth Workshop on Innovative Use of NLP for Building Educational Applications*, pages 335–340, New Orleans, Louisiana. Association for Computational Linguistics.

Matthew Honnibal, Ines Montani, Sofie Van Landeghem, and Adriane Boyd. 2020. spaCy: Industrial-strength Natural Language Processing in Python.

Gareth James, Daniela Witten, Trevor Hastie, and Robert Tibshirani. 2013. *An Introduction to Statistical Learning: with Applications in R*, second edition. Springer Texts in Statistics. Springer.

Tomoyuki Kajiwara and Mamoru Komachi. 2018. Complex word identification based on frequency in a learner corpus. In *Proceedings of the Thirteenth Workshop on Innovative Use of NLP for Building Educational Applications*, pages 195–199, New Orleans, Louisiana. Association for Computational Linguistics.

Emmanuel Keuleers, Michaël Stevens, Paweł Mandera, and Marc Brysbaert. 2015. Word knowledge in the crowd: Measuring vocabulary size and word prevalence in a massive online experiment. *Quarterly Journal of Experimental Psychology*, 68(8):1665–1692.

Reinhold Kliegl, Michael E. J. Masson, and Eike M. Richter. 2010. A linear mixed model analysis of masked repetition priming. *Visual Cognition*, 18(5):655–681.

Victor Kuperman, Denis Drieghe, Emmanuel Keuleers, and Marc Brysbaert. 2013. How strongly do word reading times and lexical decision times correlate? Combining data from eye movement corpora and megastudies. *Quarterly Journal of Experimental Psychology*, 66(3):563–580. Publisher: SAGE Publications.

Victor Kuperman and Julie A. Van Dyke. 2013. Reassessing word frequency as a determinant of word recognition for skilled and unskilled readers. *Journal of Experimental Psychology: Human Perception and Performance*, 39(3):802–823. Place: US Publisher: American Psychological Association.

Christiane Maaß. 2020. *Easy Language – Plain Language – Easy Language Plus*. Frank & Timme, Berlin.

Christiane Maaß, Isabel Rink, and Silvia Hansen-Schirra. 2021. Easy language in germany. In Ulla Vanhatalo Camilla Lindholm, editor, *Handbook of Easy Languages in Europe*, pages 191–218. Frank & Timme, Berlin.

S. Mathey. 2001. The influence of visualization of orthography on the recognition of written words. *Canadian Journal of Experimental Psychology = Revue Canadienne De Psychologie Experimentale*, 55(1):1–23.

Boris New, Ludovic ferrand, Christophe pallier, and Marc brysbaert. 2006. Reexamining the word length effect in visual word recognition: New evidence from the English Lexicon Project. *Psychonomic Bulletin & Review*, 13(1):45–52.

Kai North, Tharindu Ranasinghe, Matthew Shardlow, and Marcos Zampieri. 2024. MultiLS: An end-to-end lexical simplification framework. In *Proceedings of the Third Workshop on Text Simplification, Accessibility and Readability (TSAR 2024)*, pages 1–11, Miami, Florida, USA. Association for Computational Linguistics.

Kai North and Marcos Zampieri. 2023. Features of lexical complexity: insights from l1 and l2 speakers. *Frontiers in Artificial Intelligence*, 6.

Kai North, Marcos Zampieri, and Matthew Shardlow. 2023. Lexical complexity prediction: An overview. *ACM Comput. Surv.*, 55(9).

Jenny A. Ortiz-Zambrano and Arturo Montejo-Ráez. 2020. Overview of ALexS 2020: First Workshop on Lexical Analysis at SEPLN. In *Proceedings of ALexS 2020: First Workshop on Lexical Analysis at SEPLN*, volume 2664 of *CEUR Workshop Proceedings*. CEUR-WS.org.

Gustavo Paetzold and Lucia Specia. 2016. SemEval 2016 task 11: Complex word identification. In *Proceedings of the 10th International Workshop on Semantic Evaluation (SemEval-2016)*, pages 560–569, San Diego, California. Association for Computational Linguistics.

Sandra Pappert and Bettina M. Bock. 2020. Easy-to-read german put to the test: Do adults with intellectual disability or functional illiteracy benefit from compound segmentation? *Reading and Writing*, 33(5):1105–1131.

Fabian Pedregosa, Gaël Varoquaux, Alexandre Gramfort, Vincent Michel, Bertrand Thirion, Olivier Grisel, Mathieu Blondel, Andreas Müller, Joel Nothman, Gilles Louppe, Peter Prettenhofer, Ron Weiss, Vincent Dubourg, Jake Vanderplas, Alexandre Passos, David Cournapeau, Matthieu Brucher, Matthieu Perrot, and Édouard Duchesnay. 2018. Scikit-learn: Machine learning in Python. *Preprint*, arXiv:1201.0490.

Peng Qi, Yuhao Zhang, Yuhui Zhang, Jason Bolton, and Christopher D. Manning. 2020. Stanza: A python natural language processing toolkit for many human languages. *Preprint*, arXiv:2003.07082.

Irina Rets and Jekaterina Rogaten. 2021. To simplify or not? facilitating english l2 users' comprehension and processing of open educational resources in english using text simplification. *Journal of Computer Assisted Learning*, 37(3):705–717.

Valentino Santucci, Filippo Santarelli, Luciana Forti, and Stefania Spina. 2020. Automatic classification of text complexity. *Applied Sciences*, 10(20):7285.

Laura Schiffl. 2022. *Lexikalische Komplexität in der Leichten Sprache: Effekte von Länge, Frequenz und Wiederholung auf die visuelle Wortverarbeitung einer heterogenen Zielgruppe*. PhD dissertation, Johannes Gutenberg-Universität Mainz, Mainz.

Sascha Schroeder, Kay-Michael Würzner, Julian Heister, Alexander Geyken, and Reinhold Kliegl. 2015. childLex—Eine lexikalische Datenbank zur Schriftsprache für Kinder im Deutschen. [childLex—A Lexical Database for Print Language for Children in German.]. *Psychologische Rundschau*, 66(3):155–165. Place: Germany Publisher: Hogrefe Verlag GmbH & Co. KG.

Pauline Schröter and Sascha Schroeder. 2017. The Developmental Lexicon Project: A behavioral database to investigate visual word recognition across the lifespan. *Behavior Research Methods*, 49(6):2183–2203.

Matthew Shardlow. 2013. A comparison of techniques to automatically identify complex words. In *51st Annual Meeting of the Association for Computational Linguistics Proceedings of the Student Research Workshop*, pages 103–109, Sofia, Bulgaria. Association for Computational Linguistics.

Matthew Shardlow. 2014. A survey of automated text simplification. *International Journal of Advanced Computer Science and Applications(IJACSA), Special Issue on Natural Language Processing 2014*, 4(1).

Matthew Shardlow, Richard Evans, Gustavo Henrique Paetzold, and Marcos Zampieri. 2021. SemEval-2021 task 1: Lexical complexity prediction. In *Proceedings of the 15th International Workshop on Semantic Evaluation (SemEval-2021)*, pages 1–16, Online. Association for Computational Linguistics.

Robyn Speer. 2022. rspeer/wordfreq: v3.0.

R Development Core Team. 2025. R: A Language and Environment for Statistical Computing.

Sowmya Vajjala and Taraka Rama. 2018. Experiments with universal CEFR classification. In *Proceedings of the Thirteenth Workshop on Innovative Use of NLP for Building Educational Applications*, pages 147–153, New Orleans, Louisiana. Association for Computational Linguistics.

Eric Velleman and Thea van der Geest. 2014. Online test tool to determine the cefr reading comprehension level of text. *Procedia computer science*, 27:350–358.

Tal Yarkoni, David Balota, and Melvin Yap. 2008. Moving beyond Coltheart's N: A new measure of orthographic similarity. *Psychonomic Bulletin & Review*, 15(5):971–979.

Seid Muhie Yimam, Chris Biemann, Shervin Malmasi, Gustavo Paetzold, Lucia Specia, Sanja Štajner, Anaïs Tack, and Marcos Zampieri. 2018. A report on the complex word identification shared task 2018. In *Proceedings of the Thirteenth Workshop on Innovative Use of NLP for Building Educational Applications*, pages 66–78, New Orleans, Louisiana. Association for Computational Linguistics.

Marcos Zampieri, Shervin Malmasi, Gustavo Paetzold, and Lucia Specia. 2017. Complex word identification: Challenges in data annotation and system performance. In *Proceedings of the 4th Workshop on Natural Language Processing Techniques for Educational Applications (NLPTEA 2017)*, pages 59–63, Taipei, Taiwan. Asian Federation of Natural Language Processing.

A Sustainability Statement

All model development, training, and evaluation were conducted on an `Apple M2` laptop (8 cores), yielding minimal carbon impact beyond ordinary laptop use. Each training run, including the hyperparameter optimization, completed in under 30 minutes.

B `XGBClassifier`: Hyperparameter Space

Hyperparameter	Distribution
`classifier__n_estimators`	$\mathcal{U}\{100, 500\}$
`classifier__max_depth`	$\mathcal{U}\{5, 12\}$
`classifier__learning_rate`	$\mathcal{U}[0.2, 0.5]$
`classifier__subsample`	$\mathcal{U}[0.75, 1]$
`classifier__colsample_bytree`	$\mathcal{U}[0.6, 1]$

Table A1.1: The hyperparameter space used for drawing 5,000 random samples during the five-fold cross-validation of `XGBClassifier`.

C DeveL: Supplementary Analysis

This appendix reports the supplementary analysis of the lexical decision child dataset in DeveL, which includes recognition times from 1152 German nouns collected from 800 children from school grades 1–6 (Schröter and Schroeder, 2017). As shown in Figure A2.1, the noun recognition times from children also showed a positive relationship with the complexity measure generated by the CWI model: more complex nouns elicited longer recognition times.

The statistical analysis of the child data was performed separately from the adults, in order to use co-predictors for the CWI complexity measure that were appropriate for children. As with the adult analysis, we sought to identify the effect of the complexity measure above and beyond the linguistic variables previously shown to predict recognition times in the DeveL dataset by Schröter and Schroeder (2017). For this purpose, we ran a linear regression model with CWI complexity as a predictor together with the following variables: noun length, trigram frequency, noun type frequency, noun lemma frequency, and orthographic neighborhood size.

The predictors noun length and trigram frequency were identical to those used in the analysis of the adult groups. Noun length was operationalized as the number of letters in each noun and trigram frequency was the sum of the frequencies of a sequence of three letters within a noun, treating the word beginning and end as separate letters. But in contrast with the adult groups, the type frequency and lemma frequency predictors, as well as the orthographic neighborhood size predictor, were based on the childLex corpus, which is derived from a set of ten million tokens drawn from 500 popular German children's books (version 0.16, December 2015, see Schroeder et al., 2015). This allowed using frequency estimates that are more reflective of the lexicon of children at earlier stages of reading development.

The dependent measure in the model was the recognition time estimated for each noun in the child group. We predicted that nouns with higher CWI complexity should increase processing difficulty and therefore elicit longer recognition times.

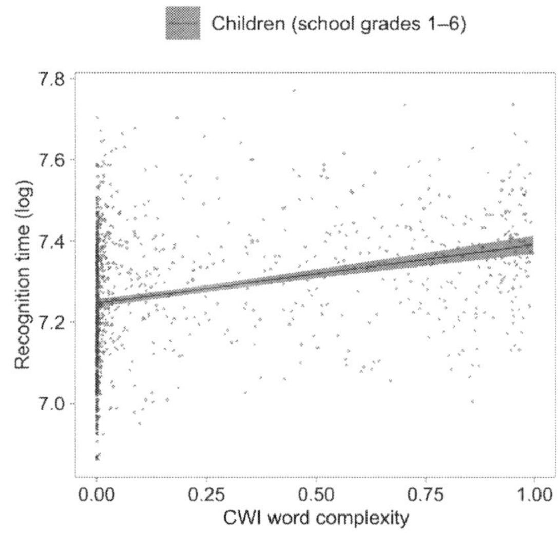

Figure A2.1: Relationship between CWI complexity and recognition time for the 1152 German nouns in the child DeveL dataset (Schröter and Schroeder, 2017). Lines show the effect of word complexity estimated without any covariates in a linear regression model with log-transformed word recognition time as the dependent variable. Ribbons show 95% confidence intervals. Dots correspond to the mean recognition time of each noun in the child group.

The results of the statistical model showed the expected effects of noun length, frequency, and orthographic neighborhood on recognition times (Table A2.1). Crucially, the effect of CWI complexity was significant after adjusting for these variables: recognition time increased with increasing complexity. These results demonstrate that the CWI

	Estimate	Std. Error	t-value	p-value
Intercept (child group)	7.279	0.004	1794.832	0.000*
Length: child	0.045	0.005	8.840	0.000*
Trigram frequency: child	–0.000	0.000	–8.713	0.000*
Type frequency: child	–0.023	0.003	–7.129	0.000*
Orthographic neighborhood size: child	–0.035	0.013	–2.640	0.008 *
CWI complexity: child	0.041	0.015	2.790	0.005*

Table A2.1: Output of the statistical model in the child data. The model used CWI word complexity as a predictor, together with noun length, trigram frequency, noun type frequency, and orthographic neighborhood size. R model structure: `lm(log(Noun recognition time) ~ Length + Trigram frequency + Type frequency + Orthographic neighborhood size + CWI complexity)`. Effects significant at the alpha .05 level are marked with asterisks. Further details of the model: $R^2 = 0.26$, Adjusted $R^2 = 0.25$, Number of observations = 1152.

complexity measure predicted noun recognition difficulties in children from different stages of reading development, and that it continued to do so after being adjusted for the effects of frequency, length, and neighborhood size reported in previous research (Schröter and Schroeder, 2017).

Democracy Made Easy: Simplifying Complex Topics to Enable Democratic Participation

Nouran Khallaf[1], Stefan Bott[2], Carlo Eugeni[1], John O'Flaherty[3], Serge Sharoff[1], Horacio Saggion[2]

[1]School of Languages, Cultures and Societies, University of Leeds, United Kingdom
[2]Department of Engineering, Universitat Pompeu Fabra, Spain
[3]The National Microelectronics Applications Centre (MAC) Ltd, Ireland

Abstract

Several groups of people are excluded from democratic deliberation because the language used in this context may be too difficult for them to understand. Our iDEM project aims to reduce existing linguistic barriers in deliberative processes by developing technology to facilitate the translation of complicated text into Easy-to-Read formats that are more suitable for many people. In this paper, we describe classification experiments for detecting different types of difficulties which should be amended in order to make texts easier to understand. We focus on a lexical simplification system that can achieve state-of-the-art results with the use of a free and open-weight large language model for the Romance Languages in our project. Moreover, a sentence segmentation system is introduced to produce text segmentation for long sentences based on training data. Finally, we describe the iDEM mobile app, which will make our technology available as a service for end-users of our target populations.

1 Introduction

Representative democracy is based on delegating policy matters to elected representatives, while the deliberative democratic process aims at involving the stakeholders directly (Bächtiger et al., 2018). Modern democratic institutions aim at a greater focus on stakeholders' involvement. However, this has the requirement of clearer language, which is accessible to the stakeholders, especially in cases where the stakeholders face challenges in understanding, for example, in such cases as people with intellectual disabilities or non-native speakers. The demand for better communication is also reflected in the international treaties, in particular, the Universal Declaration of Human Rights, in its Article 19, affirms everyone's right to seek and receive information.

Moreover, particularly important in this context is the United Nations Convention on the Rights of Persons with Disabilities (CRPD), which includes *accessibility* as one key enabler for a more inclusive society. That is, the ability of any product, service, content, environment, etc., to be used by people with the widest range of abilities (including linguistic and cognitive abilities). The CRPD also considers accessibility as, for example, an enabler for democratic participation rights such as freedom of expression and self-determination. Consequently, a lack of accessibility can be linked to a risk of exclusion for persons who cannot participate equally due to linguistic barriers.

The focus of our paper is on providing an introduction into technologies developed in the context of our project, iDEM[1] [2]: in the area of intersectionality and equality in deliberative and participatory democratic spaces, iDEM aims at making information more accessible and inclusive in the context of democracy and in particular in deliberative and participatory processes. More specifically, in this paper, we will discuss:

1. A tool for assessing sentence-level complexity and predicting appropriate simplification strategies;
2. Applications of these tools to real-world corpora, including the United Nations Parallel Corpus and Europarl;
3. A text simplification pipeline powered by Large Language Models (LLMs), focusing on lexical simplification and Easy-to-Read (E2R) sentence segmentation.

The rest of the paper is structured as follows:

[1]Innovative and Inclusive Democratic Spaces for Deliberation and Participation
[2]https://idemproject.eu/

Proceedings of the 1st Workshop on Artificial Intelligence and Easy and Plain Language in Institutional Contexts (AI & EL/PL), pages 108–124, June 23, 2025

Section 2 provides an overview of the iDEM project. Section 3 reviews related work on complexity assessment and text simplification. Section 4 details our sentence complexity classifier and simplification approach, including the evaluation results. Section 5 outlines the mobile application in development, while Section 6 discusses current limitations. Finally, Section 7 offers concluding remarks.

2 Project Overview

The iDEM Project in the area of intersectionality and equality in deliberative and participatory democratic spaces aims at making information more accessible and inclusive in the context of democracy and, in particular, in deliberative and participatory processes. In the first phase of the project we have investigated, using a theoretical approach, current marginalization from deliberative processes of diverse underrepresented groups due to language skills in order to understand what are the linguistic barriers which hamper their participation. By working with different associations, iDEM adopts a user-centered approach in use case design and data collection and annotation to ensure maximum impact in the community, thus contributing to making democracy more accessible and inclusive. An innovative iDEM service (e.g., mobile app) is being implemented to host the developed language technologies to support on-demand simplification in Catalan, English, Italian, and Spanish. In the current phase of the project, we are developing the underlying natural language processing technology as well as fine-tuning the use cases to test and evaluate our proposed approach to a more inclusive deliberative democracy. The interested reader is referred to (Saggion et al., 2024b) for an overview of the project.

3 Related Work

3.1 Easy-to-Read

Since the late nineties, many organisations have raised awareness about fundamental information being written in a way that is too difficult to understand for many people. Initiatives to palliate this deficit include "Plain Language" (U.S. Government, 2011) and "Easy-to-read" (Inclusion Europe, 2009). They are two different methods whose overall objective is to make information more accessible. They proposed guidelines for how to write more accessible texts; however, applying them to produce accessible material heavily depends on well-trained human editors and, therefore, considerably limits the production of easy-to-read or plain language texts.

Compared to standard language, easy-to-read language is a simplified version for the sake of readability for specific audiences (Caro, 2017). In this paper, we adopt E2R over Plain Language because its structured guidelines form the foundation of diverse and adaptable translation strategies designed to make information accessible to people with reading difficulties, including people with intellectual disabilities. They have little command of the language and poor literacy.

Empirical research in the field is uncommon (González-Sordé and Matamala, 2024), especially when compared to fields such as automatic text simplification. Although the topic has gained greater scholars' attention in recent years, sometimes research reports on apparently contradictory findings (Fajardo et al., 2014) between guidelines and actual text understanding by target E2R populations; moreover, even guidelines appear to take on different aspects with little agreement between them (Maaß, 2020). With the advances that natural language processing has achieved in recent years, interest in the automatic adaptation of texts to plain language or E2R has intensified (Alarcon et al., 2021; Da Cunha Fanego, 2021; Saggion, 2024).

3.2 Complexity Identification

The first focus of our research within iDEM is on theoretically understanding the factors that contribute to the complexity of a text or the sentences within this text. The guidelines described in the previous section are directed to human editors and often leave much room for interpretation and are hard to operationalise, for example the instruction to avoid difficult words. We are interested in combining theoretical insights with data-driven analysis and classification.

In previous work, computational studies typically overlook insights from translation studies, particularly the various strategies proposed (Vinay and Darbelnet, 1971; Newmark, 1988; Chesterman, 1997; Zabalbeascoa, 2000; Molina and Hurtado Albir, 2002; Gambier, 2006), focusing on the systematic processes involved in translating a source text into a target text across languages. Translation studies provide a complementary approach in examining strategies used in intra-lingual translation, where a source text is translated into a target text in the same language. Eugeni and Gambier (2023) argue that such transfers habitually achieve a complete correspondence between source and target texts. One key task in order to transform sentences into E2R is lexical simplification, i.e., simplifying individual words or short phrases independent of the effect of such simplifications on the overall sentence coherence. For instance, Paetzold and Specia (2016) developed methods that specifically targeted complex word identification (CWI), which detects difficult words and suggests simpler alternatives. These techniques usually ignore how such simpler words would fit the general sentence structure.

Datasets developed to evaluate lexical simplification, e.g., SemEval-2012 Task 1 (Specia et al., 2012), ALEXSIS (Ferrés and Saggion, 2022), TSAR 2022 (Saggion et al., 2022) or MLSP 2024 (Shardlow et al., 2024) have aided a focus on single word-level replacements. Though helpful, these datasets primarily cover single word substitutions in isolation rather than more general context-sensitive simplifications. As a result, simplifications generated with the assistance of these tools sometimes sound unnatural, which needed a post generative model to refine sentence coherence. This issue was also highlighted by Shardlow (2014), who reviewed various lexical simplification approaches and noted that, while effective for readability, they frequently ignore sentence coherence and grammatical correctness.

Corpora for sentence simplification includes ASSET (Alva-Manchego et al., 2020) that provides multiple quality simplifications per sentence. However, ASSET still focuses to some extent on fine-grained lexical or phrase-level modifications and lacks annotations for deeper grammatical or discourse-level modifications. Similarly, WikiLarge (Zhang and Lapata, 2017) provides large parallel sentence pairs for training simplification models but does not explicitly annotate the simplification strategies, making it difficult to study in detail exactly how sentences are simplified. The Simplext corpus (Saggion et al., 2015) provides full document simplifications following E2R guidelines for the Spanish language without indication of transformation type while PorSimples (Aluísio and Gasperin, 2010) provides document simplification in Portuguese covering several operations.

3.3 Text Simplification

Our focus for this paper is on lexical simplification; for an overview of full text simplification approaches and methods, the reader is referred to (Saggion, 2017). Several past approaches to lexical simplification used traditional count-based word-vectors and available dictionaries for modelling word semantics and to select simple word replacements for complex words (Biran et al., 2011; Bott et al., 2012); in later work, word embedding were used, which is learned from huge text collection (Glavaš and Štajner, 2015). More recently, large-scale language models such as BERT and its variations have been applied to predict substitution candidates for complex words. For example, LS-BERT (Qiang et al., 2020) uses the masked language model (MLM) of BERT to predict a set of candidate substitution words and their associated probability. In this context, the MLM predicts substitute words which are ranked for simplicity using: probabilities, a language model, a paraphrase database, word frequency and word semantic similarity with the target word. Very recent work presented in the TSAR 2022 (Saggion et al., 2022) and MLSP 2024 (Shardlow et al., 2024) evaluation frameworks have demonstrated that Large Language Models (LLMs) are in fact the best performing models for the lexical simplification. Techniques such as "prompting" are used to condition the LLMs to produce a simplification or to suggest alternative words. Note, however, that these models underperform when simplifying low-resourced languages. We define 'low-resourced languages' as those with limited digital text corpora (e.g., Catalan vs. English), impacting LLM performance as noted in Section 4.4. Despite advances in lexical simplification (e.g., TSAR 2022, MLSP 2024), key gaps remain: (1) How can simplification strategies be systematically categorised beyond lexical substitution? (2) What taxonomies exist for intra lingual translation, and how do they apply to automation? Section 4.2 addresses these by proposing a strategy taxonomy, testing it on institutional corpora, and leveraging LLMs without prompt engineering—a less-explored approach due to its complexity (Shardlow et al., 2024).

4 Natural Language Processing for Easy-to-Read Translation

4.1 Datasets

We use a range of datasets across different components of our system[3]. The primary dataset used

[3]Where applicable, datasets are available on request from the authors or are publicly accessible through the cited sources.

for complexity assessment and simplification strategy classification comprises 76 parallel texts collected from Scottish care services, UK political manifestos (2024), and Disability Equality Scotland newsletters. These cover diverse topics such as healthcare, environmental policies, disability advocacy, and accessibility. The texts were manually aligned at the sentence level, resulting in 4,166 words in 206 original ("complex") sentences and 3,259 words in 210 simplified counterparts. Despite the reduction in word count, the number of sentences increased slightly, reflecting a key simplification strategy that is splitting longer sentences to improve readability. We additionally use a French dataset of 370 manually aligned sentence pairs. The original texts were retrieved from the Réfugiés.info website and were anonymised to remove any personally identifiable information (PII) (Team, 2025). These parallel sentence pairs provide training data for our simplification strategy classifier (Section 4.2).[4]

For evaluating our system on larger, multilingual corpora, we use the European Parliament (Koehn, 2005) and the United Nations Parallel Corpus (Ziemski et al., 2016). These are publicly available and provide high-quality sentence-aligned translations in English, Spanish, and Italian. We applied our multilingual classifier to these datasets to analyse simplification needs across languages (Section 4.3).

For lexical simplification, we use few-shot prompting on pre-trained Salamandra models with trial data from the MLSP 2024 shared task (Shardlow et al., 2024), covering English, Spanish, Italian, and Catalan (Section 4.4).

Finally, for sentence segmentation in Spanish according to E2R standards, we accessed a private annotated dataset provided by Calleja et al. (2024). This dataset includes 3,826 training, 484 validation, and 1,452 development sentences, each annotated with E2R-compatible cut points (Section 4.6).

4.2 Complexity Assessment

The simplification strategy prediction task aims to determine the types of transformations needed to make a sentence more accessible. Table 1 provides examples of these transformations.

Our taxonomy is informed by Inclusion Europe's guidelines (Inclusion Europe, 2009), intralingual translation practices into E2R (Hansen-Schirra et al., 2020), and a qualitative analysis of our dataset. While previous taxonomies in Translation Studies have offered valuable models for interlingual and diamesic translation, they lack the granularity needed to describe all strategies observed in E2R practice. On the other hand, typologies in Automatic Text Simplification (ATS) are based on corpus analysis (Bott and Saggion, 2014) or on edit operations that mainly deal with adding, deleting, replacing, and moving words Cardon et al. (2022). However, texts translated in E2R language clearly show that professionals in the field apply many more operations that pertain to the field of pragmatics and semiotics, focused on how concepts are distributed and or explained to help the user understand them.

To address this gap, our framework adapts insights from both domains. Based on Inclusion Europe's three levels of simplification—lexical, syntactic, and semantic—we define eight macro-strategies that range along a continuum from additive operations (e.g., *Explanation*) to reductive ones (e.g., *Omission*). These are outlined in Table 2 comprises 8 macro-strategies (excluding transcript since it is a non-simplification operation), 8 strategies, and 30 micro-strategies. For the full set of strategies, see Table 10 (Appendix E).

Cross-linguistic differences in simplification strategies are also relevant. In our multilingual experiments, we observed variations in dominant strategies across English, Spanish, and Italian, which suggests that language-specific features influence how simplification is operationalised. This will be further explored in Section 4.3.

The classifier is built by application of pre-trained transformer-based models (such as multilingual BERT (Devlin et al., 2019)) for multiclass text classification, focusing on the prediction of simplification strategies need to simplify the respective sentences. We employed Stratified 5-fold Cross-Validation for rigorous evaluation and generalisation. We took the average of the validation scores across all the folds to determine the final scores. Early stopping was also employed, wherein the training was halted if the validation loss did not see an improvement for the patience period.

Class imbalance in the data, with certain strategies being underrepresented, was a problem during training. To counter this, we used a *weighted*

[4]English dataset was annotated by a linguist with expertise in translation and text simplification, using the same predefined set of simplification strategy categories described in Appendix B; the French dataset was labelled by the Réfugiés.info editorial team following the same guidelines and category definitions.

In 2018-20 From 2018 to 2020	life expectancy at birth in Scotland was babies born in Scotland were expected to live	76.8 years for males 77 years if they were boys	and 81.0 years for females. and 81 years if they were girls.
Modulation	Explanation	Synonymy,Syntax	Synonymy,Syntax

Table 1: Segment alignment for the original (top) and simplified (bottom) sentences

Strategy	Description	Example
Omission	Removing unnecessary rhetorical or diamesic constructs.	"Sir Keir Rodney Starmer KCB KC" → "Starmer"
Compression	Simplifying grammatical/semantic constructs.	"to guide the group" → "to the group"
Syntactic Change	Adjustments between syntactic levels.	"citizens" → "people in Scotland"
Transcript	No changes made to the text.	"I love music"
Transposition	Word class change.	"our aim is" → "we want"
Synonymy	Simplifying technical or abstract words.	"conversation" → "talk"
Modulation	Redistributing information linearly.	"joins in activities... supported by family" → "He joins activities. His family helps."
Explanation	Making hidden content or terms explicit.	"co-design services..." → "co-design means sharing your ideas"
Illocutionary Change	Making implied meaning explicit.	"know your body's library" → "know your body"

Table 2: Simplification strategies required for a sentence, with examples

cross-entropy loss function. Class weights were calculated as the inverse frequency of each class:

$$w_c = \frac{1}{\text{freq}_c} \cdot \frac{N}{2} \tag{1}$$

where w_c is the weight assigned to class c, freq_c is the frequency of class c, and N is the number of samples. This approach ensured that underrepresented classes contributed more to the overall loss, so the model became more capable of predicting the minority classes.

Additionally, gradient clipping was applied during training to stabilise the optimisation. Gradient clipping limits the maximum value of gradients during backpropagation to prevent extremely large updates of model parameters that could destabilise training or lead to divergence. Mathematically, gradient clipping can be expressed as:

$$g_{\text{clipped}} = \min\left(g, \frac{g_{\text{threshold}}}{\|g\|}\right), \tag{2}$$

where g represents the original gradient vector, $g_{\text{threshold}}$ is the clipping threshold, and $\|g\|$ is the norm of the gradient vector. Gradient clipping ensures consistent updates to model parameters, improving training stability.

See the summary of hyper-parameters in Table 8 (Appendix B). The use of medium-sized PLMs (such as multilingual BERT) instead of LLMs helps with the possibility of applying the classifiers to large institutional datasets (such as the entirety of Europarl or the United Nations Corpus), as well as with the possibility of deploying the classifiers to guide the corrections.

We used standard precision, recall, and F1-score metrics (Manning et al., 2008) to evaluate model performance. Given the class imbalance, we report the weighted macro F1-score (Sokolova and Lapalme, 2009), which better reflects the classifier's ability to handle both frequent and rare simplification strategies. The fine-tuned classifier model achieved a weighted macro F1-score of 0.8089, demonstrating its ability to generalize across majority and minority classes. In particular, it outperformed the baseline majority-class strategy, which corresponds to the weighted macro F1-score of 0.096.

The F1 score of the multilingual model (trained on English, tested on French) is 0.6339, thus reflecting the need to improve its ability to generalize across languages. However, given that its errors are balanced, i.e., the model is confused with predicting Synonymy for Explanation and vice versa, see the confusion matrix in Figure 2 (Appendix C). Omission and Compression categories tend to be confused with one another, with Omission commonly predicted as Explanation or Transcript, mirroring the need to enhance the separation between removal and rewriting strategies. Modulation is also commonly confused with Synonymy, mirroring the need to strengthen sentence restructuring cues in training.

Category	English # Sent.	%	Spanish # Sent.	%	Italian # Sent.	%
			Europarl			
Total Sentences	2,005,688	100	1,788,913	100	1,928,874	100
Complex	1,932,492	96.3	1,660,631	92.8	1,868,714	96.8
Omission	59,065	3.1	23	0.001	57	0.003
Syntactic Change	254,483	13.2	11,777	0.7	21,321	1.1
Transposition	13,075	0.7	35,053	2.1	40,633	2.2
Synonymy	1,104,564	57.2	37,259	2.2	81,468	4.4
Modulation	41,802	2.2	724,469	43.6	1,004,438	54.2
Explanation	459,503	23.8	852,050	51.3	702,526	37.9
			UN Corpus			
Total Sentences	10,600,000	100	10,665,709	100		
Complex	9,628,533	96.2	9,987,750	93.6		
Omission	75,217	0.7	62	0.0006		
Syntactic Change	181,228	1.8	503,047	5.0		
Transposition	39,356	0.4	68,878	0.7		
Synonymy	4,587,340	45.0	198,479	1.9		
Modulation	445,095	4.3	5,345,515	53.5		
Explanation	4,878,679	47.7	3,871,769	38.7		

Table 3: Sentence counts and proportions of simplification strategies in institutional datasets

4.3 Experiments with assessing institutional repositories

We experimented with two institutional repositories, which include English, Italian and Spanish, some of the languages of our project, the corpus of the European Parliament (Koehn, 2005) and the United Nations Parallel Corpus (Ziemski et al., 2016). Both resources include high-quality translations, so the content of each sentence is the same. However, we can expect that the three languages differ in their traditions for maintaining linguistic complexity in such formal texts as the parliamentary proceedings. Total sentences row in Table 3 presents the amount of data in each dataset. We used sentence-aligned versions from the respective repositories and applied the multilingual classifiers described in the previous section to make predictions. If the complexity classifier detected the need to simplify the sentence, i.e., it was predicted as "Complex", we estimated the likely strategy needed for this task. As the classification model is limited to the one-label setup, out of several edit operations required for a sentence (see the example in Table 1), our current version of the model predicts the single most likely operation (*Explanation* in this example).

Table 3 shows that the majority of sentences in both datasets and across all the languages considered (English, Spanish, and Italian) require some form of simplification. For English sentences, the most common simplification operations found are (1) lexical substitution (synonymy), primarily through the choice of simpler synonyms, and (2) Explanation which provides more explanation to facilitate reading.

Conversely, for both datasets of Spanish and Italian sentences, the predominant simplification strategy is modulation, with a particular emphasis on sentence restructuring for the purpose of achieving a more linear and straightforward reading experience.

4.4 Simplifying Complex Words

As reported in recent lexical simplification challenges (i.e. TSAR 2022 (Saggion et al., 2022) and MLSP 2024 (Shardlow et al., 2024)), most recent state-of-the-art lexical simplification systems rely on decoder-only autoregressive LLMs like GPT-4 (Enomoto et al., 2024). These systems seem to systematically outperform other systems, like encoder-only language models (e.g. BERT), also because recent developments of LLMs have mostly concentrated on decoder models. Decoders are generally more flexible and have strong zero-shot or few-shot abilities. Commercial closed-weight models like GPT-4, however, carry concerns for the purpose of our project since they lack guarantees of privacy protection and generate costs by using the API. In addition, their closed nature does not usually allow us to fine-tune them.

In preliminary experiments, we found out that the LLMs of the Salamandra family [5](Gonzalez-Agirre et al., 2025) perform very well on European Languages, especially on Romance languages, and within the last group, they especially excel at the performance of Catalan. This can be explained because Salamandra models are part of the Alia initiative (Government of Spain) funded by the Spanish government with a strong focus on languages spoken in Spain. Salamandra models were trained as decoder-only, and they are also provided as instruction-tuned versions. With this, we decided to use a simple few-shot system as our first approach.

Few-shot prediction from a pre-trained model refers to the process where a model that has already been trained on a large dataset (a pre-trained model) is used to make predictions or perform tasks with no or only a few labeled examples for a new task. The *shots* are examples provided in the prompt, as opposed to being used as training data for fine-tuning. Zero-shot prediction does not provide any example. The pre-trained model is typically a decoder-only model, which produces output based on an input prompt that conditions

[5]https://huggingface.co/collections/BSC-LT/salamandra-66fc171485944df79469043a

the output. In essence, few-shot prediction from a pretrained model means leveraging a model's prior knowledge from a large dataset to perform well on a new task or dataset, even with very few labeled examples. As our pre-trained models, we used the 2 billion parameters (2B) and the 7 billion parameter (7B) versions of Salamandra.

We used the following prompt without doing refinement through prompt engineering:

> *Given the context and the specified target word in {LANGUAGE}, answer 10 simpler alternative words. Do not give less than 10 alternative words. Give different words as alternatives. {SHOT_EXAMPLES} Context: {CONTEXT} Target Word: {TARGET} Alternatives Words:*

Here LANGUAGE is a variable which is set according to the language (Catalan, English, Italian, Spanish) in which we want to produce predicted solutions. For few-shot prediction we used examples from the trial section of the MLSP data. The shot examples were selected randomly, but we made sure that unique contexts were selected. An instance of a SHOT_EXAMPLE is given here:

> *´Given the context....* Context: A continue statement will skip the remainder of the block and start at the controlling conditional statement again. Target Word: remainder Alternative Words: rest, restrictive, remaining, remainder, balance

For a 2-shot or 4-shot prompt, 2 or 4 of these different examples would be included in the prompt given to the system. The CONTEXT and TARGET variables have the same form as in the provided shot examples.

As evaluation measures, we used the same as in the MLSP shared task (see Section 3.3). Accuracy (ACC) expresses the percentage of right solutions given out of all given solutions. Here we use Accuracy@1@top1 which is defined as the percentage of instances where the first top-ranked substitute matches the most frequently suggested synonym in the gold data (*top1*). MAP@k (Mean Average Precision) uses a ranked list of generated substitutes, which can either be matched or not matched against the set of the gold-standard substitutes. The first k solutions of the ranked list are considered.

The results can be seen in Table 4. We use the same baseline here as was used in the MLSP shared task. It has to be noted that the baseline used there was very strong, since it used zero-shot prompting with the use of the chat-fine-tuned version of Llama-2-70B. This is a version with 70 Billion Parameters and thus ten times larger than the Salamandra-7B model we use here. In fact, many participating systems in the MLSP shared task could not outperform this baseline. In the tables, we mark those results with an asterisk that are higher than this baseline. As a further reference we also list the performance of the different winning systems of the shared task. These winners, however, use GPT-3 for Catalan (Dutilleul et al., 2024) and GPT-4 (Enomoto et al., 2024) for the rest of the languages, and for reasons we describe above, we cannot use them for the iDEM project.

As expected, the 2B version of Salamandra could not outperform the baseline (Table 9 in Appendix D). We attribute this to the fact that this model is too small to produce reliable results in a task that requires quite a large amount of general knowledge about language, such as synonymy and simplicity. The results from this table are still interesting because we want to use fine-tuning on Salamandra-2B in future work. The 7B version of Salamandra, on the other hand, could outperform the baseline nearly systematically in few-shot settings. Interestingly, the difference between 2-shot and 4-shot predictions is not very large. In some cases, the 4-shot predictions perform even worse than 2-shot predictions. Another observation that can be made is that Salamandra mostly excels at the three Romance languages Spanish, Catalan and Italian, while for English, it performs very close to the baseline. In this case, it means that the baseline is higher and harder to beat for English than for the other languages because of the multilingual capabilities of the baseline system or the lack thereof. These observations confirm our assumption that Salamandra is a good choice for the set of languages that we have to treat in iDEM.

4.5 Integration of Complexity Assessment and Lexical Simplification

This section presents ongoing work toward integrating two core modules of our system: complexity assessment (Section 4.2) and lexical simplification (Section 4.4). The classifier first detects complex lexical items in a sentence, and the simplification module then proposes easier alternatives. While the full pipeline has not yet been formally evaluated, we have implemented a proof-of-concept

	0-Shot		2-Shot		4-Shot		MLSP Baseline		MLSP Winner	
	ACC	MAP@3	ACC	MAP@3	ACC	MAP@3	ACC	MAP@3	ACC	MAP@3
English	0.1280	0.1912	0.4017*	0.3868	0.4035*	0.4242*	0.3877	0.4241	0.5245	0.5762
Spanish	0.0286	0.1213	0.3541*	0.5148*	0.3608*	0.3644	0.3254	0.4157	0.4536	0.6763
Catalan	0.0426	0.1390	0.2292*	0.3742*	0.2022*	0.3357*	0.1977	0.3024	0.2719	0.5003
Italian	0.035	0.1419	0.3596*	0.4108*	0.3315*	0.3868*	0.2964	0.3310	0.4762	0.5661

Table 4: Results of Zero and Few Shot Lexical Simplification Performance for a big model (Salamandra-7B). Results are compared to the state of the art as reported in the recent MLSP 2024 lexical simplification shared task. Asterisks (*) indicate the model outperformed the strong baseline of the competition.

Sentence	Easy to Read Segmentation
The way this sentence is cut is easy to read.	The way this sentence is cut is easy to read.
Validar es comprobar si un documento es fácil de comprender.	Validar es comprobar si un documento es fácil de comprender.

Table 5: Examples of segmented sentences in English and Spanish taken from Easy-to-Read guidelines.

to illustrate its feasibility. Table 6 provides multilingual examples where the complexity classifier flags difficult words, which are then simplified by the Salamandra-7B lexical simplifier. For instance, in the English sentence "The reason why hypothalamic lesions affect body fat...," the words 'hypothalamic' and 'lesions' are identified as complex and replaced with 'brain' and 'damage,' respectively—substitutions that significantly enhance readability.

In the context of the iDEM project, this integration is intended for deployment within the mobile application currently under development (see Section 5), where users with cognitive or linguistic barriers can receive real-time support in understanding complex information. Future work will involve formal evaluation, expansion to full sentences, and deeper cross-linguistic adaptation.

4.6 Segmenting Sentences for Easy-to-Read

According to E2R standards (Inclusion Europe, 2009; 153101, 2018), sentences in E2R are recommended to be short and should fit on one line on the printed page (or screen). Since this is not always possible, guidelines recommend cutting the sentence where people would pause when reading out loud. Research on sentence segmentation is somehow related to the prediction of prosodic markers in text-to-speech systems, where syntactic structure and word/token information is used (Fitzpatrick and Bachenko, 1989). Examples of how sentences should be segmented in E2R in English and Spanish are presented in Table 5.

Although datasets for sentence and lexical simplification exist (as reported above), there is a lack of publicly available datasets of E2R segmentation. We have gained private access to a dataset of segmented E2R texts in Spanish (Calleja et al., 2024). This dataset is organized into three files corresponding to train (3,826 sentences), validation (484 sentences), and development (1,452 sentences). Each sentence is explicitly marked to indicate where it should be segmented following E2R standards. We adopt a machine learning approach to sentence segmentation, developing a classifier based on linguistic information and other features such as the position of the token in the sequence (first, second, etc.) or the distance to the previous cut. We process the dataset in order to convert the original sentences into instances for learning. The instances for learning are based on the tokens (words, punctuation, numbers, etc.) in each sentence; our aim is to classify all tokens as cut-point or not. In order to create the learning instances, we linguistically analyze each sentence using a Spanish model from the SpaCy library (Honnibal et al., 2020), which produces information on parts of speech, syntactic dependencies, and named entities. We extract several features including the Parts Of Speech (POS) tag of the token, the case of the token (lower cased, upper cased), whether the token is a punctuation, whether the token is part or a named entity (begin, inside, outside), the position of the token in the sentence, the distance to the previous cut point (or -1), and the distance to the end of the sentence. The learning instances (one per token) are stored in a CSV file for use by a machine learning algorithm. We report results using a Decision Tree algorithm (Steinberg, 2009) due to its simplicity and explanatory power (i.e. set of rules). Other algorithms were less successful on our data. The learning algorithm is an instance from the De-

Lang	Context (Sentence)	Complex word (by CA)	Substitute (by LS)
Eng	The reason why hypothalamic lesions affect body fat and feeding behavior has in fact much to do with leptin signaling.	hypothalamic	brain
		lesions	damage
		affect	influence
Spa	Si este indicador baja de 1, implicaría que la empresa no está en capacidad de cubrir sus obligaciones de corto plazo con los activos líquidos que posee. (If this indicator is below 1, this implies that the enterprise is not in conditions to cover its obligations in the long run with the liquid assets it possesses.)	implicaría	significaría
		indicador	medida
		plazo	tiempo
		activos	bienes
Cat	La formació sosté que "els posicionaments excloents en vers a altres realitats educatives fonamentades amb idees polítiques distorsionen la realitat del model" català. (The formation maintains that "exclusionary positions towards other educational realities based on political ideas distort the reality of the Catalan model".)	sosté	defensa
		posicionaments	posicións
		vers	contra

Table 6: Examples of cases where the Complexity Assessment (CA) system identifies a word that needs simplification and the Lexical Simplification (LS) system simplifies it.

cision Tree implementation provided by the Scikit Learn library[6] (Pedregosa et al., 2011).

Table 7 reports segmentation results for the decision tree classifier and two baselines. The baselines are based on (i) the Parts of Speech (POS) tag, which on training data is the best predictor of the token where the sentence should be segmented, and (ii) on the most common length of the segment. As for the decision tree, two methods are applied: the oracle configuration knows about the *true* previous cuts, while the blind configuration has only access to the *predicted* previous cuts. The difference between oracle and blind configurations are expected. The difference in performance between the decision tree and the baselines is an indication that the features are contributing to the classification performance. Future work should look at analyzing feature contribution and improving the models, and providing segmentation support for Catalan, English and Italian.

Algorithm	F1 (Cut)	F1 (No Cut)	Avg. F1
Decision Tree (Oracle)	0.43	0.89	0.66
Decision Tree (Blind)	0.26	0.91	0.58
POS Tag Baseline	0.17	0.95	0.56
Seg. Length Baseline	0.12	0.91	0.52

Table 7: Segmentation results (based on F1 measure) into Easy to Read (Spanish data). Comparison of a Decision Tree with baselines.

5 Accessing Simplification Technology through the iDEM App

The iDEM project implements and deploys a cloud-based, open-API iDEM platform to deliver text-simplification services, integrating components for complex language detection (Section 4.2) phenomena and adaptation through text simplification (Section 4.4). It supports diverse audiences, languages, and domains, and solutions are made available for deliberative participatory spaces as open-source products. The current version of the app supports iteration via typed text, speech, OCR or PDF. A participation functionality allows the user to check proposals currently being discussed and simplify them for better understanding. For example, the *Decidim* platform (Aragón et al., 2017) can be directly accessed from the app to translate, or simplify active participatory processes. Examples of the APP in action can be seen in Figures 1a and Figures 1b. Note that the current simplification technology supported by the app is not yet the one described in the paper; it still serves as a demonstrator of what it will look like in the coming months.

6 Limitations and Ethical Considerations

The studies on Complexity Assessment in section 4.2 and 4.3 argue for an analysis and simplification of a large array of factors, one of which is lexical simplification. We are aware that this is a current limitation, but future versions of the iDEM simplification tools will include a full treatment of sentence simplification. Our current simplification model, although achieving good performance in comparison with a strong baseline, does not do so with respect to the state of the art. This can be explained by our aim to keep models open and accessible to a broader community of stakeholders, i.e. lighter, open models could be afforded by more disadvantaged communities in the spirit of our project. Since our project deals with pro-

[6]https://scikit-learn.org/stable/modules/tree.html

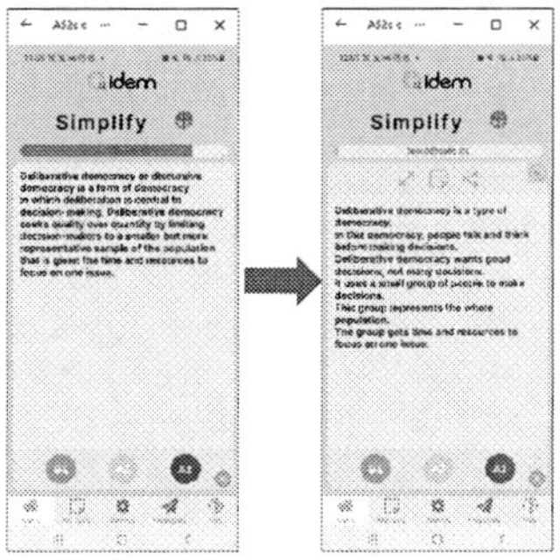

(a) English Wikipedia excerpt on deliberative democracy.

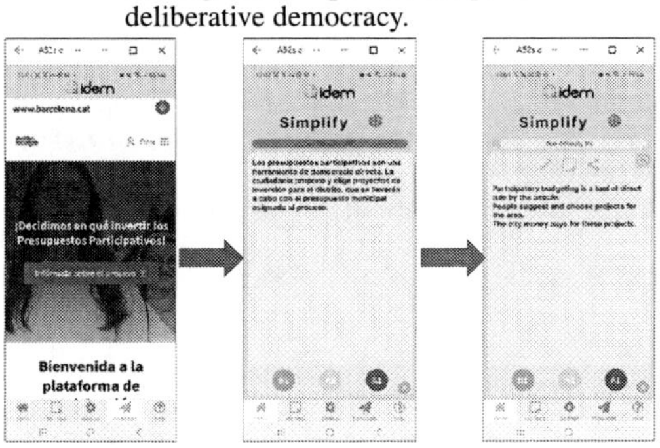

(b) Decidim platform: input in Spanish, output simplified in English.

Figure 1: Examples of cross-lingual text simplification.

viding accessible information to people who need language support, special attention has to be put in the assessment of the underlying models used as backbones for our technology as well as on the data we trained or fine-tuned our models with. An assessment of data quality and ethics has already been carried out (Saggion et al., 2024a). As for the involvement of human subjects in our case studies, we are following strict norms for data protection and ethical principles.

7 Conclusions

First, our intralingual translation-borrowed framework facilitates comparison between source and target texts more easily when the texts are simplified. Second, we proposed a taxonomy of simplification strategies inspired by intralingual translation and E2R principles, consisting of 8 macro-strategies, illustrating the cognitive complexity of intralingual translation. Such challenges underscore current automation tool limitations, as computational analyses illustrate the subtle competencies that are engaged in transcription and alteration strategies.

We applied our classifier to a parallel dataset from institutional sources and observed that Explanation and Modulation were among the most frequently predicted strategies, especially in English texts. While the classifier demonstrates promising results, a limitation of this study is that the observations were not verified through systematic manual analysis but rather were generated automatically. Therefore, further systematic validation and error analysis should be included in future work.

This first study on simplification strategies and complexity assessment underlines the importance to carry out lexical simplification. In our second study we explored lexical simplification using few-shot prompting with open-source LLMs from the Salamandra family. The most important finding is that for Romance Languages LLMs of the Salamandra family show very promising results because, in contrast to most other LLMs, they are trained on much larger amounts of data in these languages. It was important to note, that our system can obtain results similar to those obtained with commerical closed-weights LLMs without having the same disadvantage of those of being only available over APIs that generate costs and being hosted on servers for which we cannot control the protection of sensitive data. The last point is potentially important especially in a project which handles data of vulnerable populations. Further on, commercial models usually do not allow fine-tuning, since their weights are not public. Even though our current experiments do not outperform the state of the art reached by GPT-3 and GPT-4 based models, we have not experimented with fine-tuning of Salamandra models and we are confident that such an approach will give room for improvement.

Finally, we presented a proof-of-concept integration of complexity assessment and lexical simplification, demonstrating its potential for real-world applications such as accessible mobile interfaces. While formal evaluation of the full pipeline remains future work, our preliminary results suggest that strategy-aware simplification can meaningfully support inclusive democratic participation.

Acknowledgments

This document is part of a project that has received funding from the European Union's Horizon Europe research and innovation program under Grant Agreement No. 101132431 (iDEM Project). The views and opinions expressed in this document are solely those of the author(s) and do not necessarily reflect the views of the European Union. Neither the European Union nor the granting authority can be held responsible for them. The University of Leeds (UOL) was funded by UK Research and Innovation (UKRI) under the UK government's Horizon Europe funding guarantee (Grant Agreement No. 10103529).

References

UNE 153101. 2018. Lectura Fácil. Pautas y recomendaciones para la elaboración de documentos.

Rodrigo Alarcon, Lourdes Moreno, and Paloma Martínez. 2021. Lexical simplification system to improve web accessibility. *IEEE Access*, 9:58755–58767.

Sandra Aluísio and Caroline Gasperin. 2010. Fostering digital inclusion and accessibility: The PorSimples project for simplification of Portuguese texts. In *Proceedings of the NAACL HLT 2010 Young Investigators Workshop on Computational Approaches to Languages of the Americas*, pages 46–53, Los Angeles, California. Association for Computational Linguistics.

Fernando Alva-Manchego, Louis Martin, Antoine Bordes, Carolina Scarton, Benoît Sagot, and Lucia Specia. 2020. ASSET: A dataset for tuning and evaluation of sentence simplification models with multiple rewriting transformations. In *Proceedings of the 58th Annual Meeting of the Association for Computational Linguistics*, pages 4668–4679, Online. Association for Computational Linguistics.

Pablo Aragón, Andreas Kaltenbrunner, Antonio Calleja-López, Andrés Pereira, Arnau Monterde, Xabier E. Barandiaran, and Vicenç Gómez. 2017. Deliberative platform design: The case study of the online discussions in decidim barcelona. In *Social Informatics: 9th International Conference, SocInfo 2017, Oxford, UK, September 13-15, 2017, Proceedings, Part II*, pages 277–287, Cham. Springer International Publishing.

André Bächtiger, John S Dryzek, Jane Mansbridge, and Mark E Warren. 2018. *The Oxford handbook of deliberative democracy*. Oxford University Press.

Or Biran, Samuel Brody, and Noémie Elhadad. 2011. Putting it Simply: A Context-Aware Approach to Lexical Simplification. In *Proceedings of the 49th Annual Meeting of the Association for Computational Linguistics*, ACL, pages 496–501, Portland, Oregon, USA.

Stefan Bott, Luz Rello, Biljana Drndarevic, and Horacio Saggion. 2012. Can spanish be simpler? lexsis: Lexical simplification for spanish. In *Proceedings of the 24th International Conference on Computational Linguistics (COLING 2012)*, pages 357–374, Mumbai, India.

Stefan Bott and Horacio Saggion. 2014. Text simplification resources for spanish. *Lang. Resour. Evaluation*, 48(1):93–120.

Jesús Calleja, Thierry Etchegoyhen, and David Ponce. 2024. Automating Easy Read Text Segmentation. In *Findings of the Association for Computational Linguistics: EMNLP 2024*, pages 11876–11894, Miami, Florida, USA. Association for Computational Linguistics.

Rémi Cardon, Adrien Bibal, Rodrigo Wilkens, David Alfter, Magali Norré, Adeline Müller, Patrick Watrin, and Thomas François. 2022. Linguistic corpus annotation for automatic text simplification evaluation. In *Proceedings of the 2022 Conference on Empirical Methods in Natural Language Processing*, pages 1842–1866, Abu Dhabi, United Arab Emirates. Association for Computational Linguistics.

Rocío Bernabé Caro. 2017. Propuesta metodológica para el desarrollo de la lectura fácil según el diseño centrado en el usuario. *Revista Española de Discapacidad (REDIS)*, 5(2):19–51.

Andrew Chesterman. 1997. *Memes of Translation: The Spread of Ideas in Translation Theory*. John Benjamins Publishing Company, Amsterdam.

Iria Da Cunha Fanego. 2021. El sistema ARTEXT CLARO: un auxiliar per a la redacció de textos administratius en llenguatge planer. *Terminàlia*, 2(24):78–79.

Jacob Devlin, Ming-Wei Chang, Kenton Lee, and Kristina Toutanova. 2019. Bert: Pre-training of deep bidirectional transformers for language understanding. In *Proceedings of the 2019 Conference of the North American Chapter of the Association for Computational Linguistics: Human Language Technologies, Volume 1 (Long and Short Papers)*, pages 4171–4186.

Benjamin Dutilleul, Mathis Debaillon, and Sandeep Mathias. 2024. Isep_presidency_university at mlsp 2024 shared task: Using gpt-3.5 to generate substitutes for lexical simplification. In *Proceedings of the 19th Workshop on Innovative Use of NLP for Building Educational Applications (BEA 2024)*, pages 605–609.

Taisei Enomoto, Hwichan Kim, Tosho Hirasawa, Yoshinari Nagai, Ayako Sato, Kyotaro Nakajima, and Mamoru Komachi. 2024. TMU-HIT at MLSP 2024: How Well Can GPT-4 Tackle Multilingual Lexical Simplification? In *Proceedings of the 19th Workshop on Innovative Use of NLP for Building Educational Applications (BEA 2024)*, pages 590–598.

Carlo Eugeni and Yves Gambier. 2023. La traduction intralinguistique: les défis de la diamésie. *Editura Politehnica, Timisoara.*

Inmaculada Fajardo, Vicenta Ávila, Antonio Ferrer, Gema Tavares, Marcos Gómez, and Ana Hernández.

2014. Easy-to-read texts for students with intellectual disability: linguistic factors affecting comprehension. *Journal of applied research in intellectual disabilities*, 27(3):212–225. Publisher: Wiley Online Library.

Daniel Ferrés and Horacio Saggion. 2022. Alexsis: A dataset for lexical simplification in spanish. In *Proceedings of TSAR-2022*, pages 39–49.

Eileen Fitzpatrick and Joan Bachenko. 1989. Parsing for prosody: what a text-to-speech system needs from syntax. *[1989] Proceedings. The Annual AI Systems in Government Conference*, pages 188–194.

Yves Gambier. 2006. La traduction audiovisuelle : une traduction sélective. In Jorma Tommola and Yves Gambier, editors, *Translation and Interpreting – Training and Research*, pages 21–37. University of Turku, Department of English Translation Studies, Turku.

Goran Glavaš and Sanja Štajner. 2015. Simplifying Lexical Simplification: Do We Need Simplified Corpora? In *Proceedings of the 53rd Annual Meeting of the Association for Computational Linguistics and the 7th International Joint Conference on Natural Language Processing (Volume 2: Short Papers)*, pages 63–68, Beijing, China. Association for Computational Linguistics.

Aitor Gonzalez-Agirre, Marc Pàmies, Joan Llop, Irene Baucells, Severino Da Dalt, Daniel Tamayo, José Javier Saiz, Ferran Espuña, Jaume Prats, Javier Aula-Blasco, Mario Mina, Adrián Rubio, Alexander Shvets, Anna Sallés, Iñaki Lacunza, Iñigo Pikabea, Jorge Palomar, Júlia Falcão, Lucía Tormo, Luis Vasquez-Reina, Montserrat Marimon, Valle Ruíz-Fernández, and Marta Villegas. 2025. Salamandra technical report. *Preprint*, arXiv:2502.08489.

Mariona González-Sordé and Anna Matamala. 2024. Empirical evaluation of Easy Language recommendations: a systematic literature review from journal research in Catalan, English, and Spanish. *Universal Access in the Information Society*, 23(3):1369–1387. Publisher: Springer.

Government of Spain. ALIA: The public ai infrastructure in spanish and co-official languages. `https://alia.gob.es/eng/`. Accessed: March 2025.

Silvia Hansen-Schirra, Walter Bisang, Arne Nagels, Silke Gutermuth, Julia Fuchs, Liv Borghardt, Silvana Deilen, Anne-Kathrin Gros, Laura Schiffl, and Johanna Sommer. 2020. Intralingual translation into easy language – or how to reduce cognitive processing costs. In Silvia Hansen-Schirra and Christiane Maaß, editors, *Easy Language Research: Text and User Perspectives, Easy – Plain – Accessible*, volume Volume 2, pages 197–226. Frank & Timme, Berlin.

Matthew Honnibal, Ines Montani, Sofie Van Landeghem, and Adriane Boyd. 2020. spacy: Industrial-strength natural language processing in python.

Inclusion Europe. 2009. *Information for All: European Guidelines for the Production of Easy-to-Read Information*. Inclusion Europe, Brussels, Belgium. Available online at `http://www.easy-to-read.eu`.

Philipp Koehn. 2005. Europarl: A parallel corpus for statistical machine translation. In *Proceedings of the 10th Machine Translation Summit*, pages 79–86, Phuket, Thailand. Accessed: April 2025.

Christiane Maaß. 2020. *Easy language - plain language - easy language plus: balancing comprehensibility and acceptability*. Number Vol. 3 in Easy - plain - accessible. Frank & Timme, Verlag für wissenschaftliche Literatur, Berlin.

Christopher D. Manning, Prabhakar Raghavan, and Hinrich Schütze. 2008. *Introduction to Information Retrieval*. Cambridge University Press.

Lucía Molina and Amparo Hurtado Albir. 2002. Translating techniques revisited: A dynamic and functionalist approach. *Meta*, 47(4):498–512.

Peter Newmark. 1988. *A textbook of translation*, volume 66. Prentice hall New York.

Gustavo Henrique Paetzold and Lucia Specia. 2016. Semeval 2016 task 11: Complex word identification. In *Proceedings of SemEval-2016*, pages 560–569.

Fabian Pedregosa, Gaël Varoquaux, Alexandre Gramfort, Vincent Michel, Bertrand Thirion, Olivier Grisel, Mathieu Blondel, Peter Prettenhofer, Ron Weiss, Vincent Dubourg, Jake VanderPlas, Alexandre Passos, David Cournapeau, Matthieu Brucher, Matthieu Perrot, and Édouard Duchesnay. 2011. Scikit-learn: Machine learning in python. *Journal of Machine Learning Research*, 12:2825–2830.

Jipeng Qiang, Yun Li, Yi Zhu, Yunhao Yuan, and Xindong Wu. 2020. LSBert: Lexical Simplification Based on BERT. *IEEE/ACM Transactions on Audio, Speech, and Language Processing*, pages 3064–3076.

Horacio Saggion. 2017. *Automatic Text Simplification*, volume 10 of *Synthesis Lectures on Human Language Technologies*. Morgan & Claypool Publishers.

Horacio Saggion. 2024. Artificial intelligence and natural language processing for easy-to-read texts. *Revista de Llengua i Dret*, (82):84–103.

Horacio Saggion, Stefan Bott, Sandra Szasz, Nelson Pérez, Saúl Calderón, and Martín Solís. 2024a. Lexical complexity prediction and lexical simplification for Catalan and Spanish: Resource creation, quality assessment, and ethical considerations. In *Proceedings of the Third Workshop on Text Simplification, Accessibility and Readability (TSAR 2024)*, pages 82–94, Miami, Florida, USA. Association for Computational Linguistics.

Horacio Saggion, John O'Flaherty, Thomas Blanchet, Serge Sharoff, Silvia Sanfilippo, Lian Muñoz, Martin Gollegger, Almudena Rascón, José L. Martí, Sandra

Szasz, Stefan Bott, and Volkan Sayman. 2024b. Making democratic deliberation and participation more accessible: The idem project. In *SEPLN (Projects and Demonstrations)*, volume 3729 of *CEUR Workshop Proceedings*, pages 71–76. CEUR-WS.org.

Horacio Saggion, Sanja Štajner, Stefan Bott, Simon Mille, Luz Rello, and Biljana Drndarevic. 2015. Making It Simplext: Implementation and Evaluation of a Text Simplification System for Spanish. *ACM Transactions on Accessible Computing*, 6(4):1–36.

Horacio Saggion, Sanja Štajner, Daniel Ferrés, Kim Cheng Sheang, Matthew Shardlow, Kai North, and Marcos Zampieri. 2022. Findings of the TSAR-2022 shared task on multilingual lexical simplification. In *Proceedings of the Workshop on Text Simplification, Accessibility, and Readability (TSAR-2022)*, pages 271–283, Abu Dhabi, United Arab Emirates (Virtual). Association for Computational Linguistics.

Matthew Shardlow. 2014. A survey of automated text simplification. *International Journal of Advanced Computer Science and Applications*, 4:58–70.

Matthew Shardlow, Fernando Alva-Manchego, Riza Batista-Navarro, Stefan Bott, Saul Calderon Ramirez, Rémi Cardon, Thomas François, Akio Hayakawa, Andrea Horbach, Anna Hülsing, Yusuke Ide, Joseph Marvin Imperial, Adam Nohejl, Kai North, Laura Occhipinti, Nelson Peréz Rojas, Nishat Raihan, Tharindu Ranasinghe, Martin Solis Salazar, Sanja Štajner, Marcos Zampieri, and Horacio Saggion. 2024. The BEA 2024 shared task on the multilingual lexical simplification pipeline. In *Proceedings of the 19th Workshop on Innovative Use of NLP for Building Educational Applications (BEA 2024)*, pages 571–589, Mexico City, Mexico. Association for Computational Linguistics.

Marina Sokolova and Guy Lapalme. 2009. A systematic analysis of performance measures for classification tasks. *Information Processing & Management*, 45(4):427–437.

Lucia Specia, Shashi Narayan, and Carolina Gasperin. 2012. Semeval-2012 task 1: English lexical simplification. In *Proceedings of SemEval-2012*, pages 347–355.

Dan Steinberg. 2009. Cart: Classification and regression trees. Technical report.

Réfugiés.info Team. 2025. Réfugiés.info genai for public good hackathon submission. Accessed April 2025.

U.S. Government. 2011. Federal plain language guidelines. Accessed: March 2025.

Jean-Paul Vinay and Jean Darbelnet. 1971. *Stylistique comparée du français et de l'anglais*. Didier. Translated into English as *Comparative Stylistics of French and English*, 1995.

Patrick Zabalbeascoa. 2000. From techniques to types of solutions. In Allison Beeby, Doris Ensinger, and Marisa Presas, editors, *Investigating Translation*, pages 117–127. John Benjamins, Amsterdam and Philadelphia.

Wei Zhang and Mirella Lapata. 2017. Sentence simplification with deep reinforcement learning. In *Proceedings of the 2017 Conference on Empirical Methods in Natural Language Processing*, pages 584–594.

Michał Ziemski, Marcin Junczys-Dowmunt, and Bruno Pouliquen. 2016. The United Nations parallel corpus v1.0. In *Proc. LREC*, Portorož, Slovenia.

A Plain Language Summary

This paper describes how to make difficult text easier to read. It is part of the iDEM project, which aims to help more people participate in democratic processes. Some people find official or complex documents hard to read. Because of that, they might not be able to vote or take part in important discussions.

The iDEM project studies ways to make public information easier to read. By removing or replacing hard words, adding helpful explanations, and splitting text into shorter sentences. To do this, it uses computer programs. One program can detect which words or sentences are difficult. Another program can suggest simpler words to replace the difficult ones. There is also another program to split long sentences into shorter ones.

The project uses freely available language models. These models are trained to understand many languages, such as English, Spanish, Italian, and Catalan.

B Classifier Configuration

Parameter	Value
Pre-trained Model	`bert-base-multilingual`
Max Sequence Length	512 tokens
Tokenisation	Pre-trained tokenizer
Loss Function	Weighted Cross-Entropy Loss
Class Weights	Inverse frequency of labels
Gradient Clipping Threshold	1.0
Learning Rate	5×10^{-6}
Batch Size	8
Weight Decay	0.01
Number of Epochs	Up to 20 (early stopping)
Cross-Validation	Stratified 5-Fold
Early Stopping Patience	3 epochs
GPU	NVIDIA Tesla T4 (Google Colab). Occasionally V100 (our HPC cluster).

Table 8: Hyperparameters and Training Configuration for experiments in Section 4.2

C Confusion Matrix

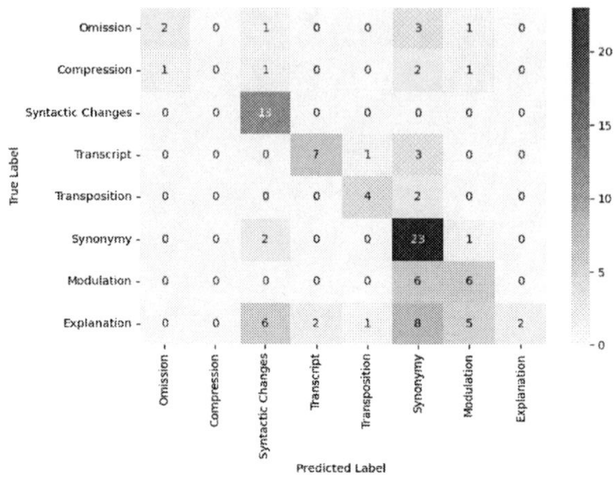

Figure 2: Confusion Matrix of the multilingual model.

D Zero and Few Shot Lexical Simplification Performance Smaller Model

	0-Shot		2-Shot		4-Shot		MLSP Baseline		MLSP Winner	
	ACC	MAP@3	ACC	MAP@3	ACC	MAP@3	ACC	MAP@3	ACC	MAP@3
English	0.2877	0.261	0.3017	0.2601	0.3315	0.2765	0.3877	0.4241	0.5245	0.5762
Spanish	0.2192	0.2608	0.2596	0.3011	0.2681	0.3356	0.3254	0.4157	0.4536	0.6763
Catalan	0.1438	0.1817	0.1438	0.1961	0.1348	0.1710	0.1977	0.3024	0.2719	0.5003
Italian	0.228	0.1983	0.2736	0.2251	0.1684	0.2006	0.2964	0.3310	0.4762	0.5661

Table 9: Results of Zero and Few Shot Lexical Simplification Performance for a small model (Salamandra-2B). Results are compared to the state of the art, as reported in the recent MLSP 2024 lexical simplification shared task.

E Classification Strategies

Strategy	**MacroStrategy**	**Explanation and Examples**	**Total**
WorExp	Explanation	Explanation of a word. e.g. "co-design services..." → "co-design services with people who use or work in them..."	
ExpExp	Explanation	Explanation of an expression. e.g. "Accessible Transport..." → "Accessible travel means making buses, trains, ferries and taxis easier to use..."	
HidGra	Explanation	Making hidden grammar explicit. e.g. "this is the music I love" → "This is the music that I love"	4
HidCon	Explanation	Making hidden content explicit. e.g. "COVID-19" → "Covid pandemic"	
ModInf	Modulation	Splitting sentence based on number of ideas. e.g. "He joins in community activities..." → "He likes to take part... He gets support..."	

(continued on next page)

(continued from previous page)

Strategy	MacroStrategy	Explanation and Examples	Total
ModLin	Modulation	Redistribution of sentence components: - **ModWord**: "...collaboration and information sharing..." → "...working together and sharing information..." - **ModGrou**: "Accessible Museums is a topic..." → "Our members think it is important to talk about Accessible Museums" - **ModClau**: "To improve community health... the Government works..." → "The Government works... to improve..."	2
PraSyn	Synonymy	Pragmatic synonyms: - **PraProp**: UN → United Nations, Nutella → chocolate cream - **PraCont**: "Sir Keir Starmer" → "the new Prime Minister"	
SemSyn	Synonymy	Semantic synonyms: - **SemStere**: ponder → think - **SemHype**: lecturers → teachers - **SemHypo**: flora → trees and flowers	3
GraSyn	Synonymy	Grammatical synonyms: - **GraPron**: "you don't see it" → "you don't see the mistake" - **GraTens**: "we have been doing" → "we have done" - **GraPass**: passive → active - **GraNega**: "not an obstacle" → "facilitated"	
TraNou	Transposition	Noun transposition. e.g. "our aim" → "we want"	
TraVer	Transposition	Verb transposition. e.g. "listening to music" → "music"	
TrAdje	Transposition	Adjective transposition. e.g. "mountainous landscapes" → "mountains"	4
TrAdve	Transposition	Adverb transposition. e.g. "behaving happily" → "was happy"	
Transcript	Transcript	A sentence is left unchanged.	
SynW2G/S/C	Syntactic Change	Word to group/clause/sentence	
SynG2W/C/S	Syntactic Change	Group to word/clause/sentence	12
SynC2W/G/S	Syntactic Change	Clause to word/group/sentence	
SynS2W/G/C	Syntactic Change	Sentence to word/group/clause	
Illocutionary Change	Illocutionary Change	Making implied meaning explicit.	1
GraSim	Compression	Grammatical simplification. e.g. "so as to" → "to"	
SemSim	Compression	Semantic simplification. e.g. condensing explanations	2
OmiEle	Omission	Omission of elements: - **OmiSubj**: "Sir Keir Rodney Starmer..." → "Starmer is..." - **OmiVerb**, **OmiComp**, **OmiClau**, **OmiSent** (e.g. full sentence removed)	

(continued on next page)

(continued from previous page)

Strategy	MacroStrategy	Explanation and Examples	Total
OmiDia	Omission	Omission of discourse elements: - **OmiFil**: "you know" → removed - **OmiRef**: "I was tight… right when..." → "I was right when..." - **OmiRhe**: "wasn't I?" → removed	2
		Total	**30**

Table 10: Macro-strategies, Strategies, Micro-strategies, and Examples with Annotated Totals

Author Index

Association for Computational Linguistics
209 N. Eighth Street
Stroudsburg, Pennsylvania 18360

ISBN 979-8-3313-2669-2

CURRAN ASSOCIATES INC.
proceedings.com